IMAGES
of America

DELL RAPIDS

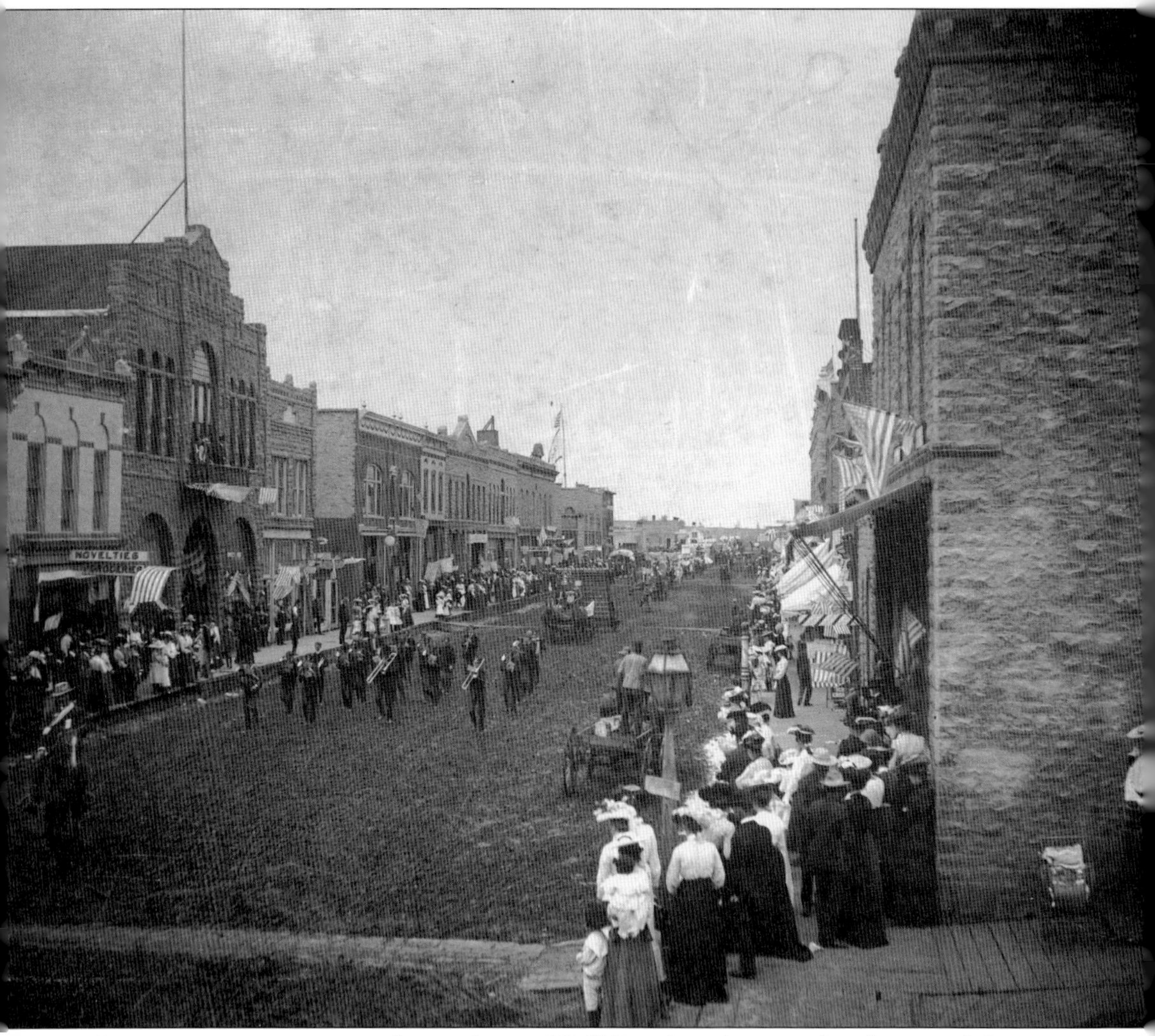

It is not uncommon to see the residents of Dell Rapids gather together for one of the many celebrations in town, whether to honor Civil War veterans on Decoration Day or Quarry Days or to support the local school on homecoming. This parade occurred in 1903 on Decoration Day, with the Dell Rapids City Band helping to lead the way. (Courtesy Dell Rapids Museum.)

On the Cover: The coming of the railroad marked a definitive period in the success of Dell Rapids. For many years, the train was a reliable source of transportation, bringing visitors and commerce to the town. Without the train, many smaller towns eventually died out. The two men standing on the railroad bridge exemplify the characteristics of Dell Rapids: courage, adventure, and reliability. (Courtesy Dell Rapids Museum.)

IMAGES
of America

DELL RAPIDS

Teri Fiegen and Luke Tatge

ARCADIA
PUBLISHING

ISBN 978-0-7385-9376-0

Published by Arcadia Publishing
Charleston, South Carolina

Printed in the United States of America

Library of Congress Control Number: 2012939802

For all general information, please contact Arcadia Publishing:
Telephone 843-853-2070
Fax 843-853-0044
E-mail sales@arcadiapublishing.com
For customer service and orders:
Toll-Free 1-888-313-2665

Visit us on the Internet at www.arcadiapublishing.com

We would like to dedicate this book to the past, present, and future residents of Dell Rapids, for their courage and inspiration. To Scott, Todd, and Kati Fiegen, who have stood beside Teri in all her searches, discoveries, and activities. To Dorothy and John Frank and Mary and Orville Tatge for their endless supply of stories, and to Donna and Lyle Tatge for their years of encouragement: thank you!

Contents

Acknowledgments 6

Introduction 7

1. Major Events and Landmarks 9
2. Notable Residents 35
3. Military 53
4. Town and Business 61
5. Churches 81
6. Public School 101
7. Health and Wellness 109
8. Recreation 117

Acknowledgments

Dell Rapids has been fortunate to have so many people who value the importance of history. Two particular individuals, Robert DeVaney and George Schwebach, shared their memories, documented the history, and eventually became a part of that history. Their efforts greatly contributed to the creation of the Dell Rapids Museum. Unless otherwise noted, all images appear courtesy of the Dell Rapids Museum.

The community support has been wonderful. We could not have compiled all the photographs and information without it. The contributions from local churches and the American Legion have proved to be invaluable, and the photographs from the Rose Stone Inn are a true treasure.

A special thank-you goes to Tom Schwebach for helping with the book. The kind words of encouragement, the corrections, the documents, the photographs, and the patient answering of the many, many questions—overall, your input is irreplaceable.

Every individual who told a story about his or her family, business, or event has contributed to this book. It is impossible to thank every individual—a few in particular are Tom Merry, Allen Brown, Carolyn Lamberty, Harvey Pederson, Darlene Schnieders, Tim Schwebach, and Bette Huss. A special thank-you goes to Thelma Busk for overall moral support.

INTRODUCTION

Through its rich history and traditions lasting more than 100 years, Dell Rapids has become a prominent city in the area because of its ongoing familial heritage, its dedication to commercial, natural, and religious endeavors, and a spirit of community identity that separates it from other small populations in the region. Settled in the late 1800s, the town has seen its share of events, and they have shaped the population—from nature's devastating fires, crippling snowstorms and blizzards, and overwhelming Big Sioux River floods to the notorious bank robberies of the 1930s and the still celebrated summertime festivals, Quarry Days and Cootie Days.

Business has boomed through the years, thanks to the devotion of locals to the pursuit of progress and success. The rock quarries have helped define the town's identity and form the structures of some of the oldest buildings in the area. And the dells themselves have fueled production at mills and dams since the early days of the city, leaving an irreplaceable mark on the town's history.

With a military history dating back to the Civil War and commemorated with well-kept statues and memorials and a dedicated American Legion post, the city also has respect and awe for those who would give their lives to serve the country. Pioneering efforts from men and women in the medical field have kept Dell Rapids residents healthy through hardship and abundance, and the hospital and clinic has kept its doors open to those in need. And with a keen interest in keeping the faith, religion has remained a pillar of the town's citizens. Dell Rapids is home to a handful of congregations, which have stayed invigorated through decades of progress and change.

While it is situated on the southeastern edge of South Dakota, on the northern brim of Minnehaha County, home to the state's most populous city, Sioux Falls, Dell Rapids has secured an identity as a town with a unique and well-documented history. Its citizens have kept the town on the map through discoveries, such as botanist Charlotte Elliott's work with bacteria in corn, Titus Unger's invention of a more efficient and easier-to-use minnow bucket, and Lucile Fargo's written works, which have kept the stories of the people of the prairie alive. But without the efforts of the town's founders, none of what has happened since would be possible.

More than 140 years have passed since Peter Morse helped bring "Dell City" to fruition in the fall of 1871, and every year since has added to the storied tale of Dell Rapids. Without the help of the early settlers' vision to build dams, bridges, and roads to suit the population, the town would never have the buildings, businesses, and memories of traditions and events kept alive through community involvement. With a focus on education and the instillation of values in the youth of the city, local schools and noted families have maintained a grip on the well-being of Dells' future citizens and those who have gone out into the world to make the town and its people proud. The future looks bright for Dell Rapids, as constant construction and progress keep the ever-expanding population in step with a changing world.

As many flock to the city, booming the city's numbers, the structure of the town will continue to evolve. But growth and succession are what has kept the city going. The foresight of its forefathers and foremothers has been the lifeblood of a community that reaches for bigger and better.

One

Major Events and Landmarks

Though it underwent a name change and a significant population boost thanks to years of business and interest growth, what was once Dell City still maintains much of its original heritage as Dell Rapids. The early industrial phase of the town's history was fueled by mills powered by the Big Sioux River and the rock quarries still in use today. Railroad companies defined the commodities business in the area and led to the commercialization of the downtown district. The arrival of the Dieson family and their widely known department store helped advance the city on the dells, which has evolved greatly with time.

With venues such as the historic Grand Opera House, the former dance pavilion, and the still-in-operation Dells Theatre, the town has seen a variety of visitors seeking top-notch arenas for performance and production. However, Dell Rapids has not avoided its share of fire-related destruction, such as the Silkensen service station fire. The town also saw a string of bank robberies in the 1930s, with the Dells' own First National Bank falling victim to the FBI's Public Enemy No. 1 in 1934. But through well-attended events and traditions like the national corn-husking contest or the annual Quarry Days, Dell Rapids has shone well beyond the state boundaries for its individual and community achievements.

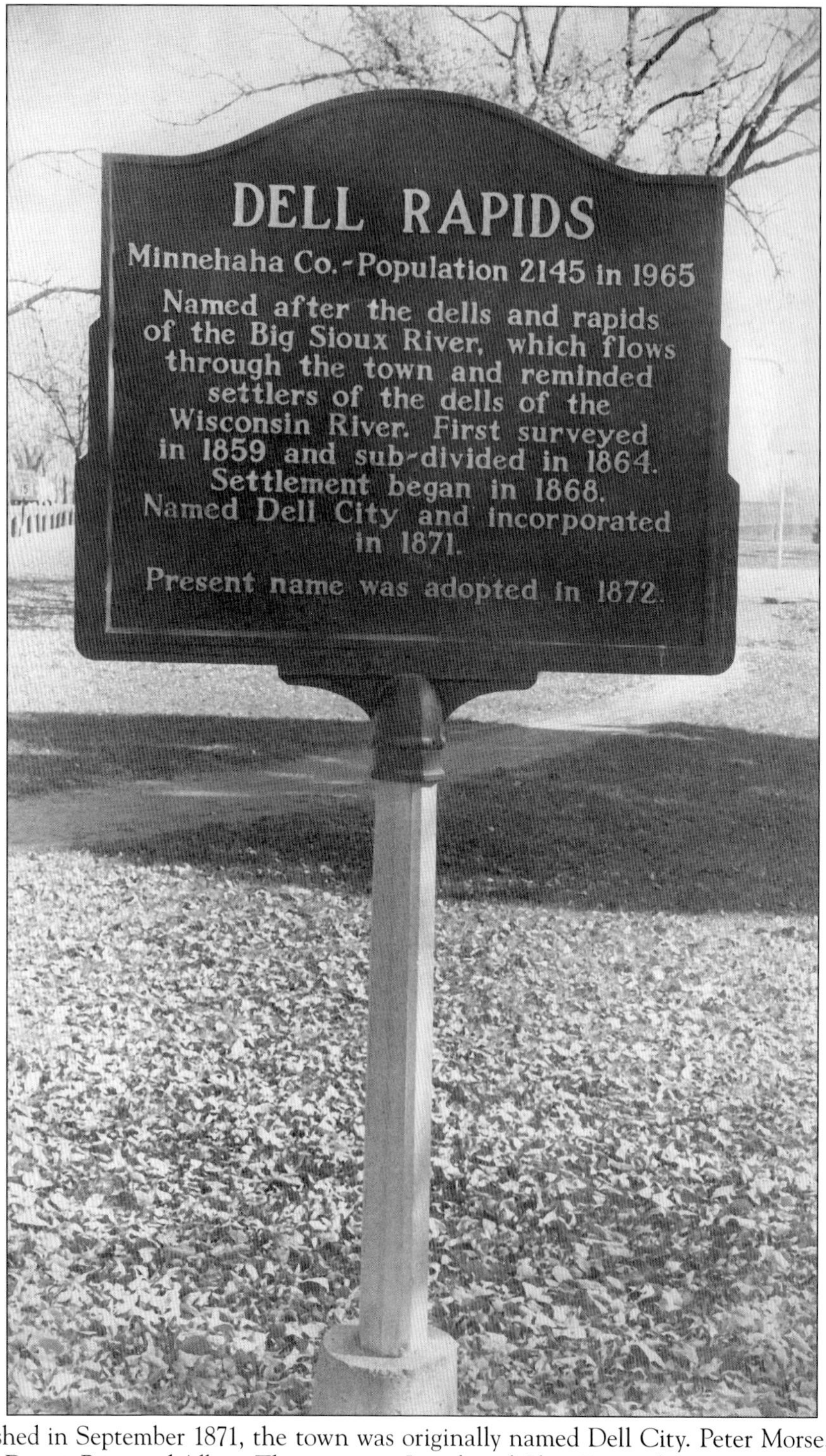

Established in September 1871, the town was originally named Dell City. Peter Morse, Byron Graves, Dennis Rice, and Albion Thorne met at Joseph and Clara Ervins' house in 1872 to rename the town. Morse suggested "Dell Rapids" with the thought that "Rapids" would give the world the idea that there was fine waterpower here.

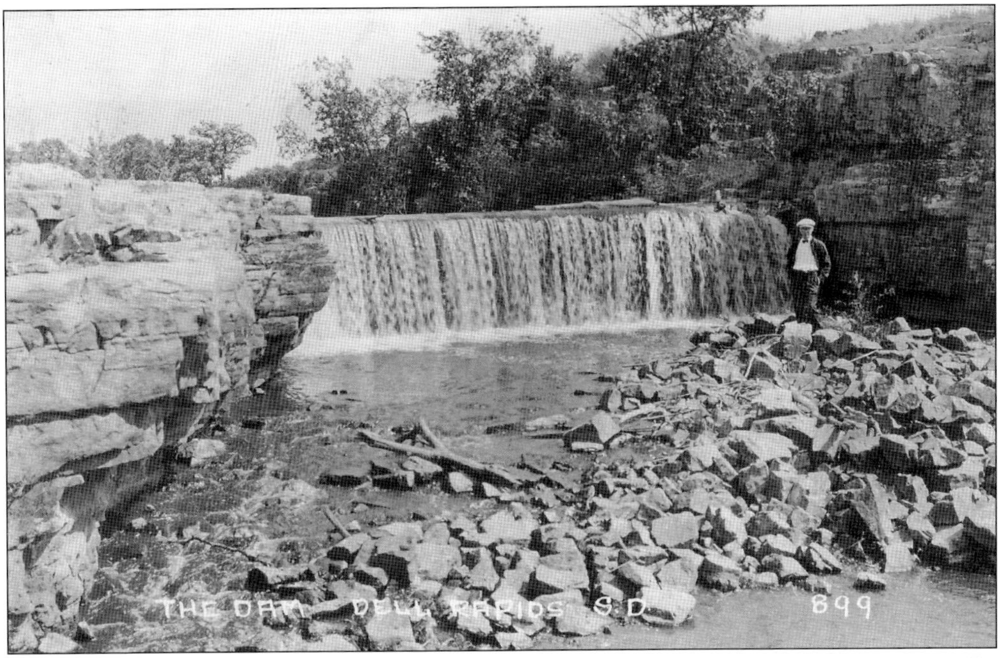

Brothers Frank and Dennis Rice began building the first dam across the Big Sioux River in 1871. Early settlers assisted in building the dam by hauling straw and equipment with oxen teams. The dam was replaced in 1877 by a new stone dam built by William Van Eps. Receiving many improvements and repairs over time, the dam continues to span the river in its original location.

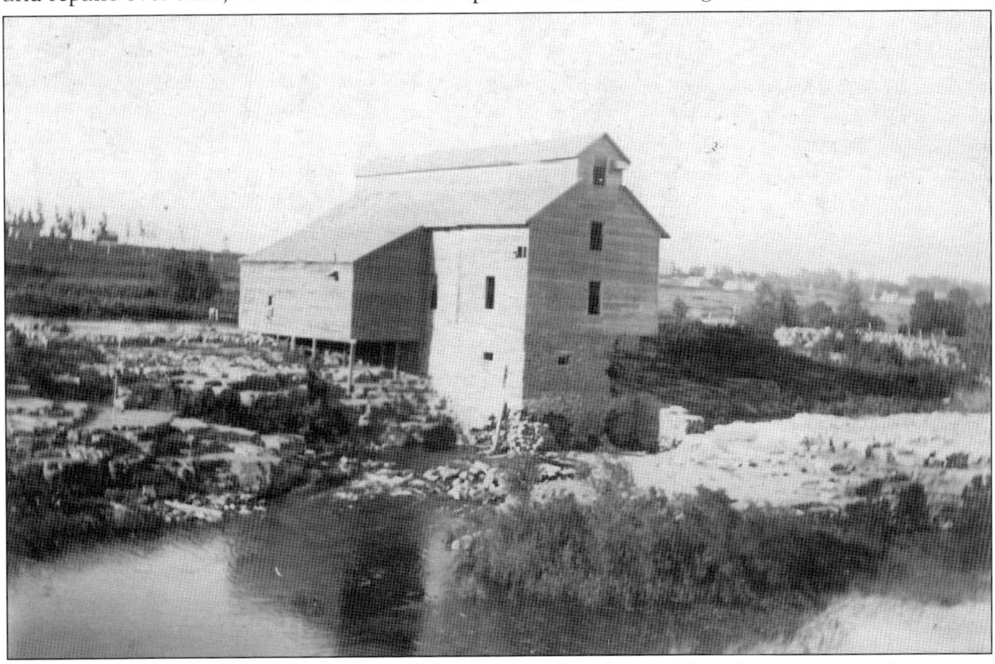

The Rice brothers completed the sawmill in 1872. At first, lumber from big cottonwood trees was milled. However, due to the lack of lumber in the area, the sawmill was replaced by a flouring mill in 1873. The Rice brothers operated the mill until August 1874, when it was purchased by William Van Eps.

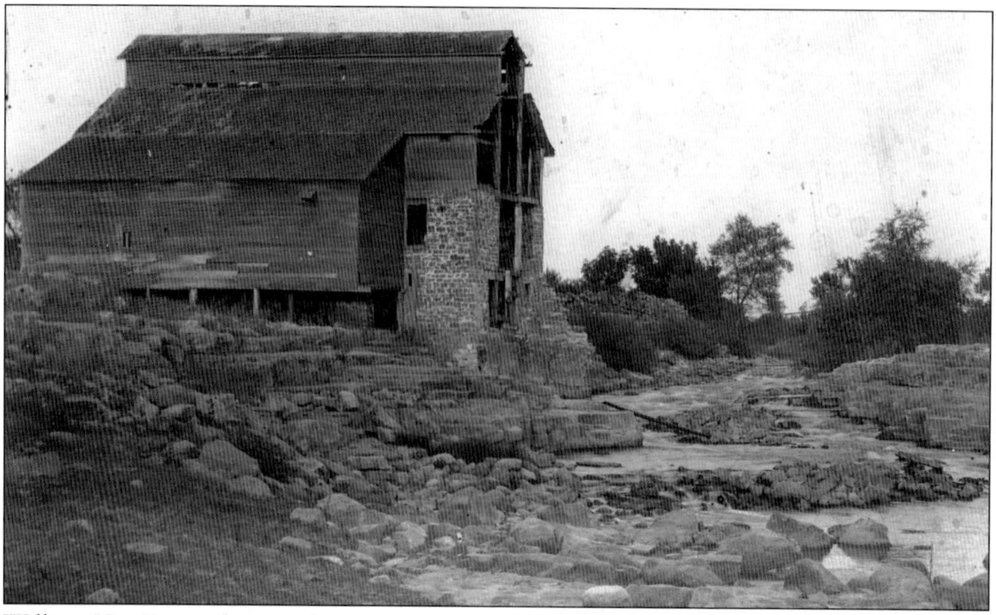

William Van Eps made several improvements to the mill and dam when he purchased the land in 1884. Edley Elliot, who was in charge of the Queen Bee Mill in Sioux Falls, later came to run the mill. In 1906, the land was sold, and the mill was torn down. One of the original stone burrs was placed in the city park by the Daughters of the American Revolution.

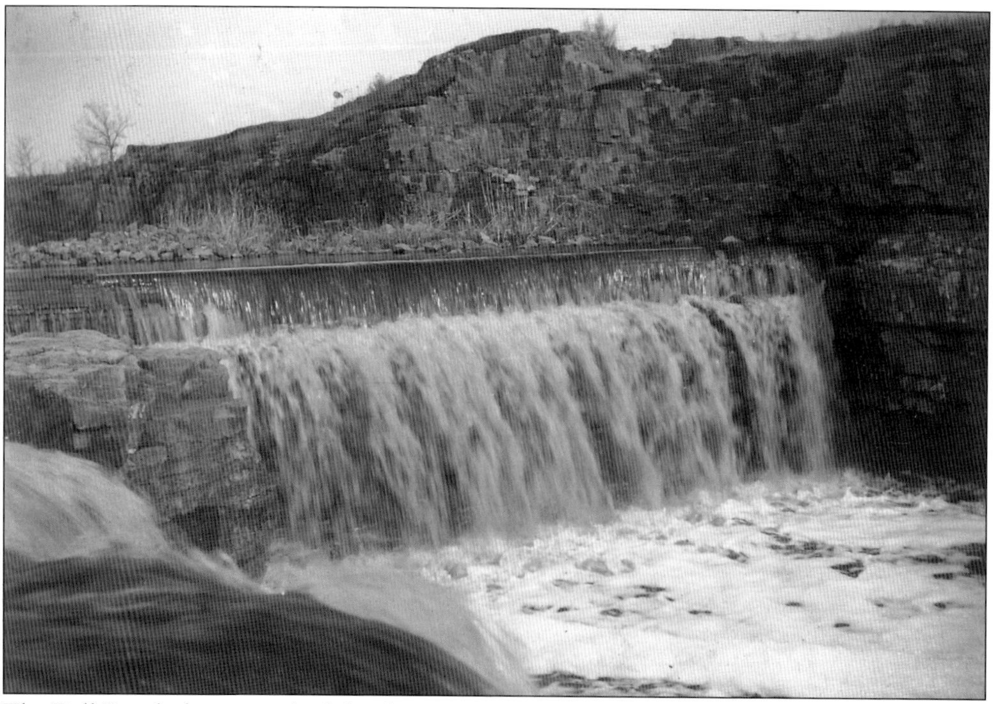

The Dell Rapids dam was rebuilt by the city in 1916 and again in 1933. The five acres near the dam continue to be a popular fishing attraction. Smallmouth bass, catfish, crappie, northern pike, perch, and walleye of all sizes can be found along the Big Sioux River. The last repairs to the dam took place in 1991.

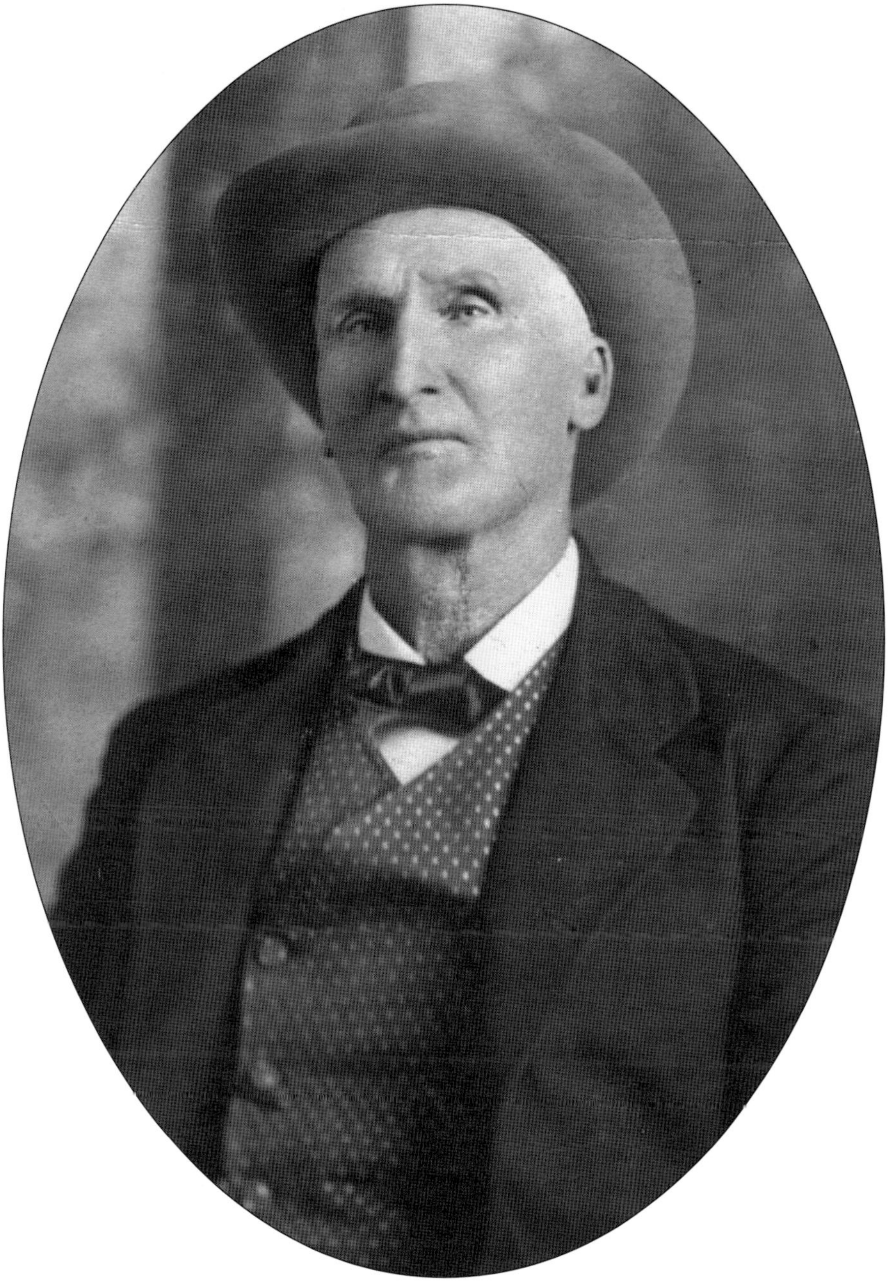

Frank Rice and his brothers, Dennis and Gilbert, settled in Iowa in a place later named after the family—Riceville. In 1868, the family moved to Osage, Iowa, where they built and operated the Cedar Valley Mills. The Rice brothers arrived in Sioux Falls in July 1871 to purchase interest in a business in town. They were unsuccessful, but they soon obtained a foothold in Dell Rapids, building a mill. Later, Frank would become a real estate agent, purchasing several hundred acres of land in Todd Township in Minnesota. Frank named and helped establish the town of Park Rapids and lived there until his death in 1910. In 1881, he built a dam on the Fish Hook River that powered a rolling stone grain mill and a sawmill. His stay in Dell Rapids was short, but the impact on the town was far greater than he could have imagined.

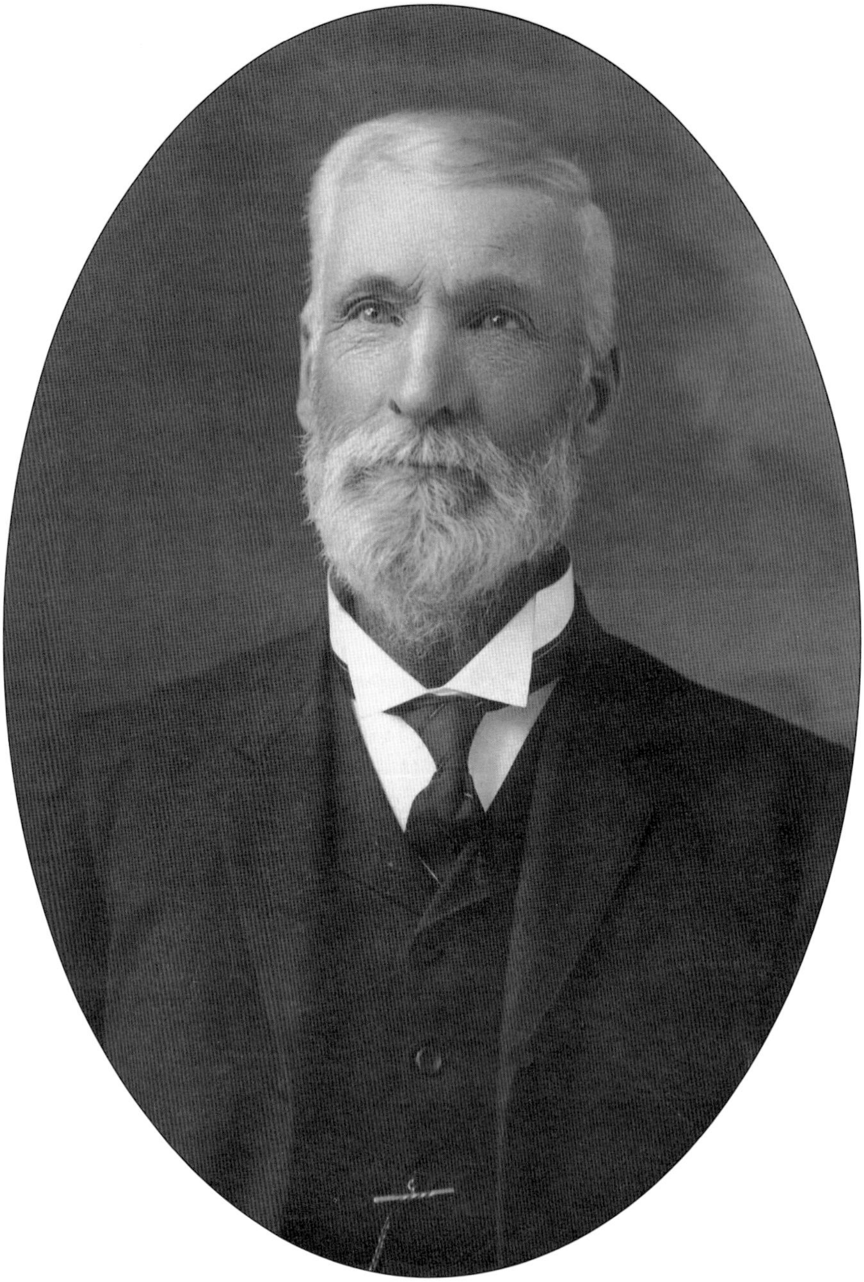

Peter Morse traveled to the area in 1871. He was very pleased with the location for a townsite and returned to Osage, Iowa, where he found Frank and Dennis Rice, two experienced mill men, and convinced them to invest in the area later known as Dell Rapids. In 1872, the Rice brothers came to Dell Rapids to build a dam and mill. They wanted to create a boom large enough to merit the county seat. They were instrumental in the establishment of Dell Rapids; however, the town never became the county seat. The Rices later moved to Minnesota and continued milling. For a brief time, Dennis Rice traveled to Texas and engaged in the land business. In his later years, Dennis lived with his daughter in Wisconsin until his death in 1921. He is buried in Osage, Iowa, where he is considered a prominent county pioneer.

Until it was torn down, the Old Mill was a popular landmark and a common recreational area. Children spent hours climbing through the timbers of the mill remains, fishing, and hiking around the cliffs nearby. Groups of young adults also saw this site as a perfect picnicking area, with gorgeous natural scenery along the Big Sioux River.

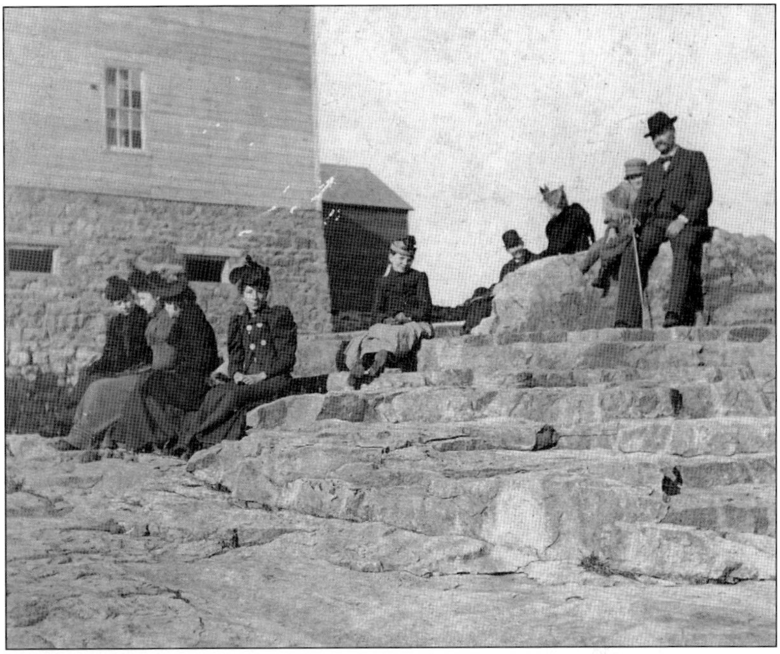

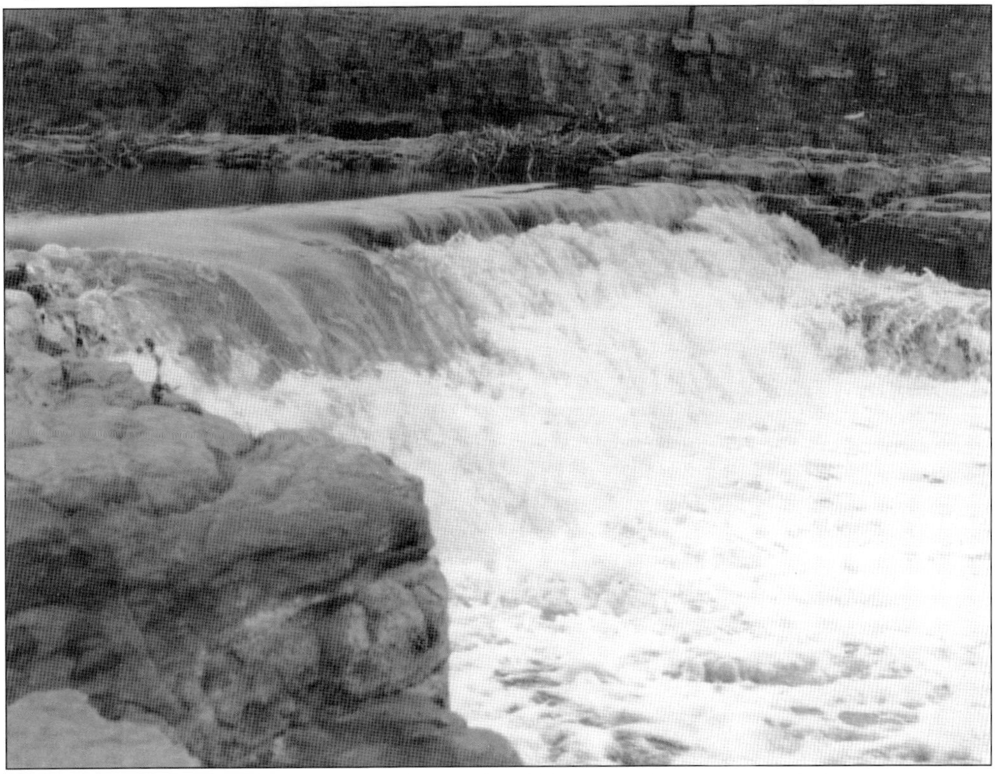

Renovation on the old dam started in September 1991, as workers uncovered what was thought to be a natural granite cap on the riverbed. The cap was part of the original dam, which had deteriorated over time. The water level behind the dam eventually increased, attracting more fishermen and boaters.

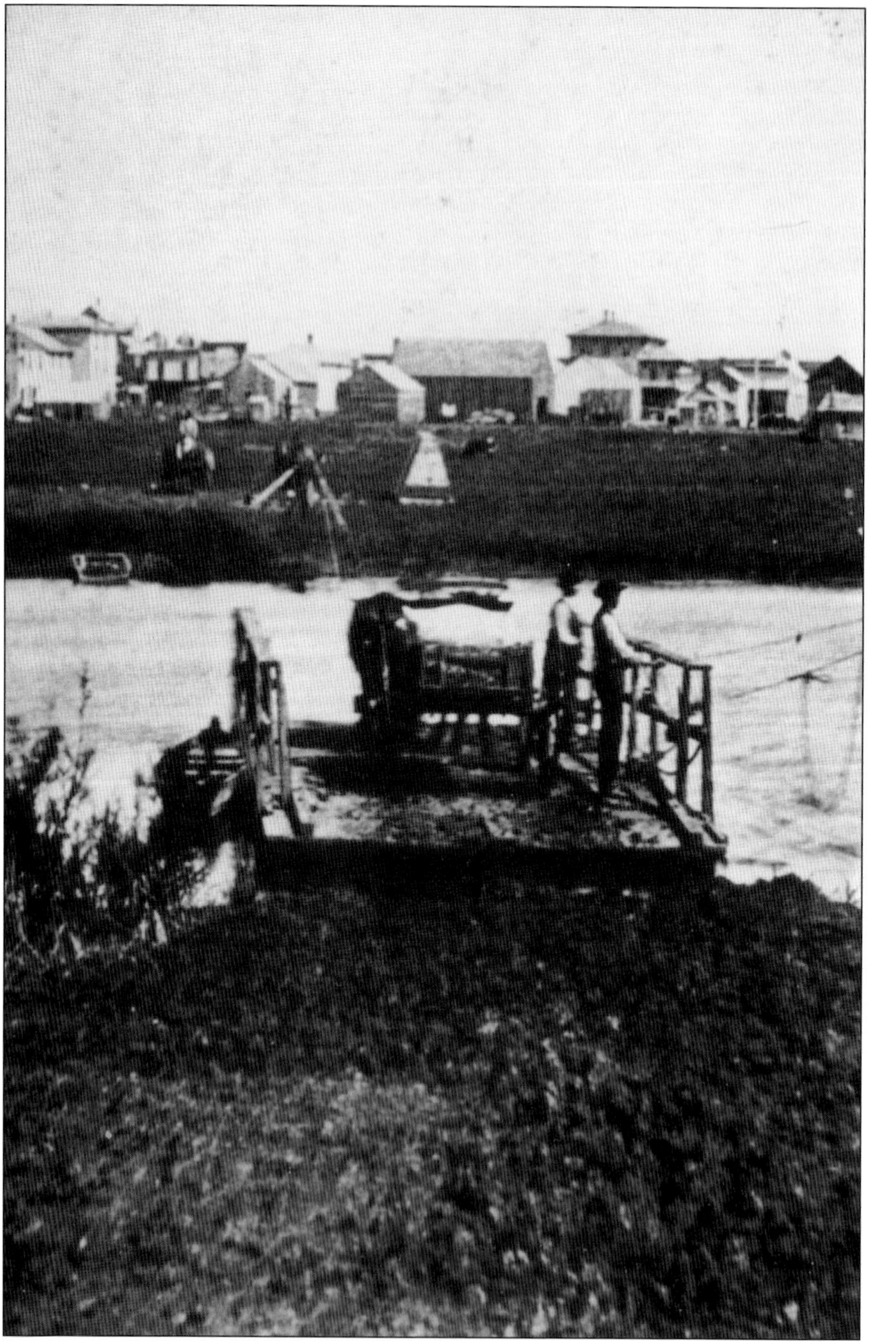

The Big Sioux was an obstacle for the early settlers. A mode of transportation across the river was needed. In 1872, $7 bought a boat, which was the only means across the river for two years. In 1874, a ferry owned by the city was built. Tommy Lyons, a paid employee, ran the ferry for the city. The ferry was located near Orleans Street and was used for years by farmers and residents living on the south side of the river. The cost of the ferry was 5¢ per individual and 10¢ for a team and wagon. By 1877, the community had gathered enough funding to build a bridge. Unfortunately, the bridge only lasted a few years; it was washed away in a devastating flood in 1881.

The old footbridge was built in 1885. It was one of three bridges spanning the Big Sioux River at Dell Rapids, located at the south end of Orleans Avenue. Liability insurance costs, along with prohibitive repair costs, forced its demolition more than 100 years later. In 1990, workers first removed the deck of the bridge before cutting the girders and dismantling the bridge on the ice.

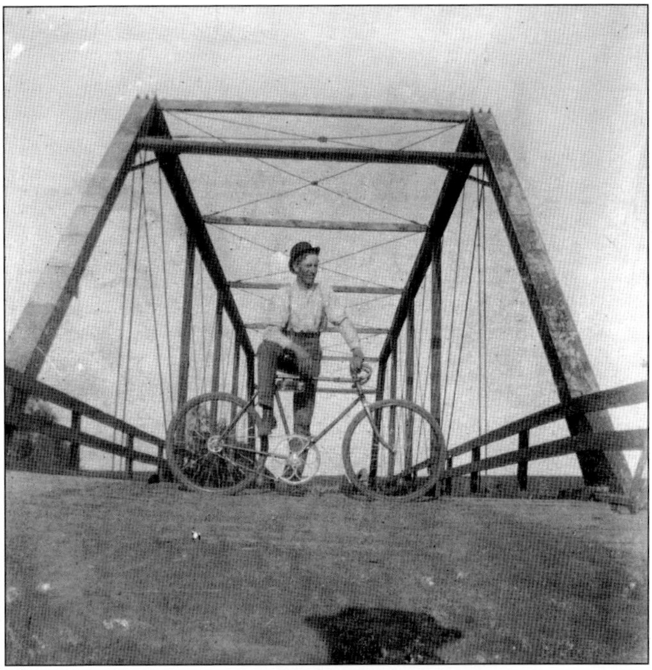

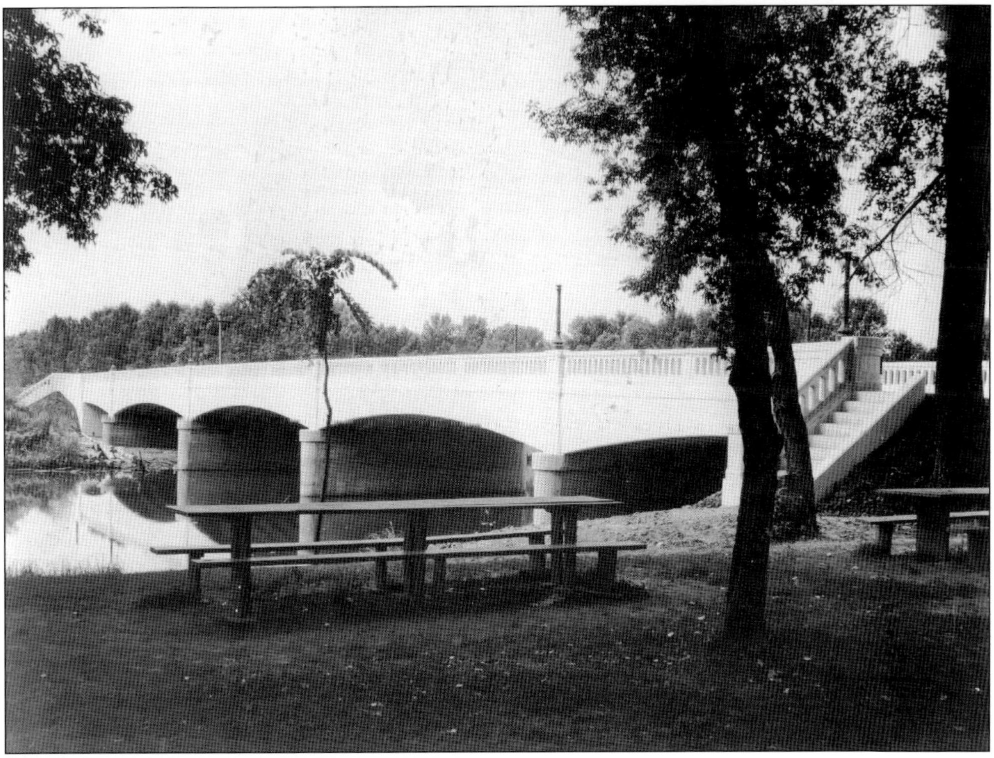

This bridge is said to be one of the most beautiful in the state. Built in 1929, it was respectfully dedicated to the early settlers of the community. For more than 80 years, it has crossed the Big Sioux River along the original State Highway 77. However, due to age and condition, it has been scheduled for replacement.

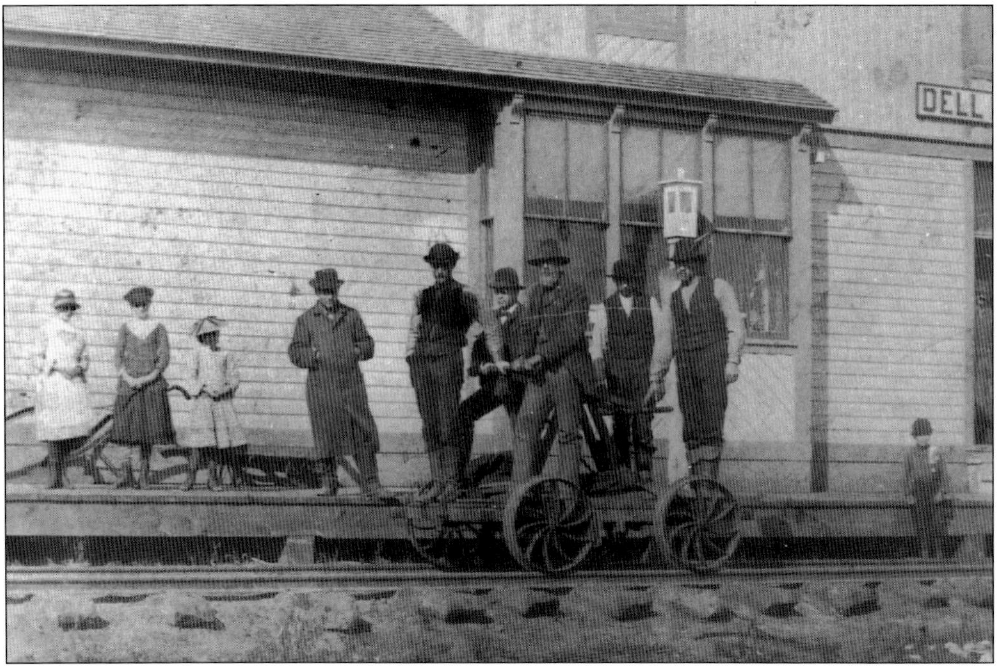

As the railroad arrived in 1880, so did many Catholics. Mike Anthony (second from left) was section foreman for the railroad for 25 years and did his part by serving Mass in his home. Anthony was the only man in Dell Rapids capable of serving Mass until 1891, when the Bells moved in and young Frank Bell assumed the duty. (Courtesy St. Mary Catholic Church.)

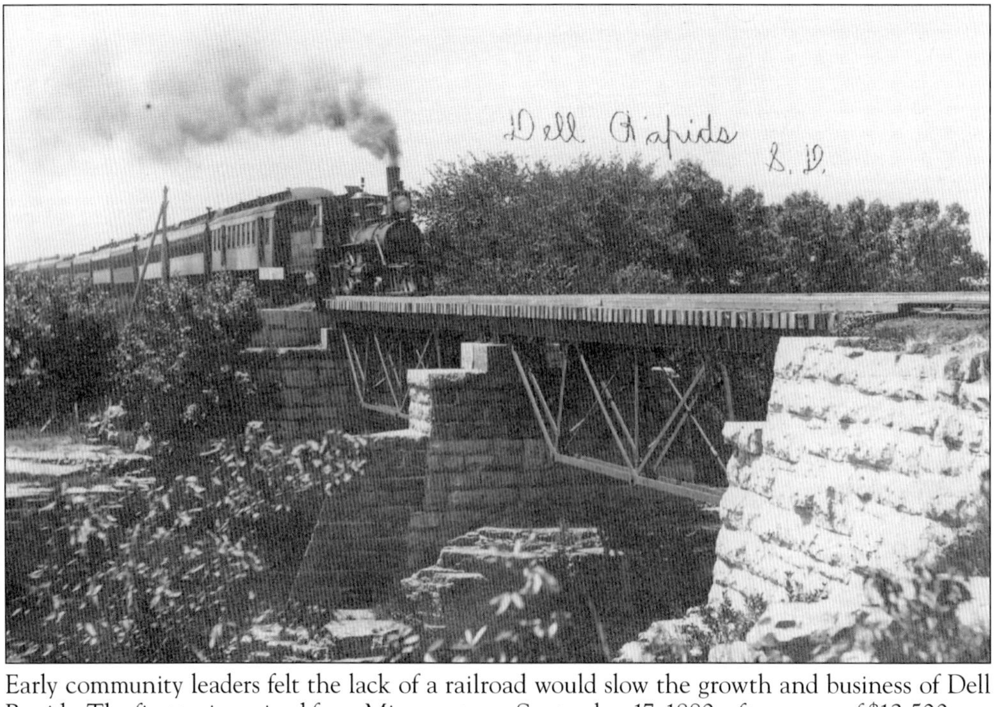

Early community leaders felt the lack of a railroad would slow the growth and business of Dell Rapids. The first train arrived from Minnesota on September 17, 1880, after a sum of $12,500 was raised as an incentive. A great celebration was held in honor of the occasion.

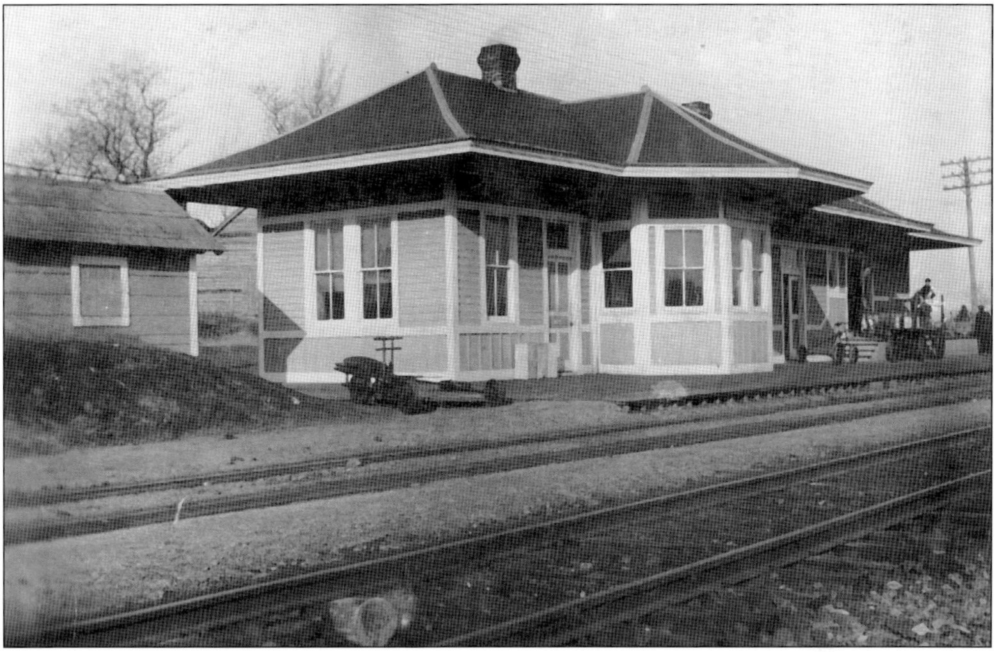

The need for a new depot increased as passenger trains came through Dell Rapids once a day by 1890. The train was given the nickname "The Galloping Goose." In addition to the passenger trains, the station also saw an increase in freight trains. The depot was 76 feet long and 24 feet wide, with 12-foot posts, and was built at a cost of about $4,200.

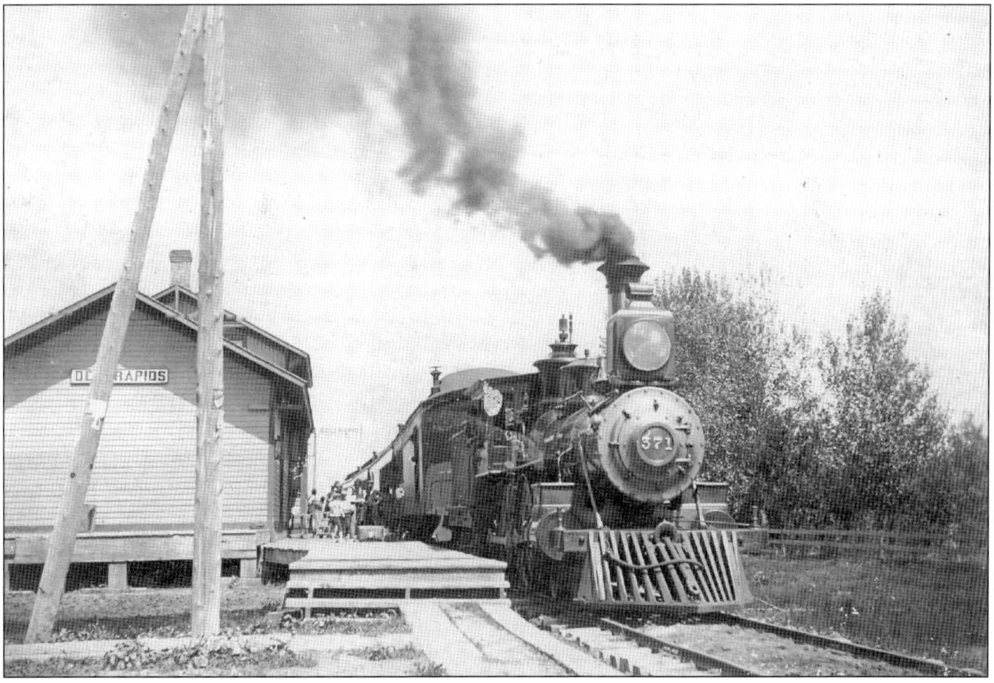

The arrival of the railroad had a major impact on the community's social and economic development. Each time a train came to town, residents would come down to the train station to see the comings and goings of the passengers and to see what new supplies had arrived.

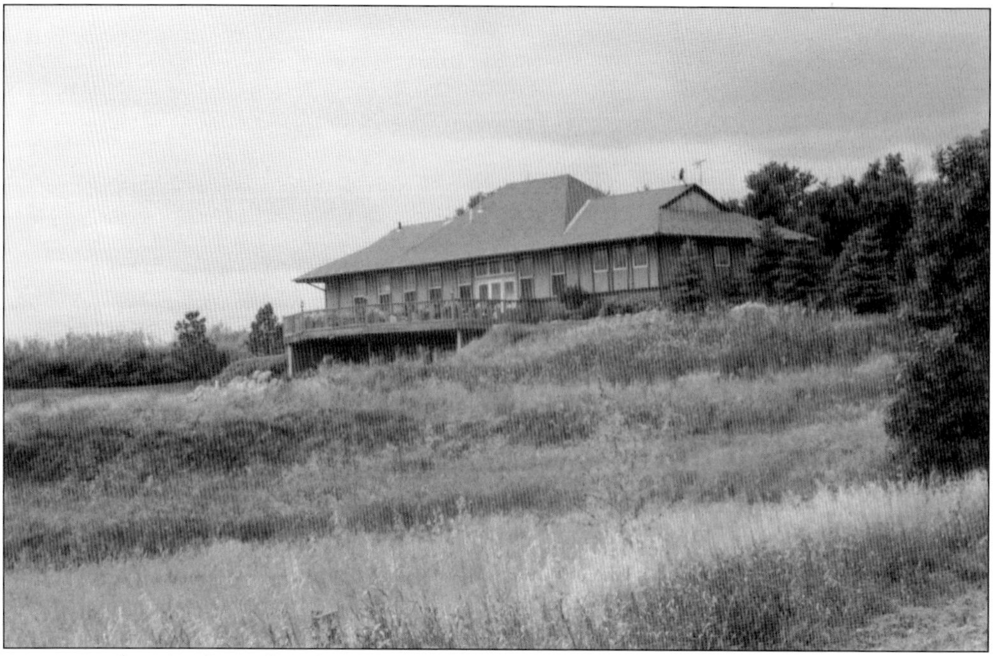

For over a decade, the Milwaukee Railroad depot located at the corner of Orleans Avenue and Third Street sat empty. Built in 1908, the depot saw its last passenger services in 1950, and the building was closed in 1978. In 1991, it was sold to Porter Williams and moved to Rowena, refurbished, and made into a comfortable private residence.

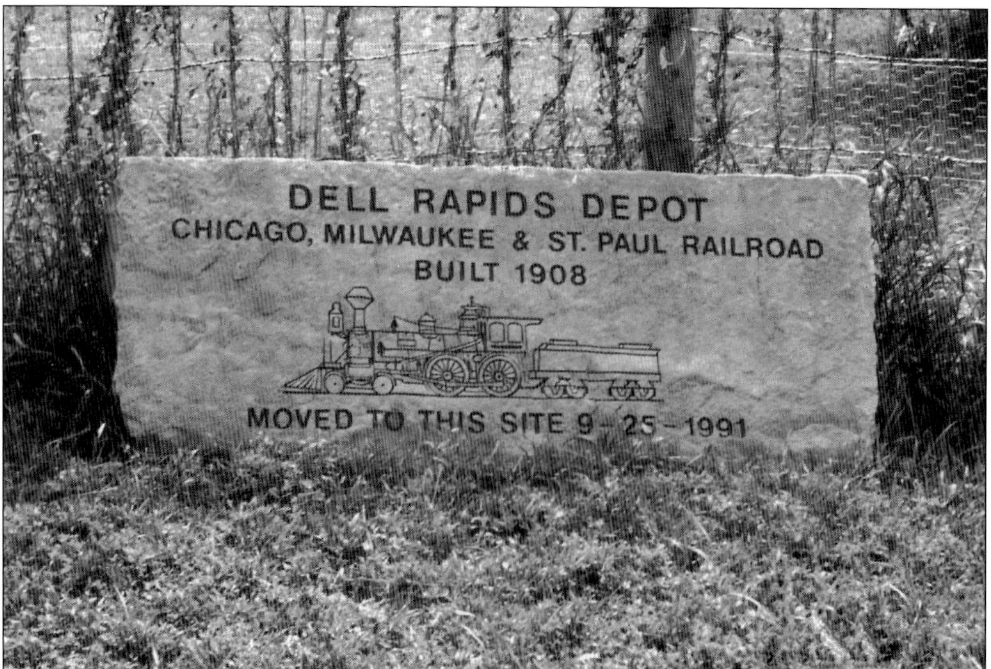

Although the depot structure sat in the same spot from 1908 until the move, it only took two days to uproot it and move it the 30 miles to Rowena. A quarry rock sign at the private residence displays the date of relocation of the railroad depot.

Attracted by the stone industry, stonecutter Ritchie Simpson (center) came to Dell Rapids in 1884 and secured full ownership of the Dell Rapids Granite Company on the east side of town. It became the largest employer in town. Simpson's payroll was a substantial help to the general business conditions of the growing city. Also pictured are his daughters Mary (left) and Nellie Simpson.

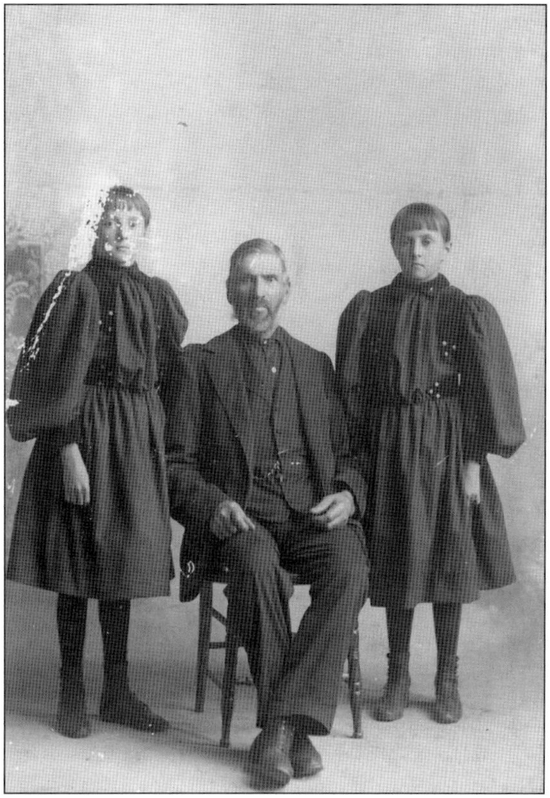

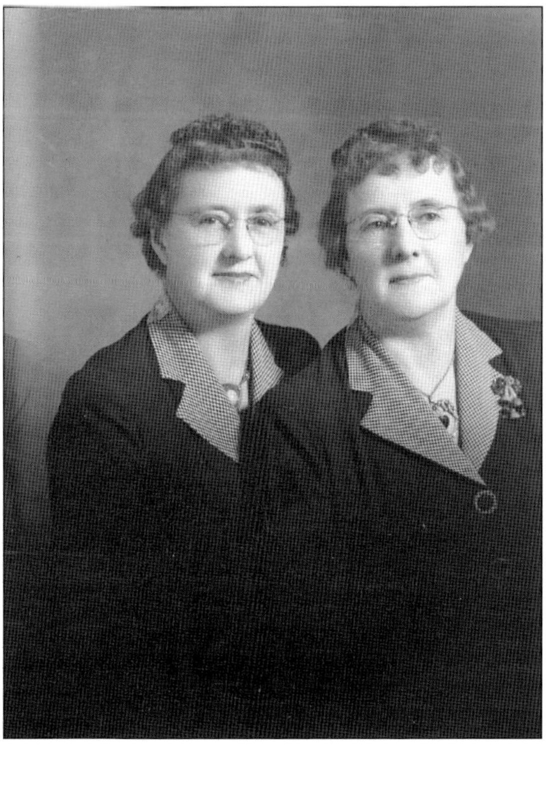

The Simpson Stone Company owned and operated the "East" Quarry from 1885 to 1927. The Simpson twins, Mary (left) and Nellie, were born on November 4, 1885. After the death of their father, Ritchie Simpson, in 1914, they operated the Simpson Stone Company until it was leased to the L.G. Everist Company of Sioux City, Iowa, in 1927.

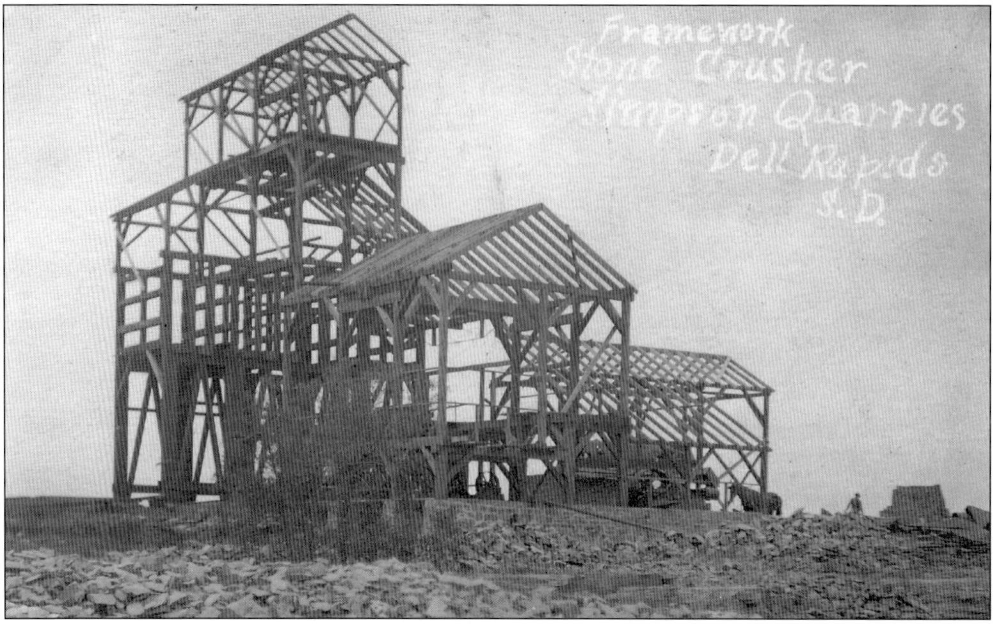

In 1911, stone-crushing machinery was installed to produce crushed rock. Before mechanization and the Depression in the 1930s, much of the hard labor was performed by hand and most of the stone was used for roads and streets. Because of its color and quality, the rock was also used in the building of the Cook County Courthouse, the J.C. Penney Company headquarters building in Dallas, and in many buildings in Minneapolis.

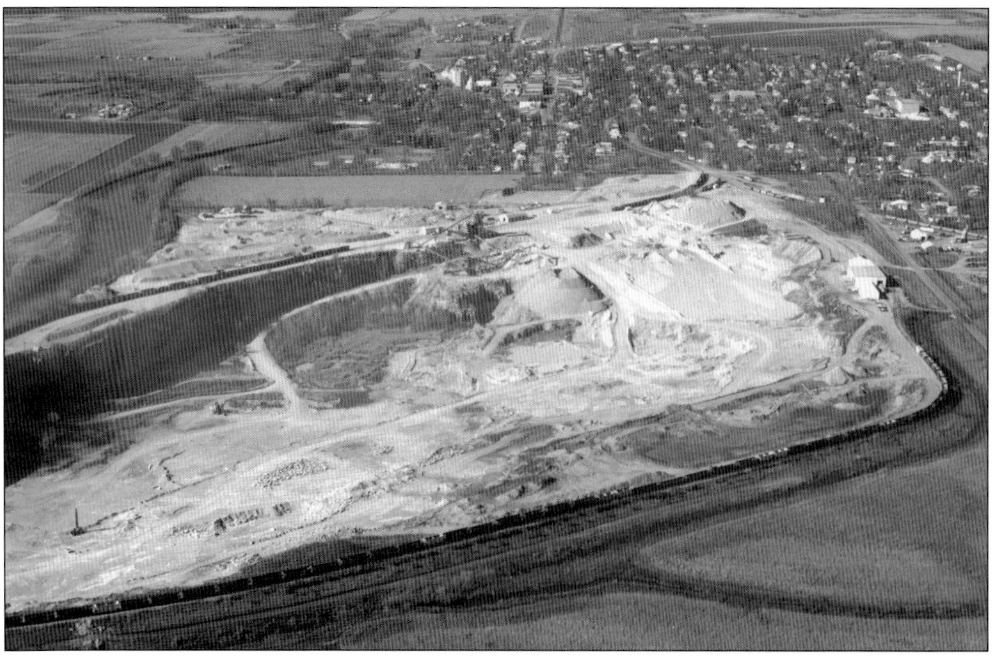

Dell Rapids was once the home of four quarries producing beautiful and durable stones. The first rock was quarried from a site at the west edge of town. In 1969, when 30 billion gallons of water ran into the east quarry pit, the costly quarry prevented devastating flooding in Dell Rapids and portions of Sioux Falls.

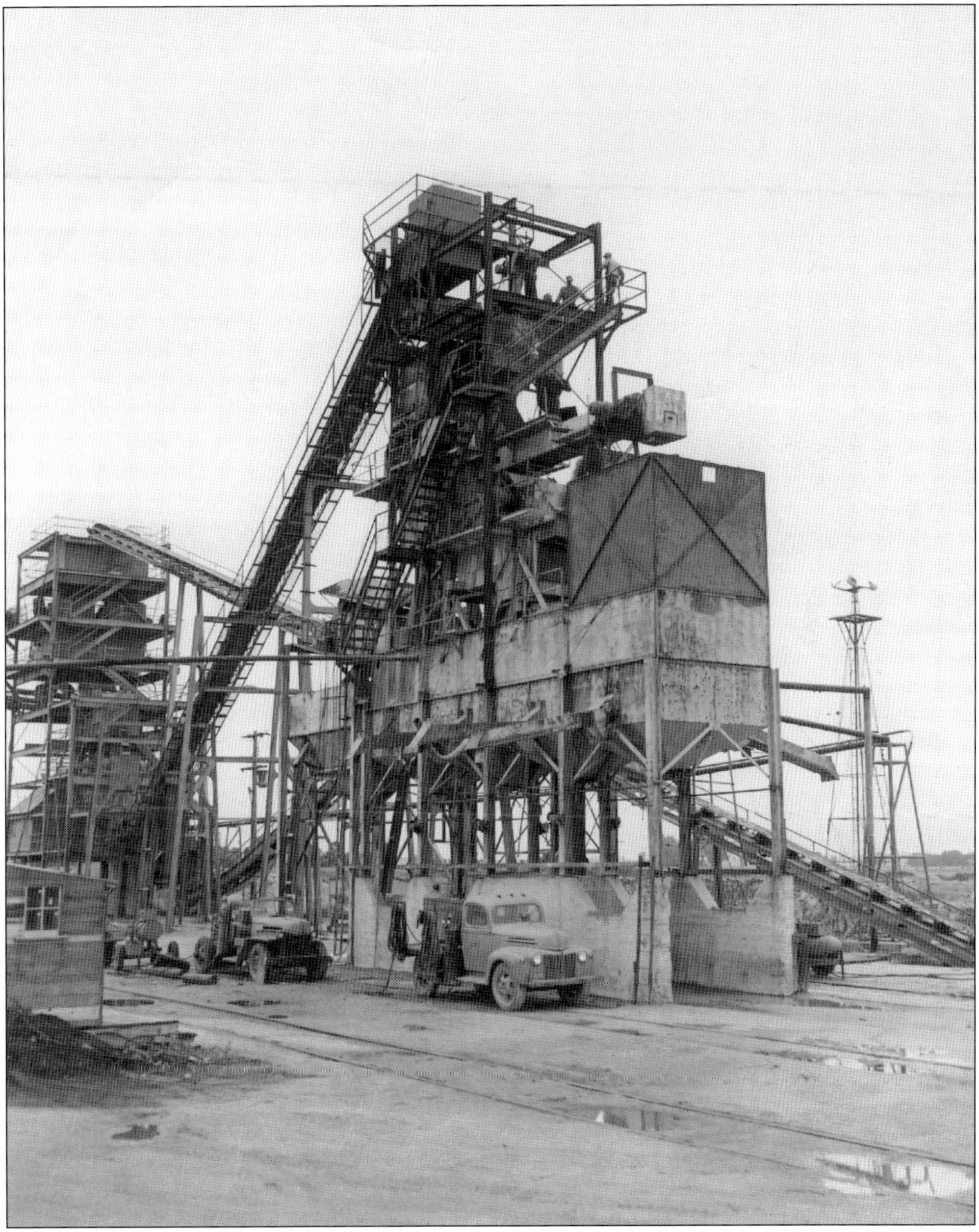

At one time, the quarries employed 500 men. These men worked long, hard hours pounding 25-pound rock hammers against one of the most durable materials in the world. Working at the quarry was not without its hazards. The use of dynamite proved deadly when a piece of flying debris stuck Arthur Stengel, killing him. Dan Welch lost his right hand and eye in a separate blasting accident. Another more common hazard of the time was the quality of air in the pits. In 1929, when Simpson sold to L.G. Everist, 29 men were reported to have quarry TB or quarry consumption. Men with this disease were literally coughing their lungs out, trying to expel years of inhaled rock dust. Conditions were improved with the mechanization of the East Quarry in 1948 and the installation of a dust control system in 1974. Safety has become a priority over the years, nearly eradicating life-threatening conditions and accidents. (Courtesy L.G. Everist Inc.)

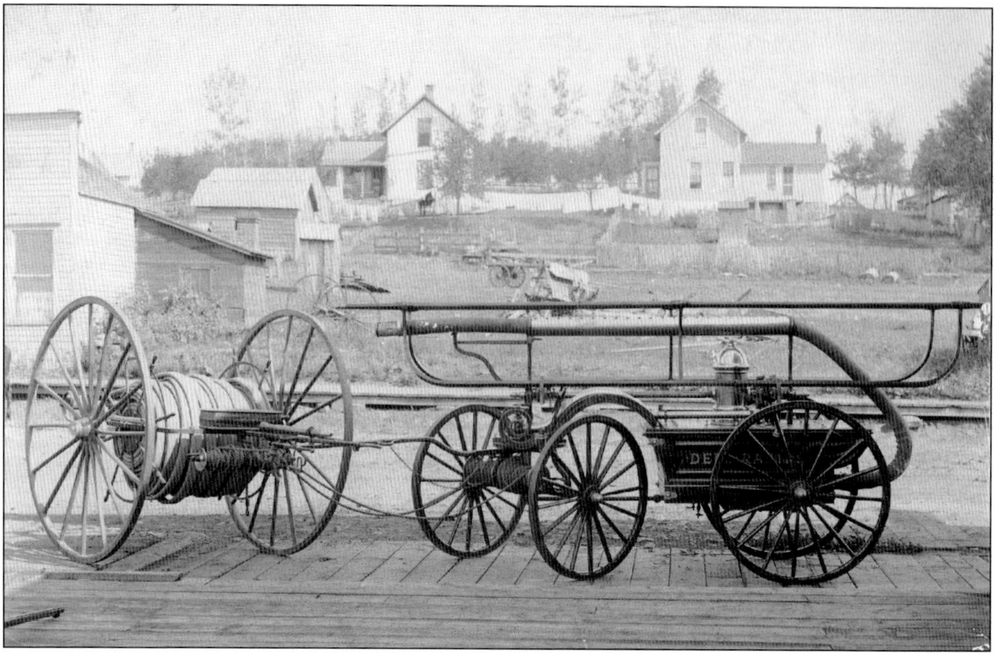

On February 14, 1888, a fire hit the business district and men were called out on three separate occasions to extinguish the blaze. Many buildings were destroyed. The fire was the catalyst for creating an ordinance mandating that all downtown buildings be made of fireproof materials. As a result, many of the commercial buildings in the district were built with stone.

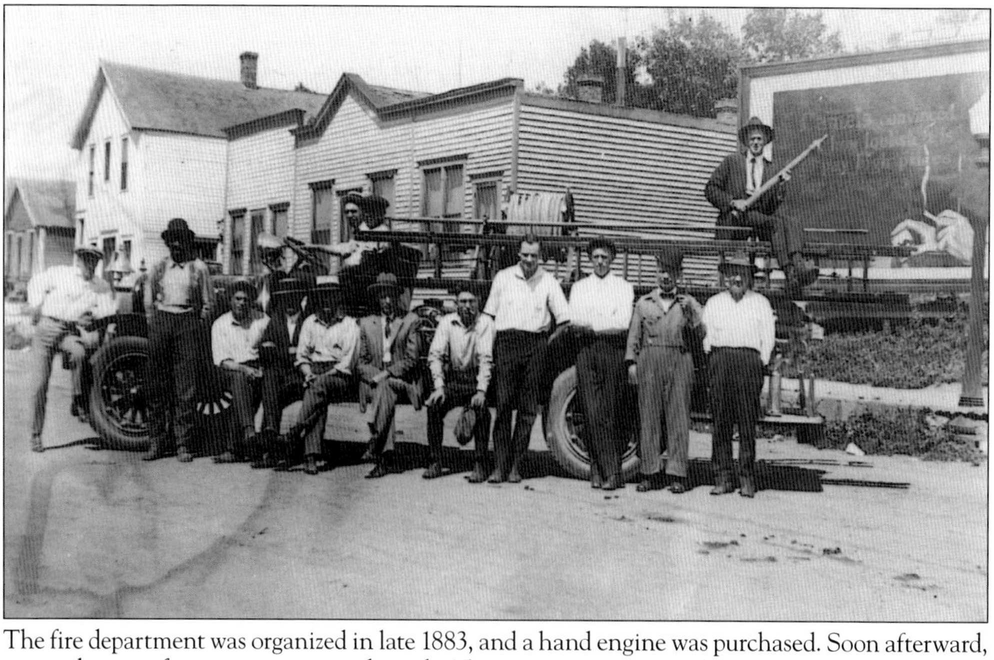

The fire department was organized in late 1883, and a hand engine was purchased. Soon afterward, two volunteer fire companies, each with 15 men, were organized, as were engine and hose companies. The department gradually lost most of its manpower and finally ceased operations in 1887. The town went for seven years without fire protection until 1894, when a new 18-member crew took over.

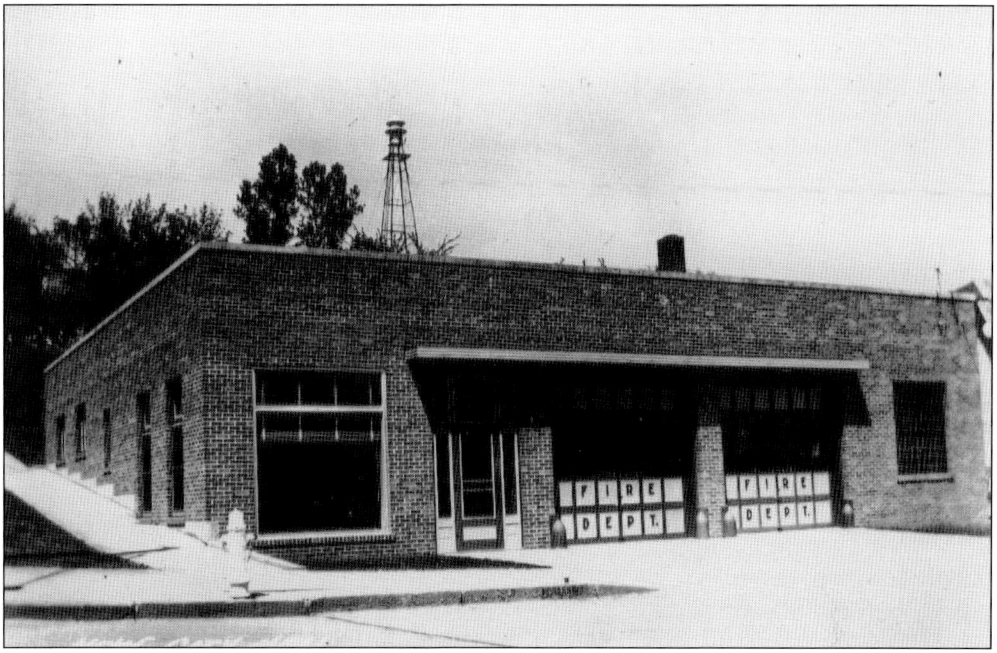

The new city hall and fire station was built in 1948. It is 60 feet by 62 feet, constructed of brick and tile, and divided into several rooms to accommodate the city administrative offices, the auditor's office, council chambers, and the city jail, on the east side. A large vault has been built for the protection of all city records.

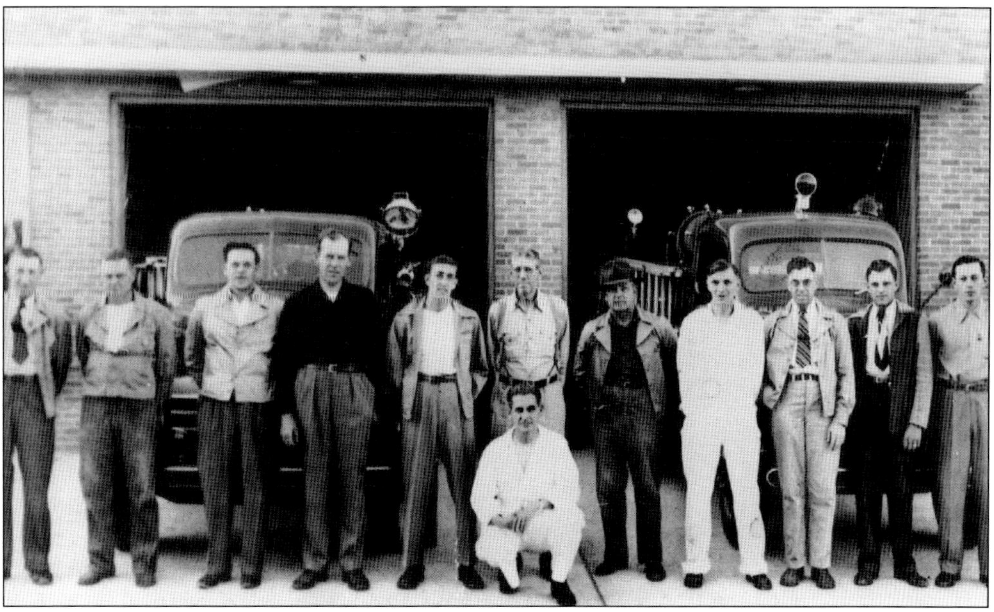

The 1948 Dell Rapids Fire Department includes, from left to right, Frank Schuster, John Fairhurst, Cecil Graves, Leonard Hegg, Jack Munk, Adolph Harders, Guy Munk, John Larson, Claude Munk, Melvin Munk, Howard Merry, and Webster Drummond (kneeling). The fire department now averages approximately 225 calls a year and is the oldest established volunteer fire department in rural Minnehaha County.

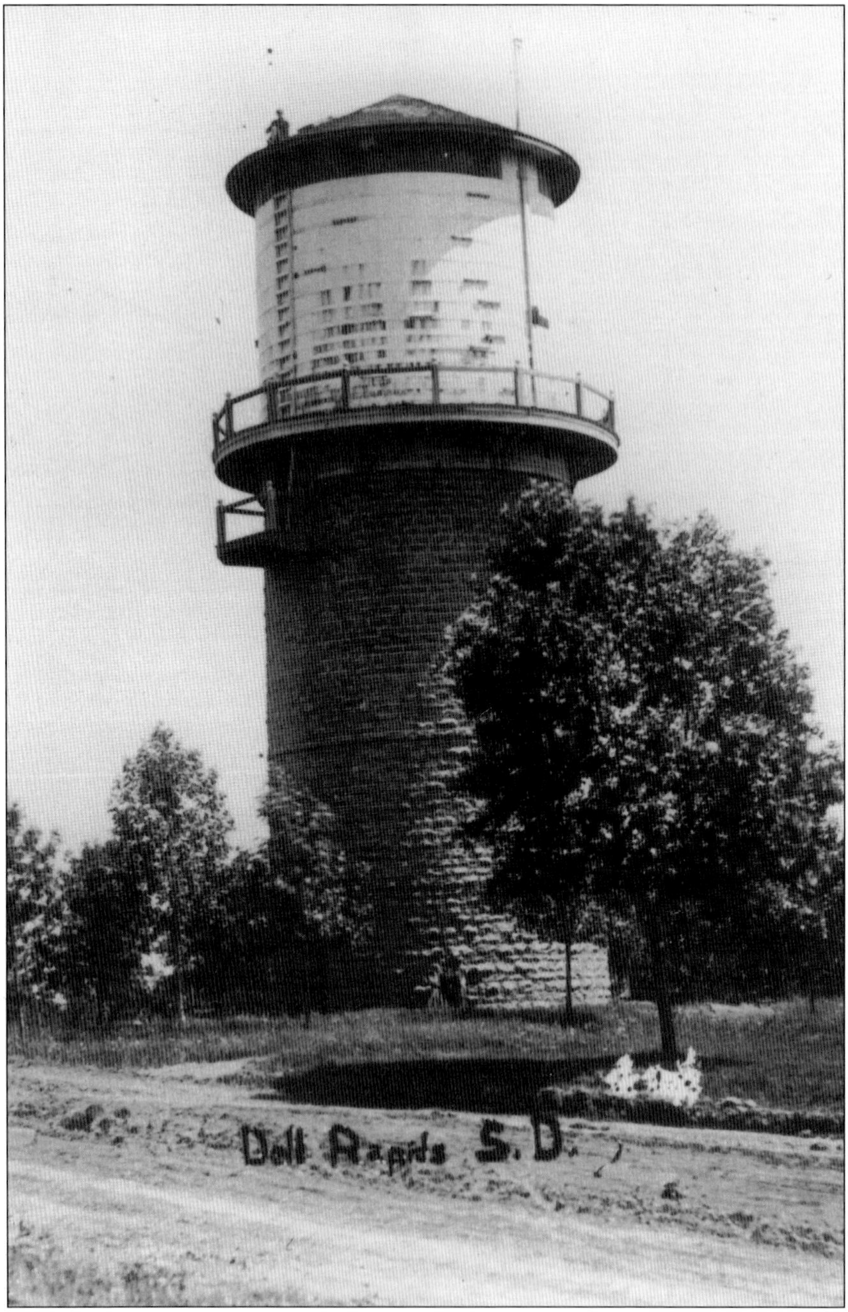

The old Dell Rapids quarried-rock water tower, built in 1894 and engineered and designed by C.W. Hubbard and S.B. Howe, is one of three of its type in the United States. The tower's base is 30 feet in diameter, and the structure is 44 feet high. The tank at the top is made of redwood horizontal staves. Only the stone base remains, at Tenth Street and Orleans Avenue in Dell Rapids. The water tower was saved with funding provided by Ralph Wilson, the city council, and the Dell Rapids Historic Society, and was listed in the National Register of Historic Places on February 23, 1984. A commemorative bronze plaque was put in place at the water tower by local Eagle Scout Joseph Holles.

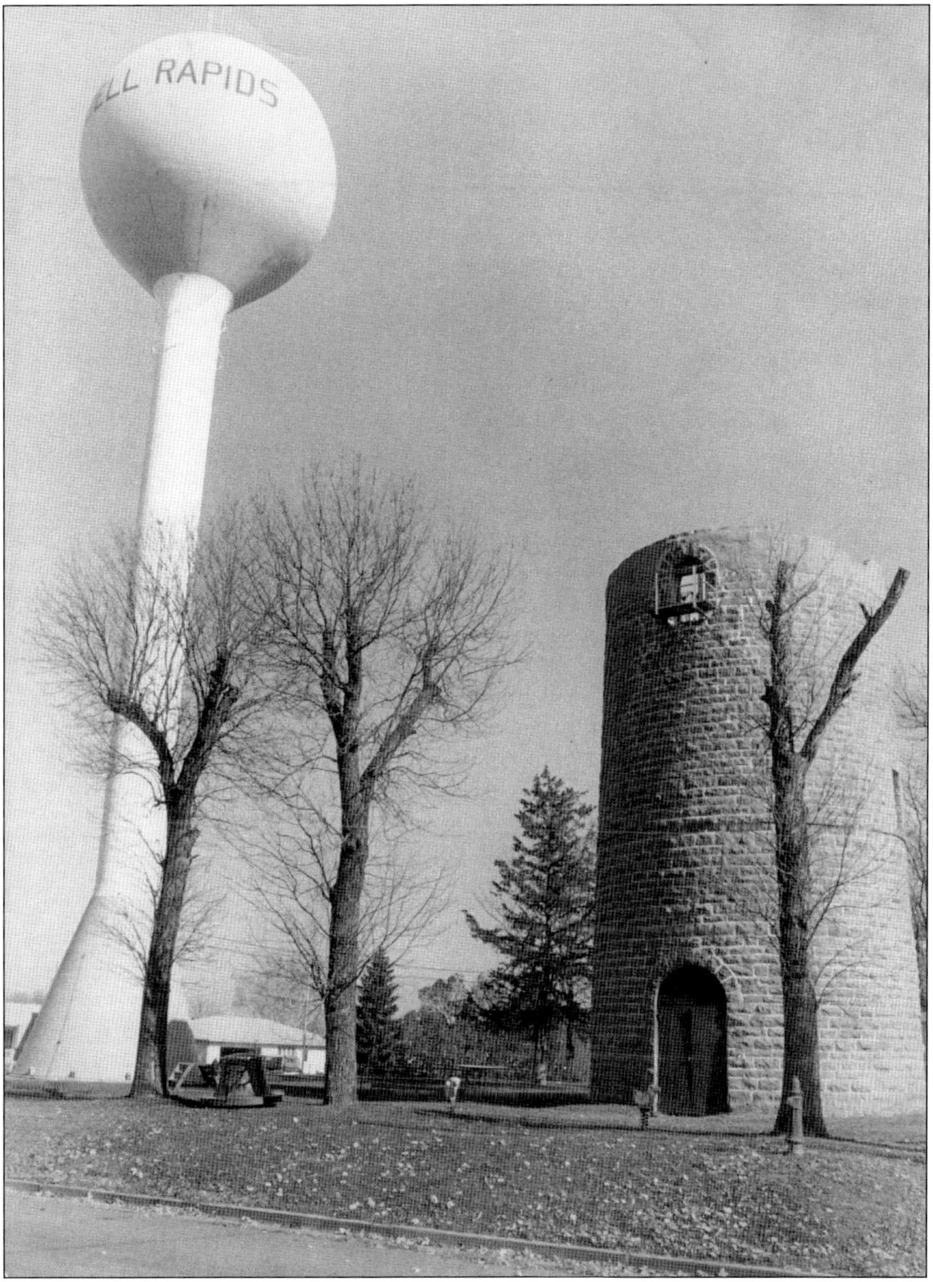

The newly created waterworks system in 1894 had about three miles of mains and 25 fire hydrants, providing an excellent fire protection system. Simon Peters was the first to procure a lawn sprinkler and hose; by 1895, many in town had followed suit. In 1894, the capacity of the water plant was far in excess of the city's demand, with a 2,500-barrel capacity. Water was originally obtained from a spring near the Sioux River and a large well, or reservoir, was dug into solid rock, from which the water was pumped. Currently, the city operates two elevated water towers as part of a water distribution system. The 150,000-gallon tower built in 1962 is located next to the original water tower on Tenth Street. In 2003, an additional tank with a 500,000-gallon capacity was built on the north end of town.

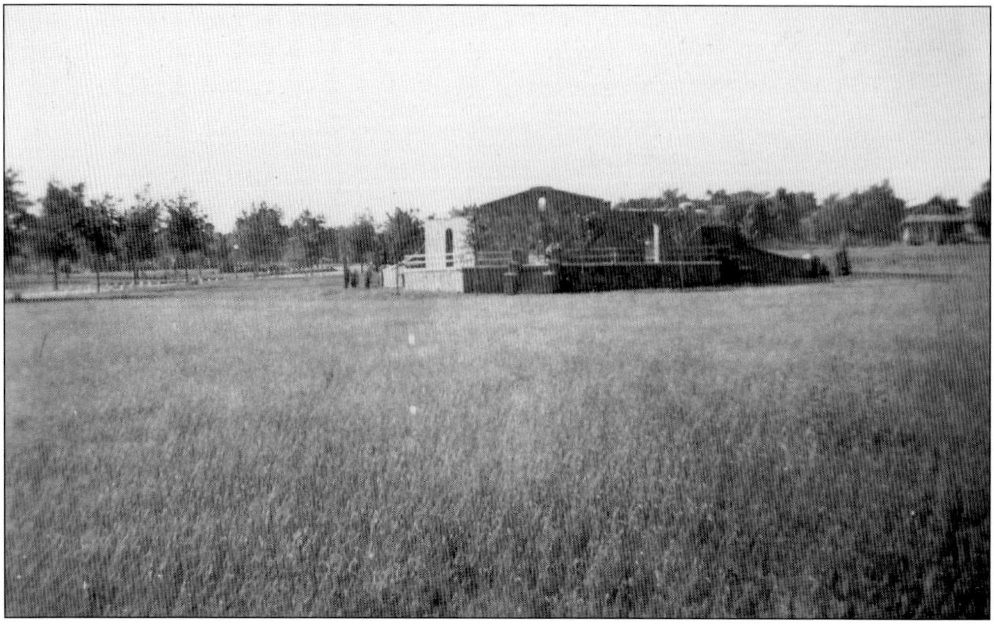

The historic amphitheater was constructed in the Dell Rapids City Park in 1936 as a project of the Works Progress Administration (WPA). Workers included local stonecutters Joe Putnam and Ed Leum. In 2001, the amphitheater was placed on Preserve South Dakota's "Places in Peril" list and is now listed in the National Register of Historic Places. The structure continues to be a popular focal point for many summertime activities.

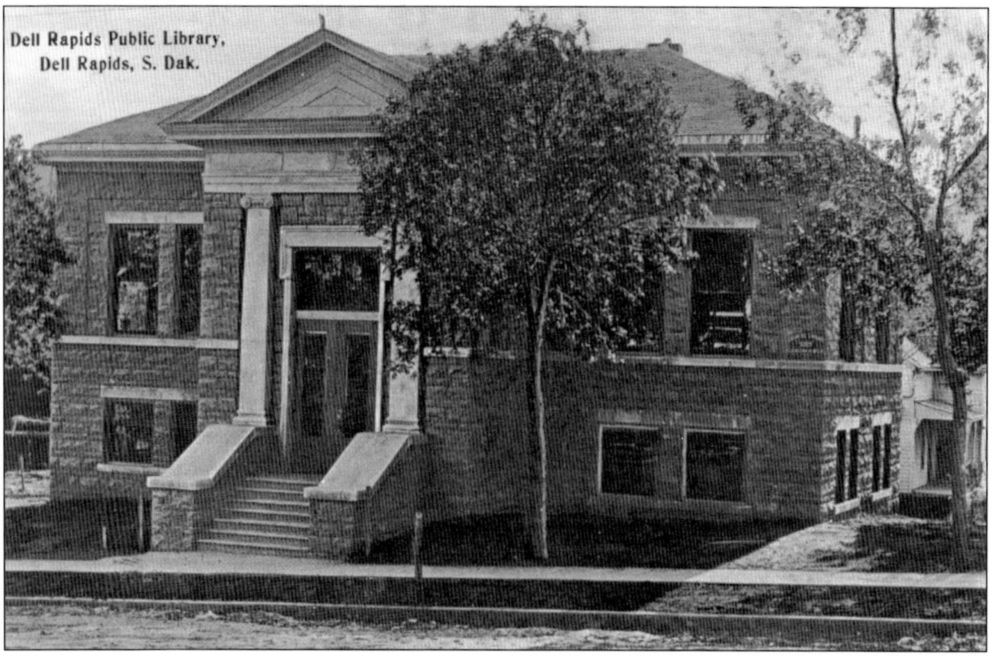

The Dell Rapids Public Library, a Carnegie library, was the culmination of a 10-year effort by the leading women in Dell Rapids to have a modern library constructed in town. Industrialist Andrew Carnegie offered $6,000 toward the building if the city would pledge $500 annually for operating expenses. The library was dedicated on March 16, 1910.

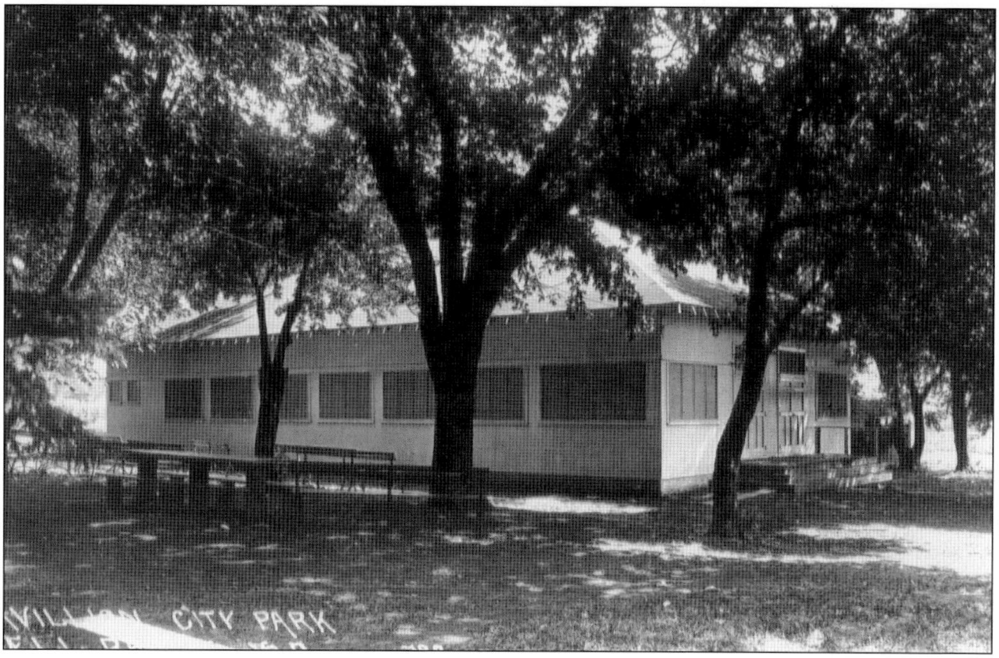

The first pavilion was built in 1917. In 1947, the dance hall burned to the ground, and a new one was constructed. Dances, weddings, and roller-skating made it a hotspot for hosting well-known artists such as Lawrence Welk. Eventually, the building closed and came to house a factory for plastic bathtubs in the 1970s before catching fire in 1979. In 2010, it was inducted into the South Dakota Rock and Roll Hall of Fame.

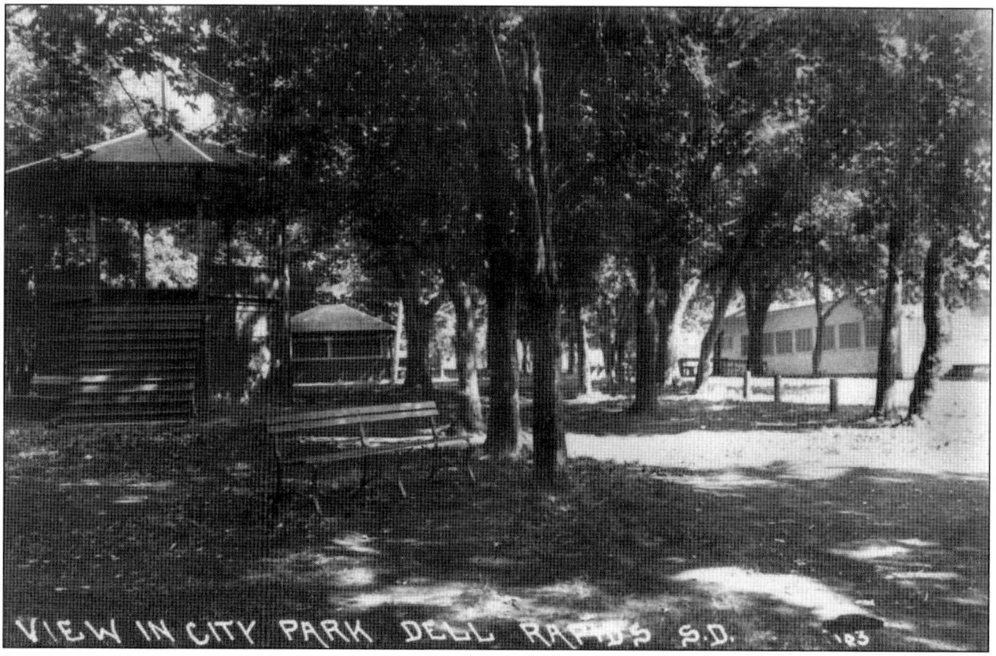

In 1913, the city purchased 20 acres of land to be designated for the city park. The setting near the Big Sioux River made the site attractive and the perfect location for city events. Picnic grounds, a bathing beach, and the bathhouse were among the first areas to be built.

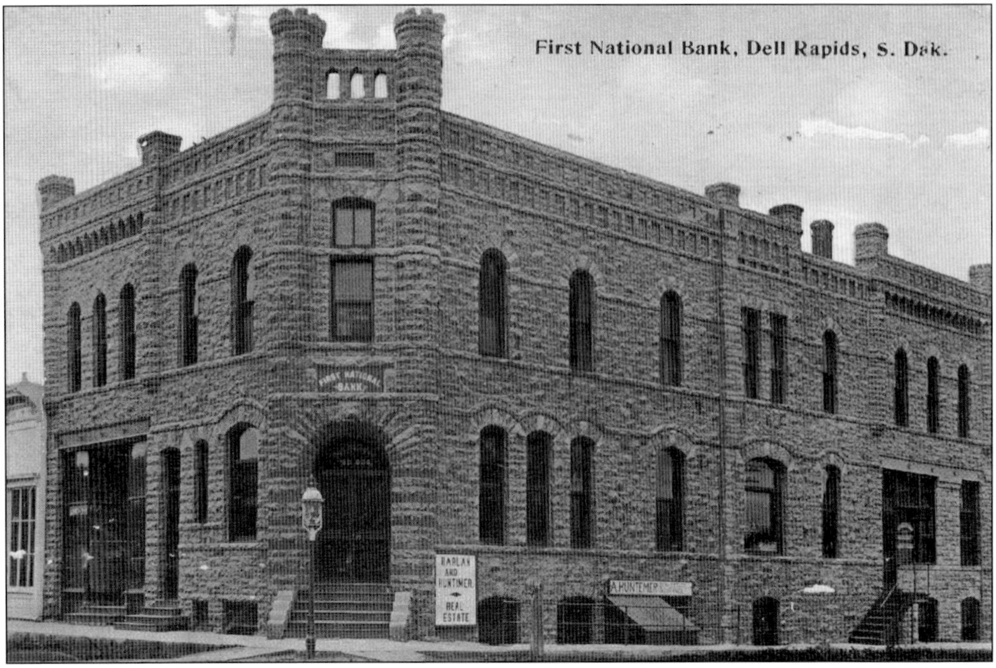

The 1930s were a time of well-known bank robberies and gangsters, such as Al Capone, Bonnie and Clyde, and John Dillinger. Although crime was not a common problem locally, Dell Rapids was not immune from criminal activity. The most infamous and talked about was the First National Bank robbery on November 7, 1934.

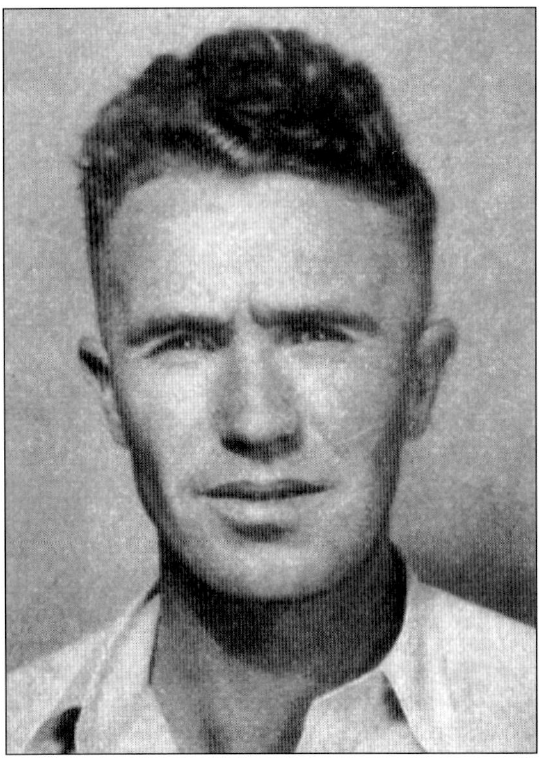

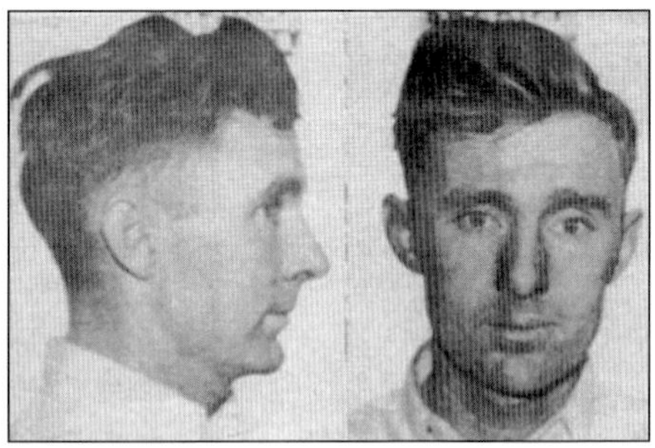

Fugitives Maurice Denning (above) and Thomas Limerick (left) robbed First National Bank in 1934. Limerick was captured in 1935 and was killed on May 23, 1938, in an attempt to escape from Alcatraz prison. After the Dillinger gang had been eliminated, Denning was named the FBI's Public Enemy No. 1, but he was never captured and is considered one of the most successful bank robbers in history.

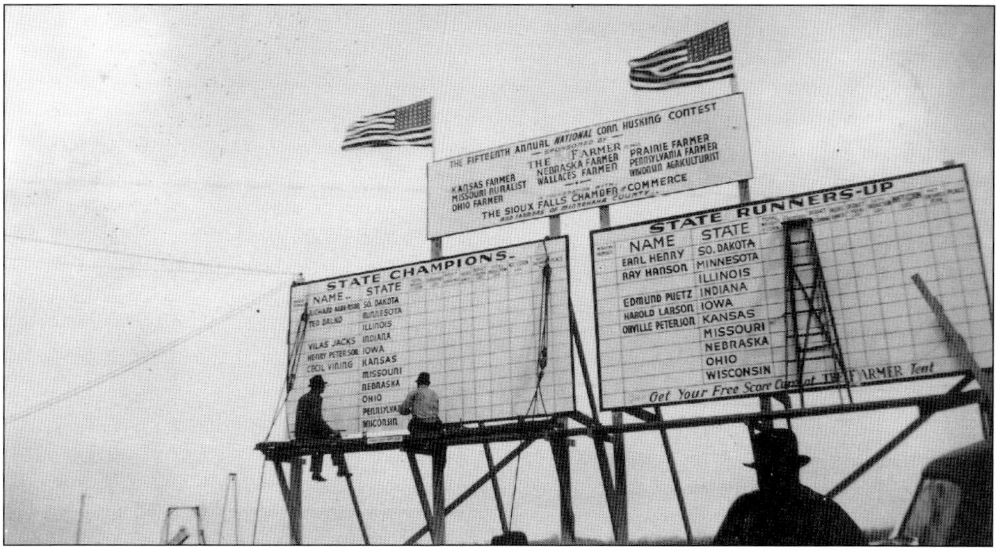

In 1938, the National Corn Husking Contest was held at the Neil Jensen farm one mile north and one mile east of Dell Rapids. Admission and parking were free, and the event attracted nearly 125,000 people to the area. Local and county officers, state patrol, and the National Guard were called upon to help with traffic. There was a long line of tents called "Tent City" erected on the 80 acres adjoining the contest field. Food and beverages were available at 80 concession stands, and the event itself lasted 80 minutes. Years later, more than 250 people attended a dedication ceremony for the historical marker located on the Jensen Farm, many of them wearing ribbons stating "I Was There."

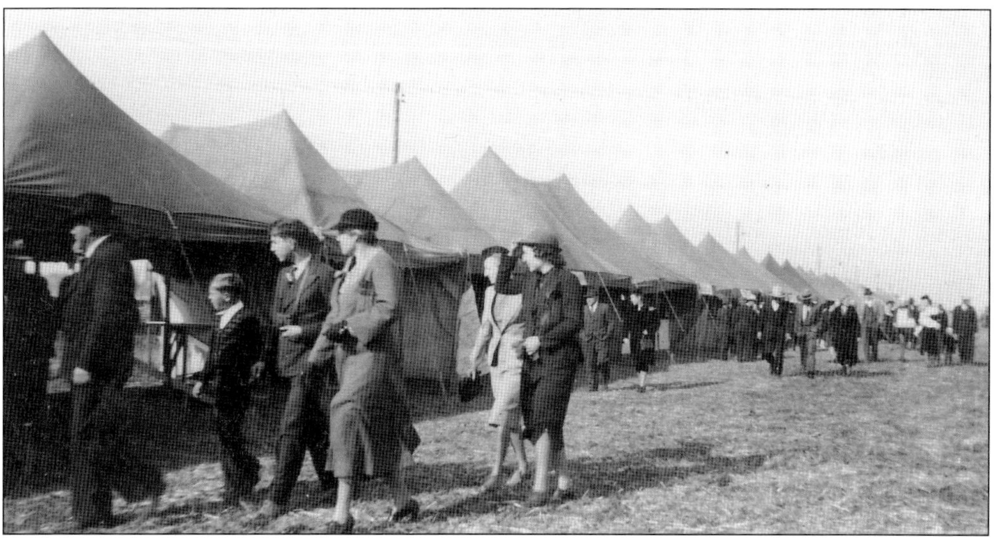

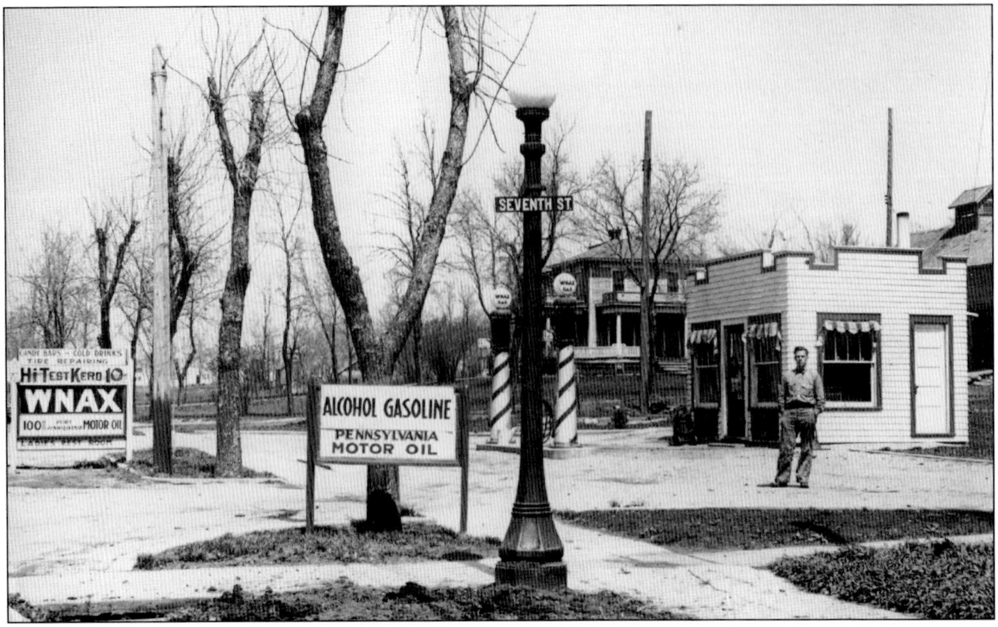

In one of the most destructive fires in Dell Rapids history, the Hollis Silkensen service station, on Highway 77 at the corner of Seventh Street, was completely burned on Thursday, April 27, 1944. Silkensen and Donald Anderson were servicing Dr. L.L. Dunn's car in the driveway when the fire broke out. One of the men entered the station for something, and, as he entered, there appeared to be a flash at the rear of the large tank truck that was in the building at the time. In an instant, the blaze spread to all parts of the interior. The fire department had been summoned, but the blaze had gained such headway it was impossible to save the building or contents. Above, Theron Graves, an employee of Silkensen's, stands in front of the station as it looked before the fire.

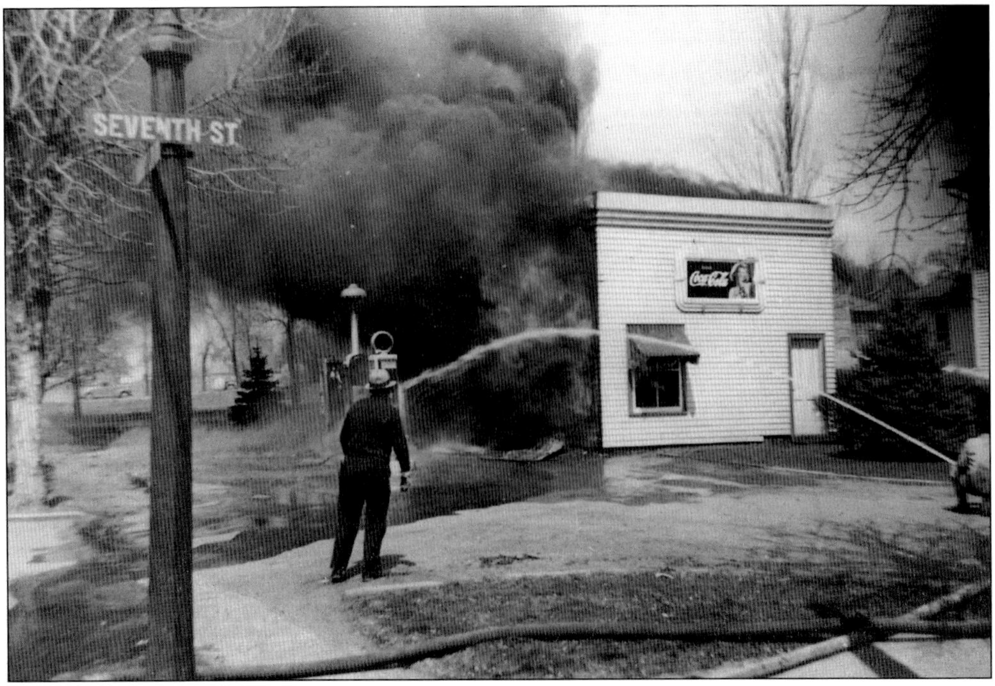

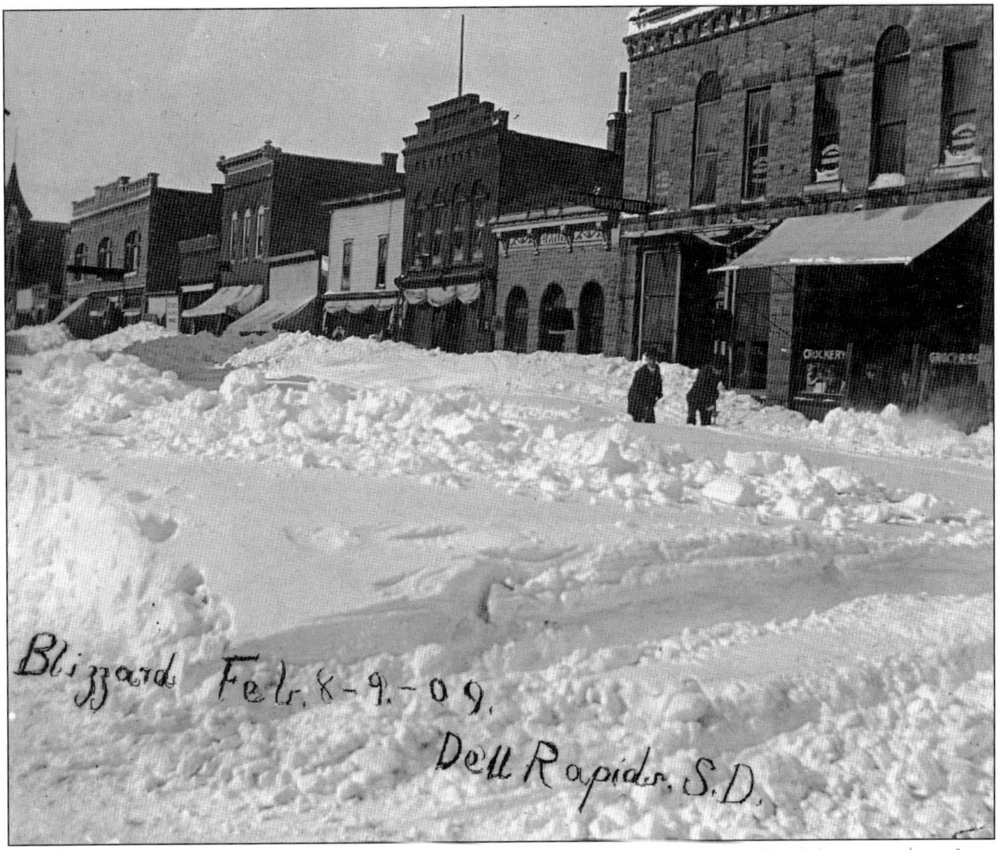

Workers did not have equipment comparable to present-day tractor-powered bulldozers and graders; horses and ox-teams were hitched onto small scrapers and plows. The two men above use simple shovels to clear the snow. Many were unable to drive a team into town, making foot traffic the only way to commute, so the sidewalks were cleared of snow before the streets.

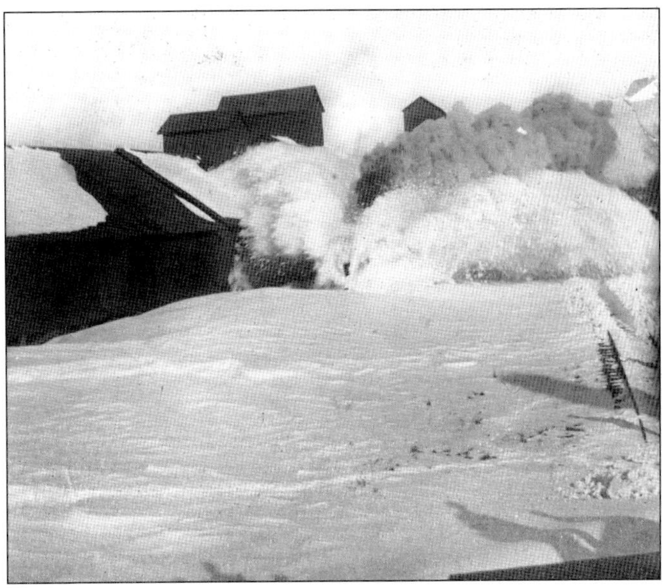

The snowstorm of 1909 affected many individuals, families, and businesses in the Dell Rapids area. The sheer force and power of a locomotive is shown as it clears the snow from the railroad tracks for continued normal operations.

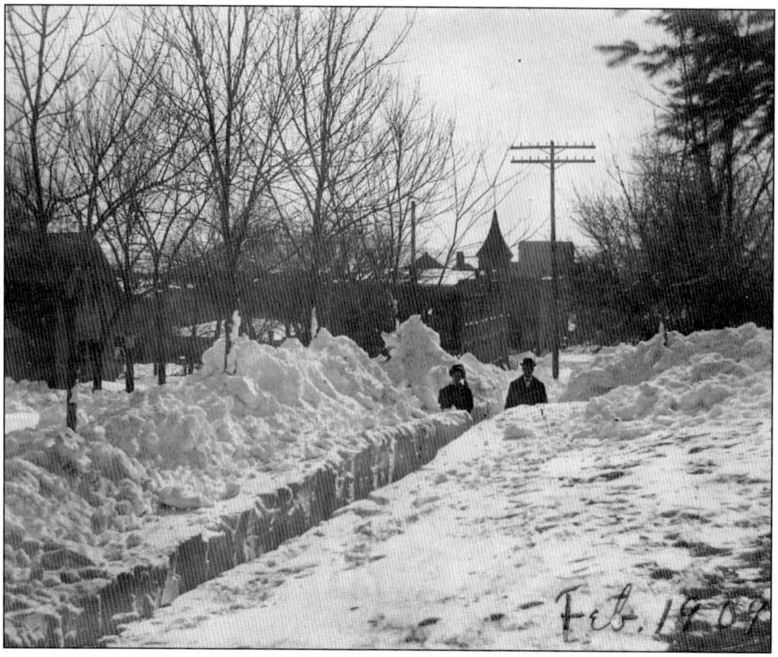

The hefty amount of snowfall in the February 8–9, 1909, blizzard took many days to clean up. This scene one block north of Main Street shows the depth and limitlessness of the snowdrifts. Narrow paths were carved into the huge drifts, making passages limited but accessible to walkers.

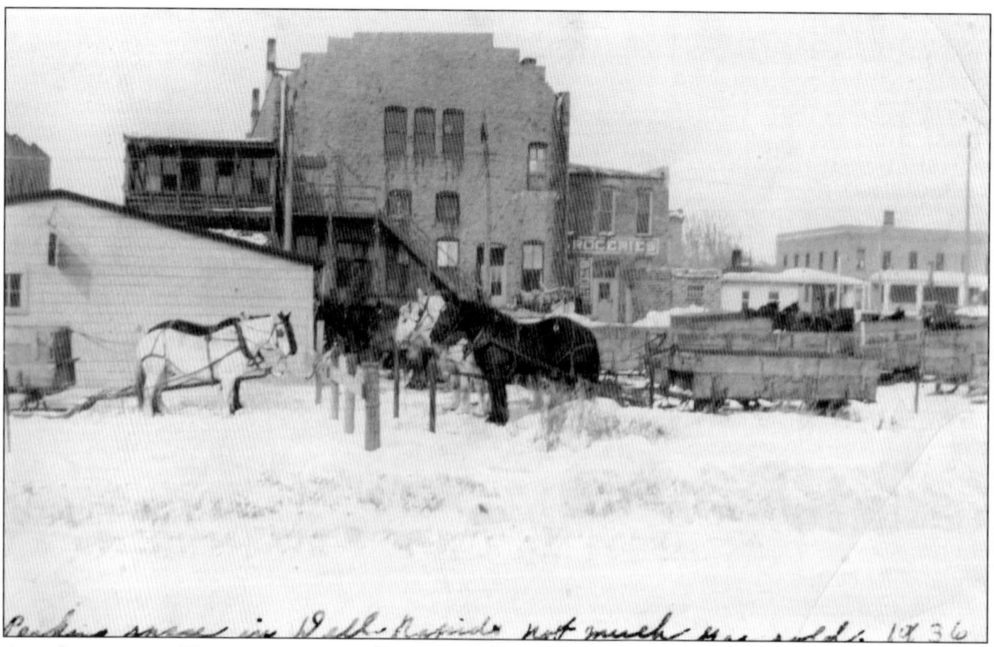

Another memorable snow event took place in the winter of 1935–1936. Most of the rural roads were blocked by large, hard snowdrifts for weeks at a time. Larry Nelson was a freshman at the high school at the time and remembers his father taking him to town in a bobsled pulled by a team of horses.

Two

Notable Residents

There has never been a shortage of memorable citizens in Dell Rapids. To this day, many descendants of pioneers live in the town built on the foundation of families. From Peter Morse's interest in the natural advantages of a town on the Big Sioux to the early settlers and business owners, the city has thrived through the decades because of its talented, dedicated residents. Among the most noted citizens were the Johnsons, who kept a hardware business in the family for more than four decades; Civil War veteran Robert Sloan Alexander, who became a prominent figurehead in the town's leadership; the O'Learys, who brought entertainment to the city with their redesign of the Grand as a movie theater; and the Krauses, who helped found the local law firm, which still operates to this day as the longest continuously running business in the town's history. Thanks to familial ties that stood the test of time and passing businesses down through generations, Dell Rapids has maintained a healthy berth throughout its history as a productive midsize town in the state of South Dakota.

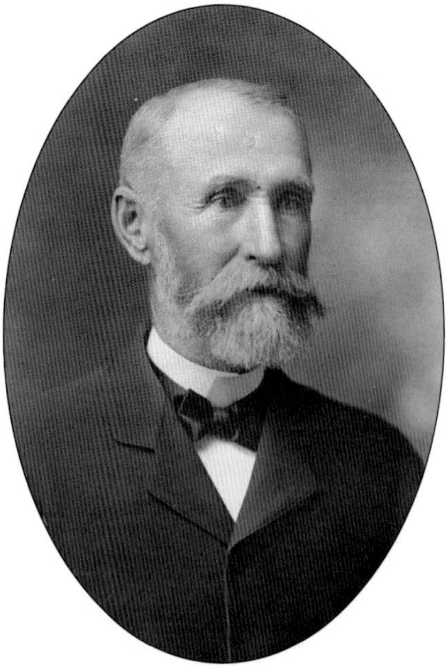

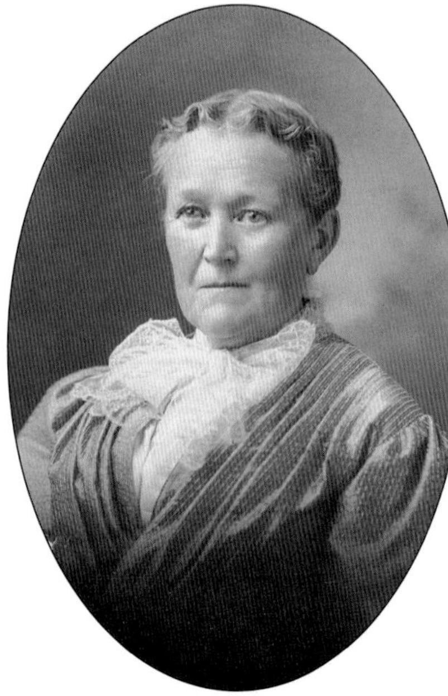

In June 1871, Peter Morse, then a resident of Osage, Iowa, arrived in the Dell Rapids area while on an exploring expedition in the Sioux Valley. Although he was not the first to discover the dells, he was the first to consider the natural advantages they offered for a future town. It was not long afterward that his wife, Phoebe Hinman Morse, and family followed, making Dell Rapids their home.

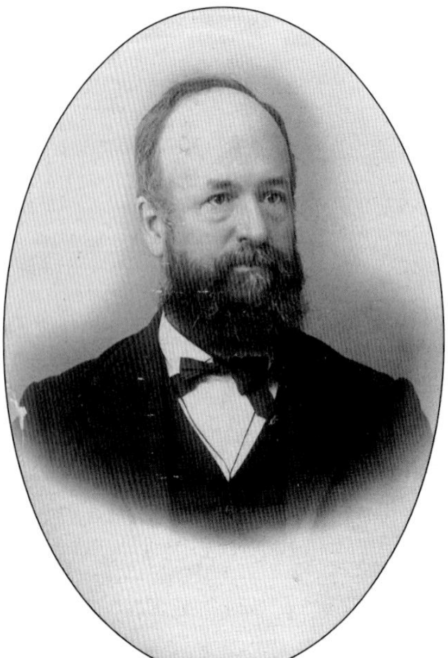

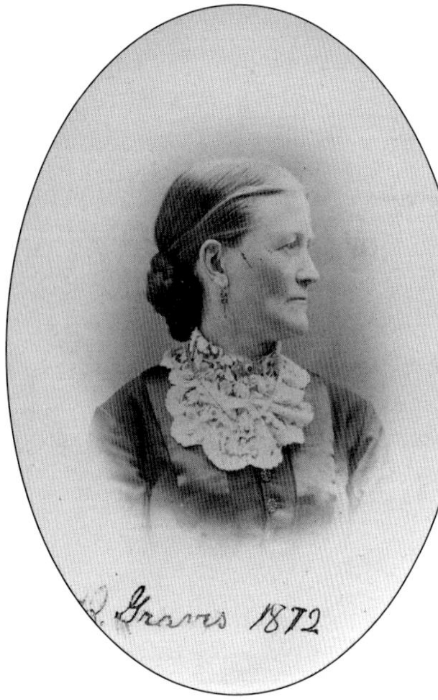

Byron and Lydia Graves built the first store in town near the mill site in 1872. Landowners near the mill wanted the business district to be located nearby, and a compromise was made. Due to his limited supply of merchandise and the business district relocation, Graves's store did not succeed. He continued to help establish the town by sitting on multiple committees and living out his life here.

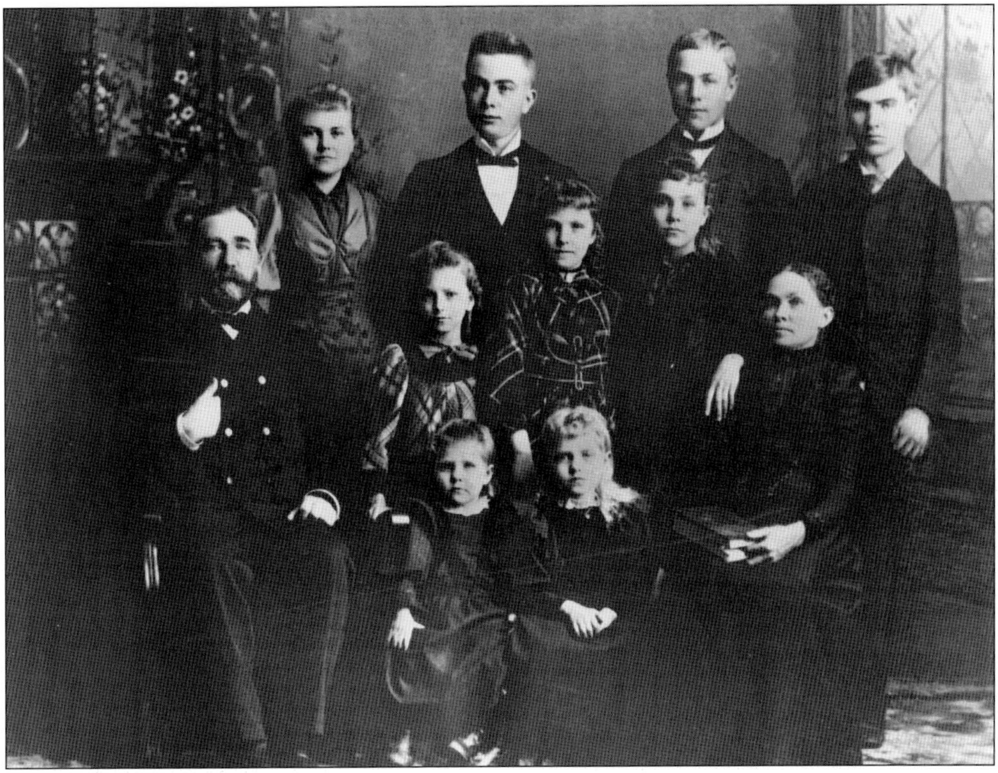

In 1879, Carl Johnson made his first trip to Dell Rapids and decided this was where he wanted to relocate. In May 1880, the Johnson family moved to Dell Rapids and ran a hardware business for 44 years. This large family photograph includes, from left to right, (first row) Louise and Judith; (second row) Carl John, Lillie, Edna, Caroline, and Margit; (third row) Inga, Christian, Martin, and Edward.

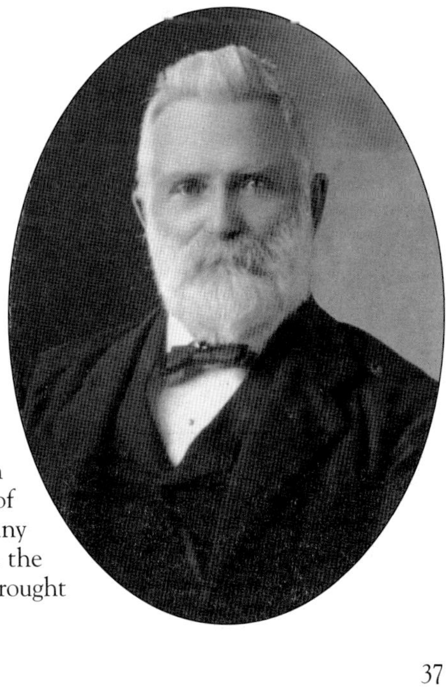

Robert Sloan Alexander, born in 1824 in Pennsylvania, gradually moved across the states until he reached Dakota Territory in 1871, living about two miles south of town. A Civil War veteran, he was a member of the Dahlgren Post in Dell Rapids. He also sat on many boards of service, including the Masonic lodge and the township board, and was part of the committee that brought the railroad to town in 1880.

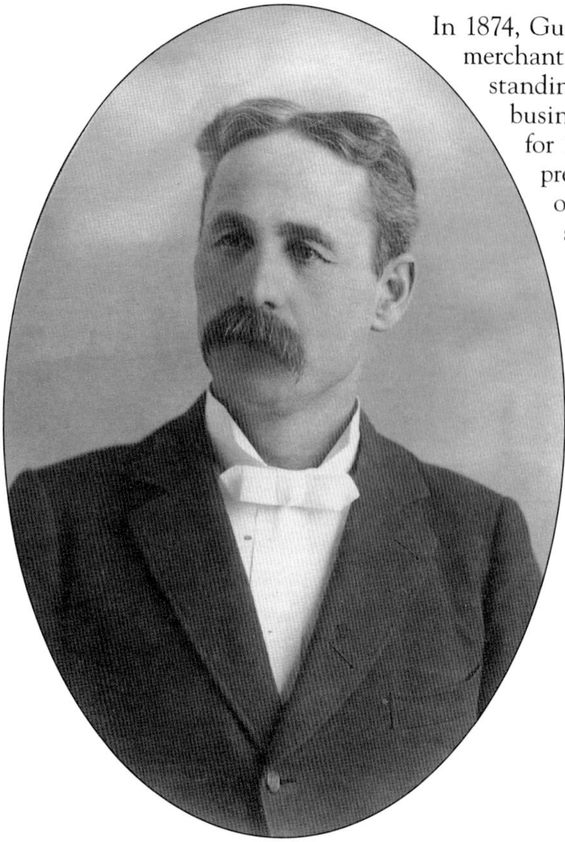

In 1874, Gustav A. Uline became the first general merchant in Dell Rapids. There were two buildings standing where the city is now. He started his business with $1,000 in goods and kept on for 17 years. In 1881, he was elected village president. In 1892, he organized and presided over the Dell Rapids State Bank. Uline is still considered one of the foremost citizens of South Dakota.

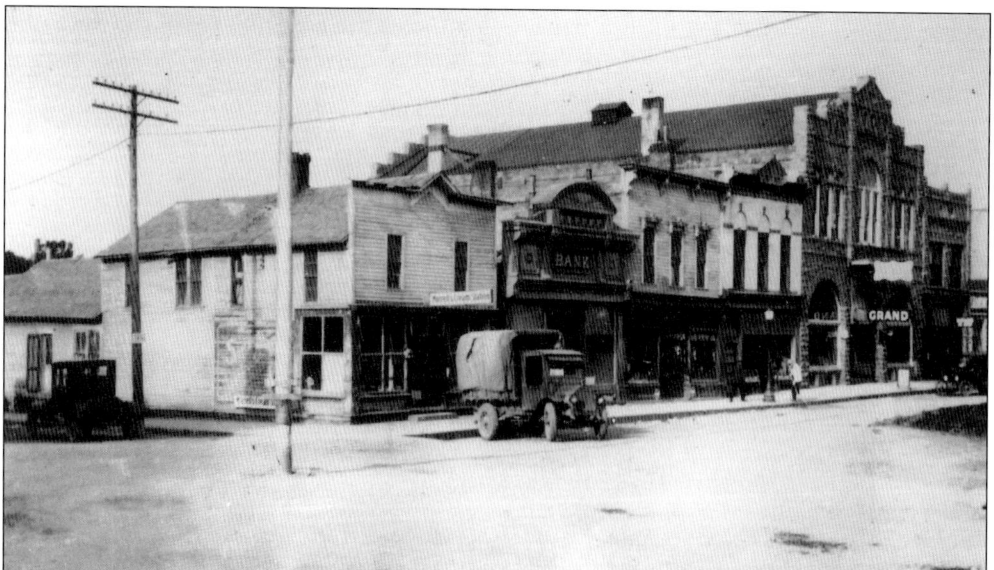

Many of the Main Street buildings have stood the test of time and remain in good standing, although a few buildings have been lost due to fire and prohibitive costs. These three buildings were located on the corner of Fourth Street and Orleans Avenue. Photographs like this one show the last remnants of these buildings and are the only proof of their existence.

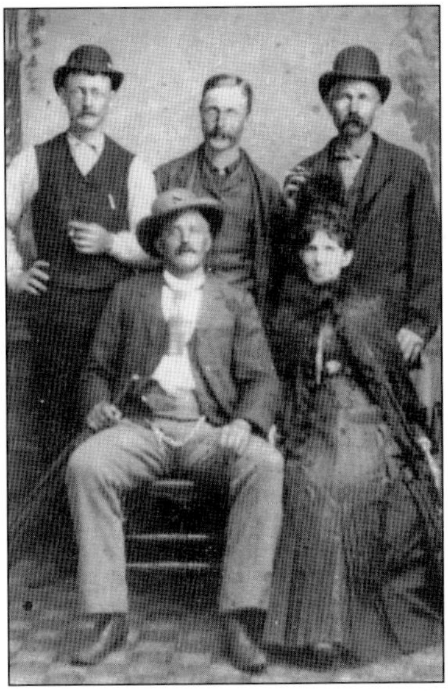

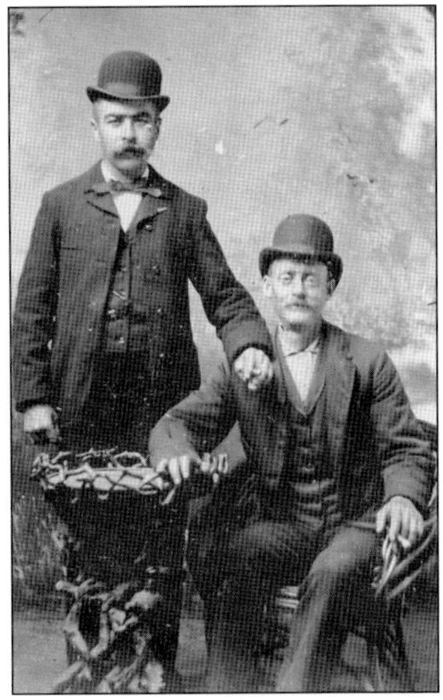

In 1912, John, Edward, and Patrick O'Leary purchased the Grand Opera House. In 1915, a motion picture machine was installed, changing the playhouse into a movie theater. The three brothers ran the opera house for several years before selling it to John Underwood. Pictured at left are (seated) Michael and Margaret O'Leary and (standing, from left to right) John, Edward, and Patrick. At right are Patrick (left) and John. (Both, courtesy Rose Stone Inn.)

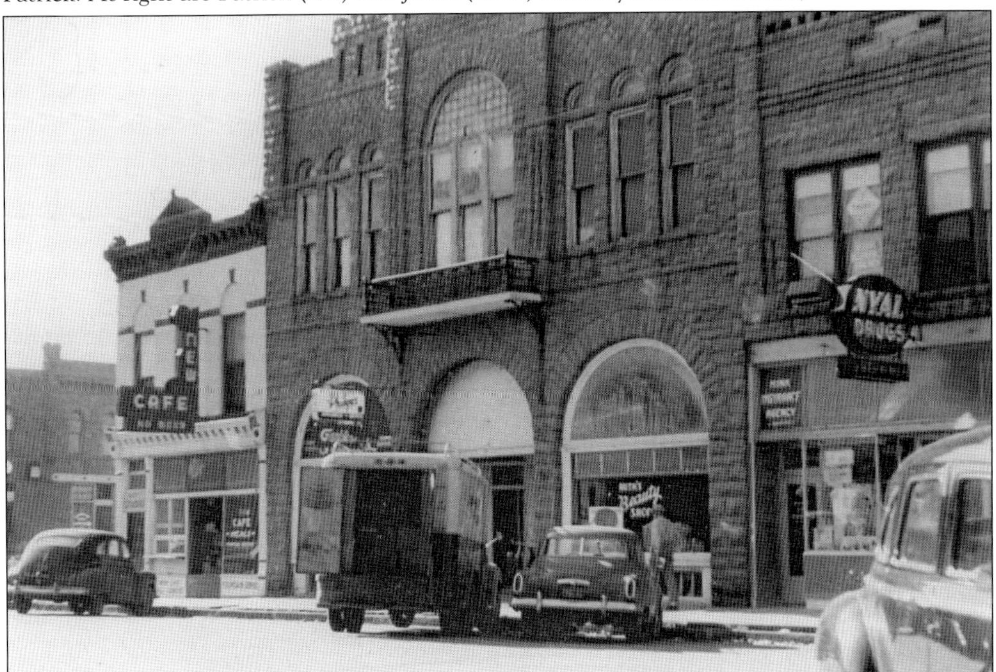

After the fire on Main Street, residents urged the building of an opera house in town. On November 5, 1888, the Grand, designed by Wallace Dow, was built by John Cooley and Michael Kenefick. The Grand has hosted many events, including professional and amateur theater, roller-skating, dances, and various businesses. The building has since been purchased by a private resident and renovated to its original appearance.

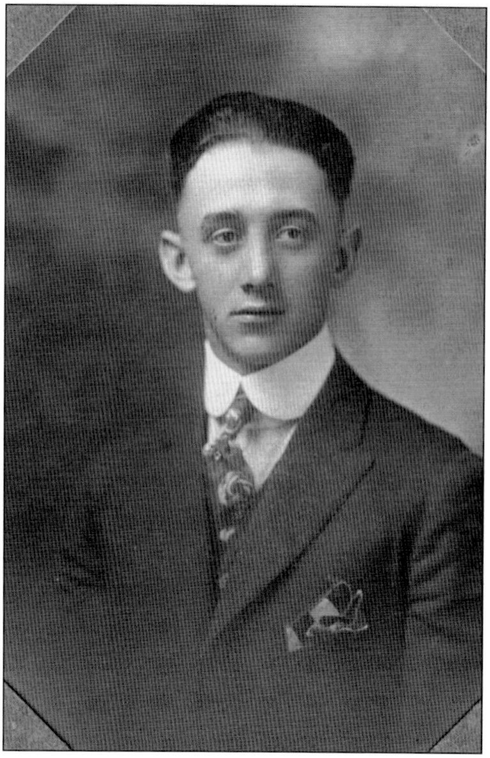

Joseph Burlingame was born in 1881 and came to Dell Rapids with his family in 1888. He was a well-driller and worked in the quarry, setting the dynamite charges. He was also an early bartender in Dell Rapids and Sioux Falls, where he moved after marrying Alida Larsen in 1936. In 1950, they relocated to Tacoma, Washington, where Joe died in 1951.

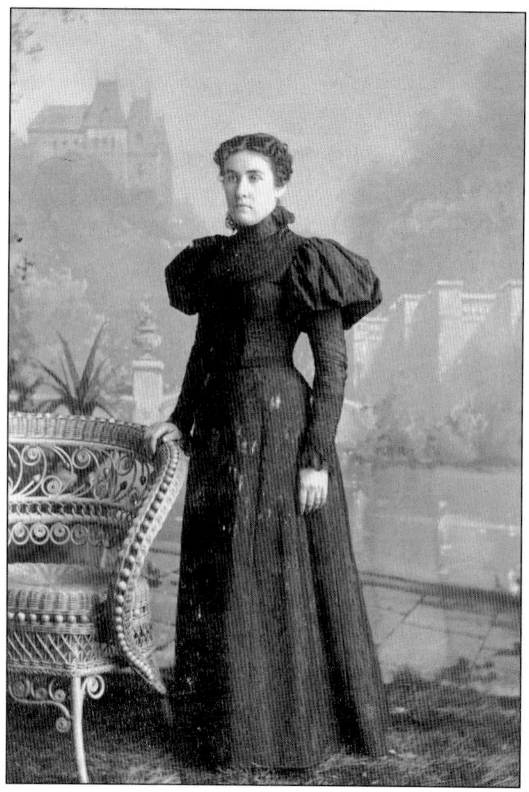

Affa Burlingame came to Dell Rapids with her parents, George and Mary Burlingame. Affa and her brothers were attending school when the devastating blizzard of 1888 tore through the Midwest. Their teacher told them to go home and when their father had found them, Affa had blisters hanging from her legs, but she survived. In 1913, Affa and her former employer, Aaron Olsen, were married in Huron.

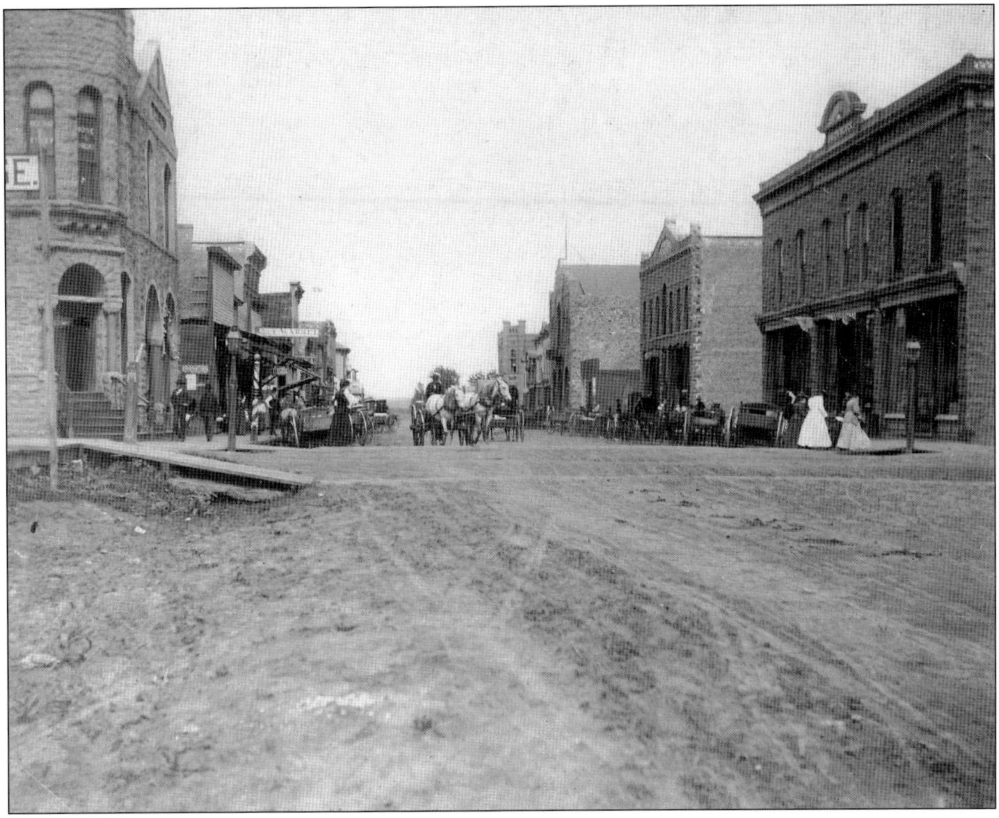

In this early, pre-1900 view of Main Street, showing early businesses and shopping, streets have yet to be paved, sidewalks are made of planks, and there are wagons parked all along the street. By this time, Main Street had been established as a vital economic and social region for residents. Many of these buildings still exist and are in the National Register of Historic Places.

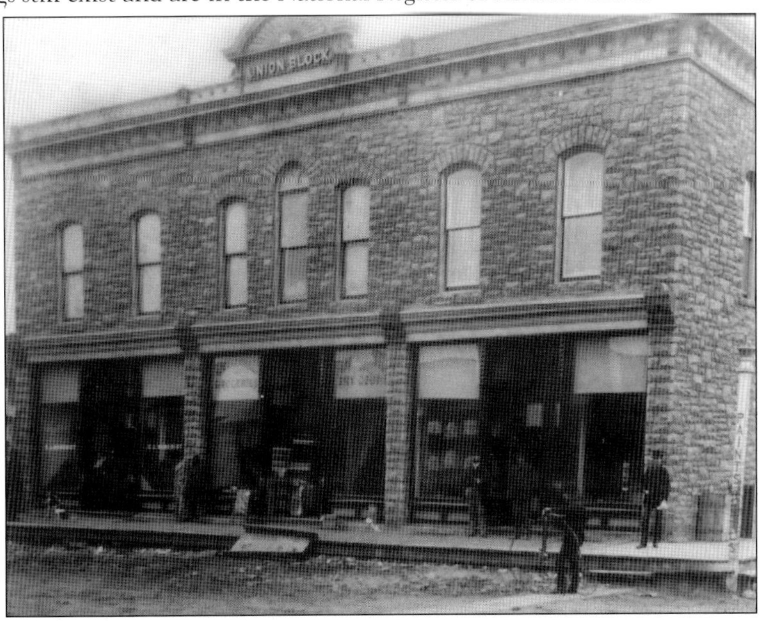

The Union Block building, measuring three bays wide, was erected in 1894. Each bay housed a separate local business, including a grocery store, clothing store, Putnam's Billiard Hall, Sheridan Pool Hall, and a saloon. The continuing cornice that rounded the building and the Union Block sign no longer exist.

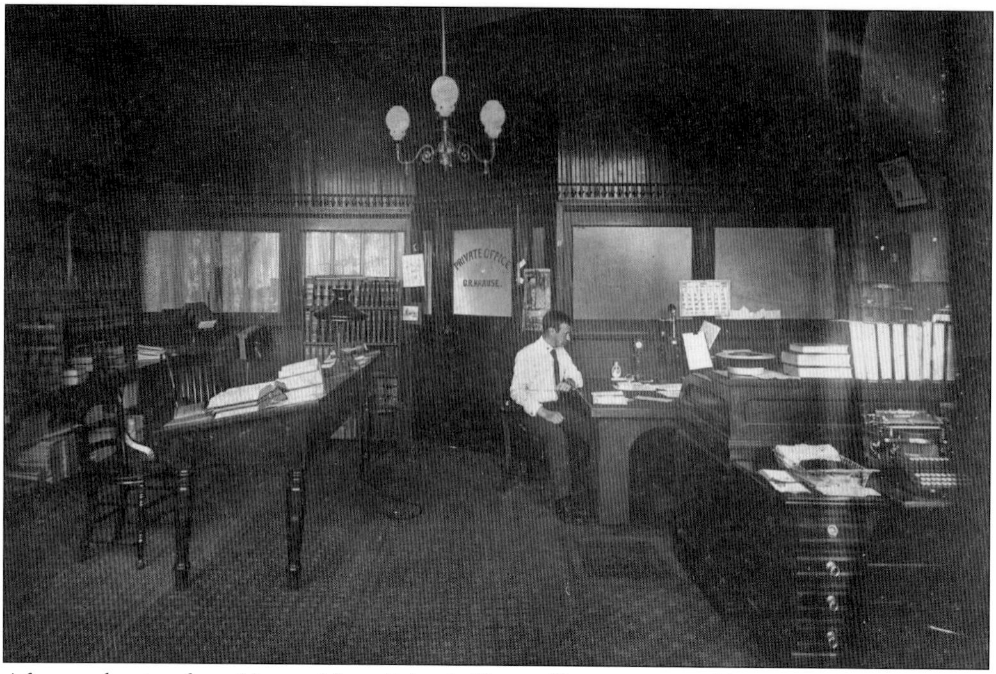

After graduation from Harvard Law School, Homer Krause returned home, and the law office of G.R. Krause became the office of Krause and Krause, Attorneys-at-Law. Gustavus Krause and his son worked together, drawing clients from all over the Midwest. Their practice was at one time the largest one in Minnehaha County, and the office is the longest-running continuous business in Dell Rapids.

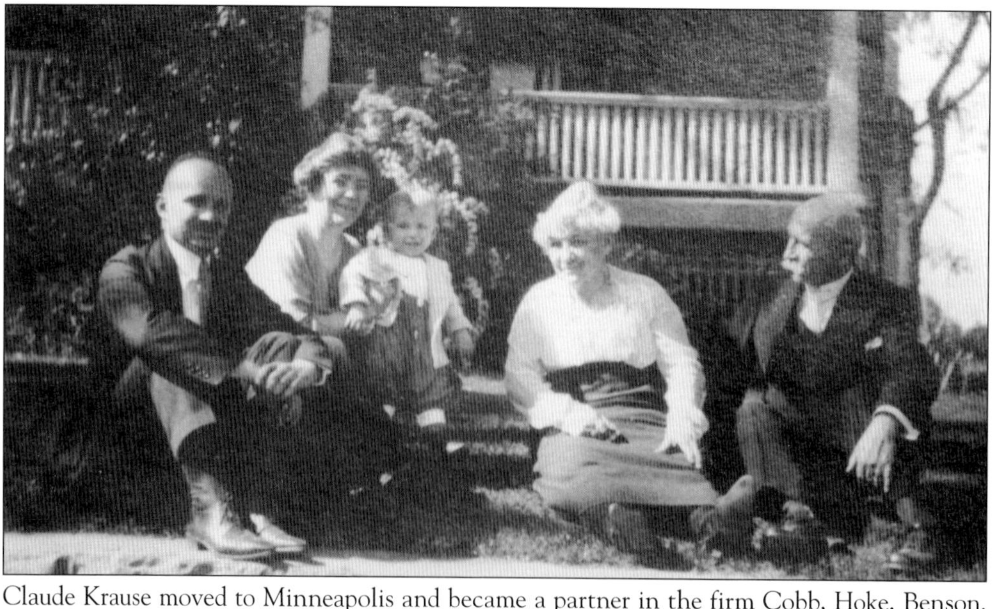

Claude Krause moved to Minneapolis and became a partner in the firm Cobb, Hoke, Benson, Krause, and Faegre. He remained in Minneapolis until his death in 1940. This photograph was taken in the summer of 1923 at the residence of Krause's parents and shows, from left to right, Claude Krause; Edna Krause, his sister-in-law; Robert Krause, his nephew; and his parents, Delia and Gustavus Krause.

Gustavus Richard Krause moved to Dell Rapids in 1886 and was a self-educated man, a student all his life. From his knowledge of real estate law, he passed the state bar examination in 1889 and became a lawyer under a grandfather clause in the state. He is the founder of the law firm that still exists in Dell Rapids today.

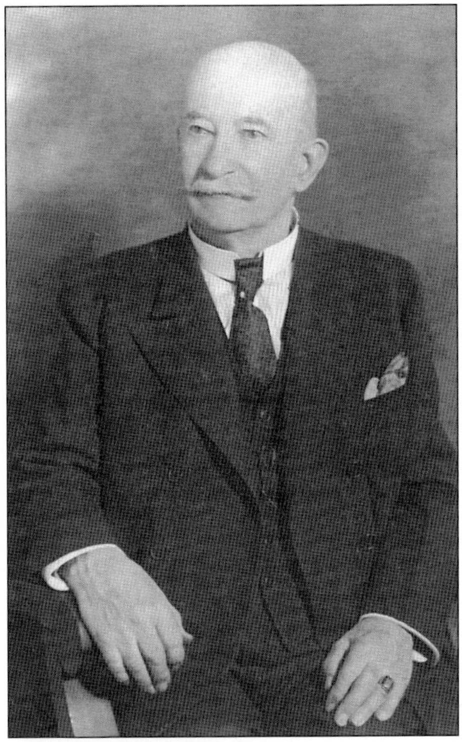

Delia Pattison Christison came to America with her parents in 1874. Delia and her husband, Gustavus Krause, came to Dell Rapids around 1890, about the same time her father, Robert Christison, a Presbyterian minister, arrived. Delia was always active in community affairs and was one of the founders of the Dell Rapids Women's Club, and, in conjunction with others, took the initial efforts in obtaining a Carnegie library for the betterment of the city.

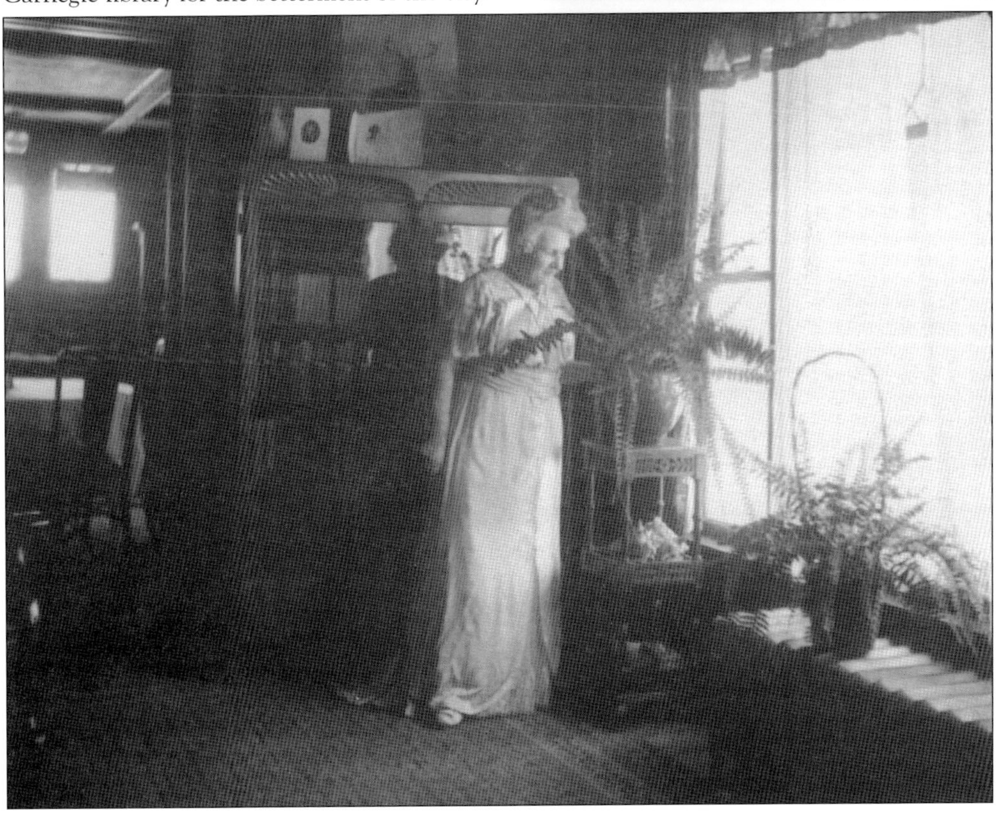

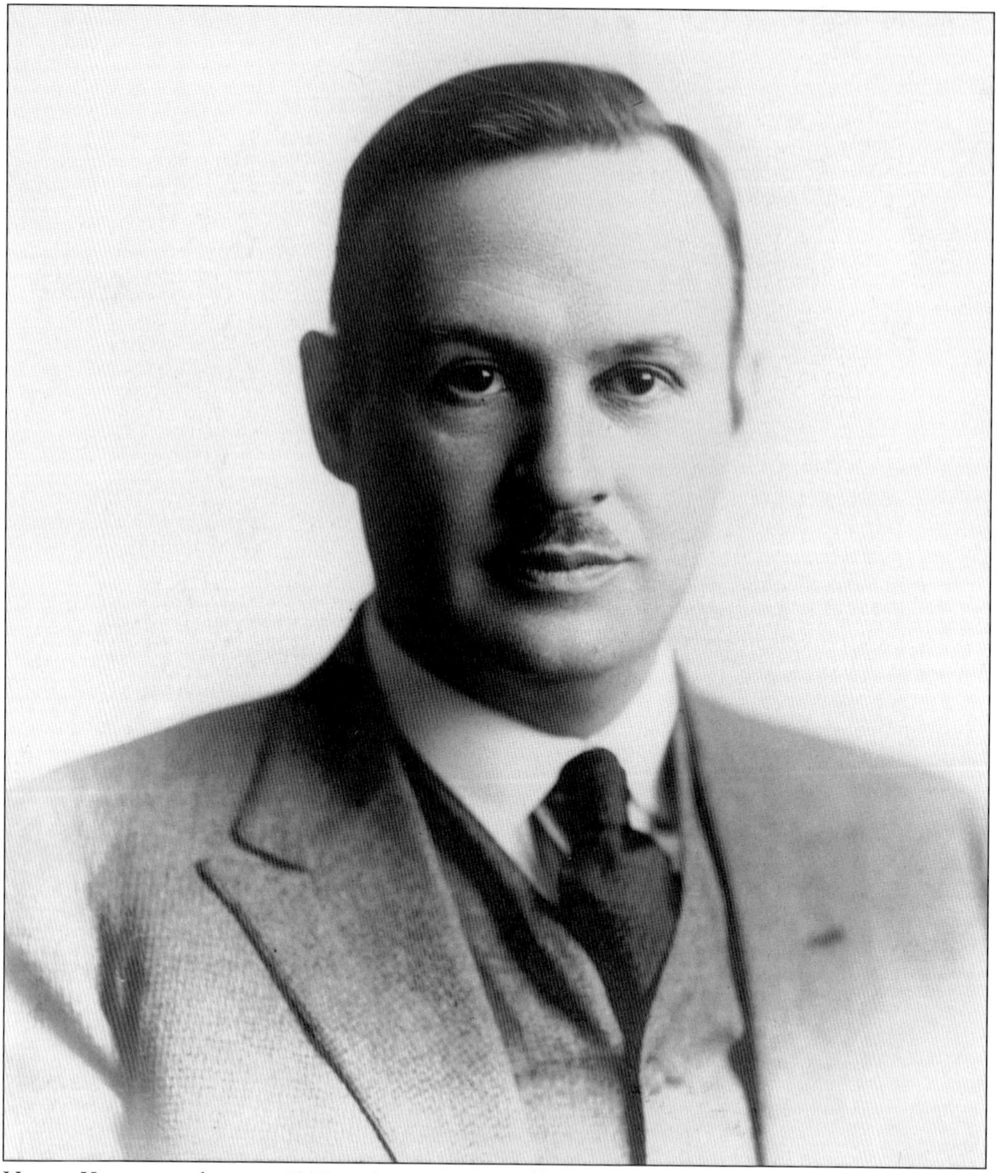

Homer Krause was born in 1883 and grew up in Dell Rapids. He graduated high school in 1901 and went on to Carleton College in Northfield, Minnesota, and then Harvard Law School. He joined his father's law firm in 1910 and became a well-known lawyer across the state of South Dakota. He married Edna Johnson, the daughter of Carl Johnson, a well-known local businessman, in 1920. Their son, Robert, was born in 1921, but Homer died of a heart attack in 1924. At the time, he was president and director of the Dell Rapids Commercial Club and was considered to be Dell Rapids' biggest booster. Members of the Minnehaha County Bar Association declared that Homer had one of the best legal minds in the state. His death was a shock to his family and the entire community.

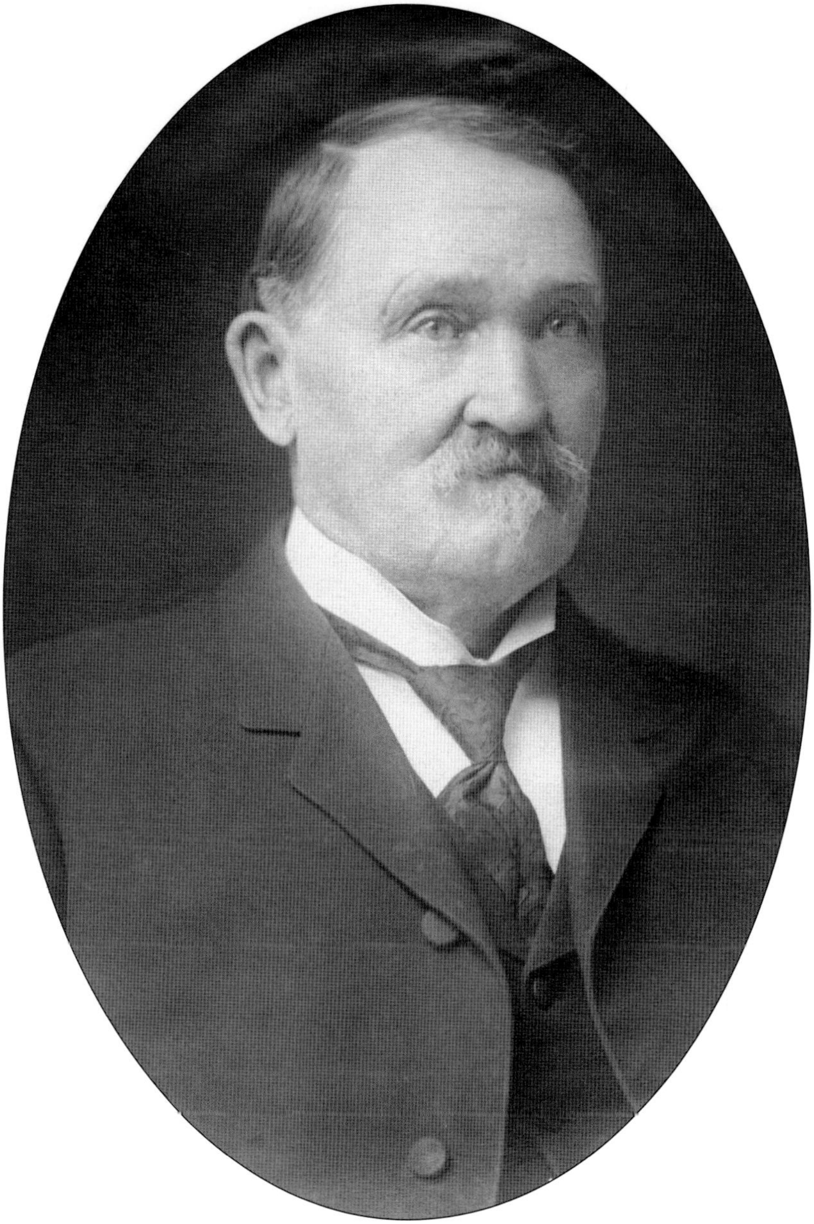

Attorney Albion Thorne, shown here in 1871, was the first postmaster in Dell Rapids; his salary was $1 per month. Thorne was born in Lisbon, Maine, in 1836. On September 9, 1862, he enlisted as a member of the Company C 23rd Maine Volunteer Infantry and was honorably discharged after 10 months of service. While engaged in the mercantile business, he began studying law and became a lawyer in 1866. Arriving in 1871, Thorne recognized the advantages and potential growth of what would become Dell Rapids. The first social event held in Dell Rapids was at Thorne's home on Christmas Day 1871. Thorne believed in public service, serving on several county boards and as district attorney for the county. He also held many principal offices in the Independent Order of Odd Fellows No. 8. Thorne tried his hand in the newspaper business, but his efforts were short-lived, and he sold the *Exponent* to Charles Griswold. Thorne remained in the area for the rest of his life.

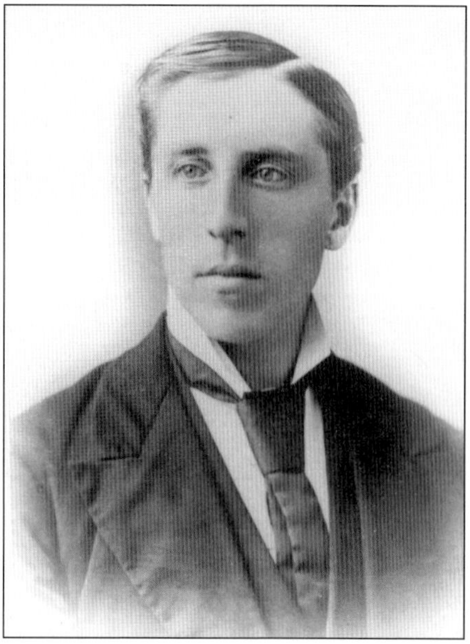
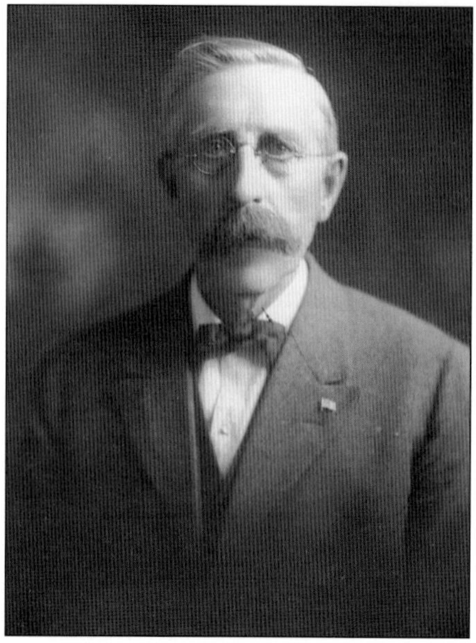

Martin Dieson settled in Dell Rapids in 1887 and ran a mercantile for many years. The first building was destroyed in the 1888 fire, but eventually his business grew and flourished, becoming a household name. He was one of the founders of the local Lutheran church and was deeply interested in civic improvement. He had been in business for 36 years when he passed away in 1923.

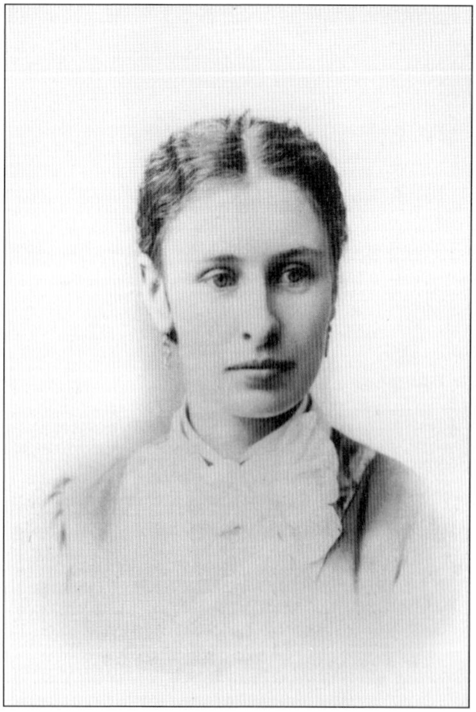
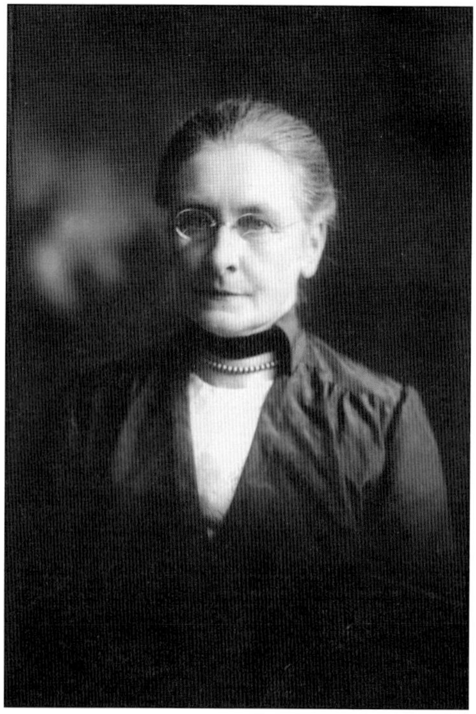

Thone Torgeson came to America with her parents in 1867. On September 7, 1881, she married Martin A. Dieson and they established a home in Houston, Minnesota, where they lived until 1887, when they moved back to Dell Rapids. Besides caring for the family's eight children, her largest interest was her church; she was an active member of the Ladies' Aid and the Legion Auxiliary.

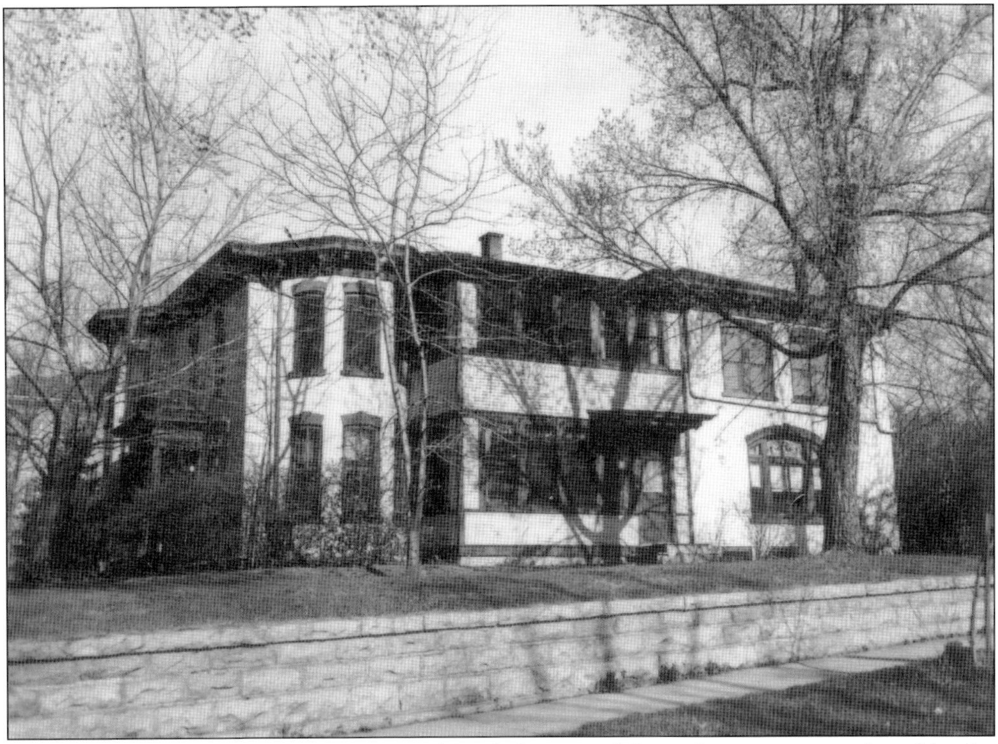

The Dieson family home on the corner of Sixth Street and State Avenue was purchased by the Dell Rapids School Board in the early 1950s and remodeled into a four-room primary school. The building served that purpose until 1982, when, along with the old high school, the building was torn down to make room for a new kindergarten section.

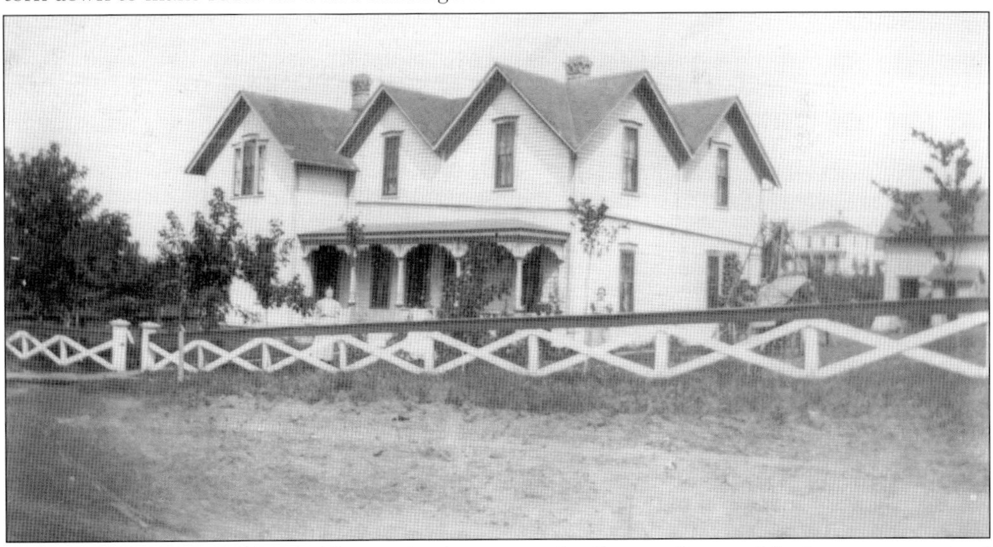

The "House of Nine Gables" held many fond memories for Georgia Dieson. The home was acquired by her father, Martin, in lieu of payment on a grocery debt. Georgia's early childhood memories include obscure hallways, a visiting ventriloquist, and church choir practices. The memories—of her mother baking in the kitchen and completing homework with her and of her father planting evergreens—made the house a home.

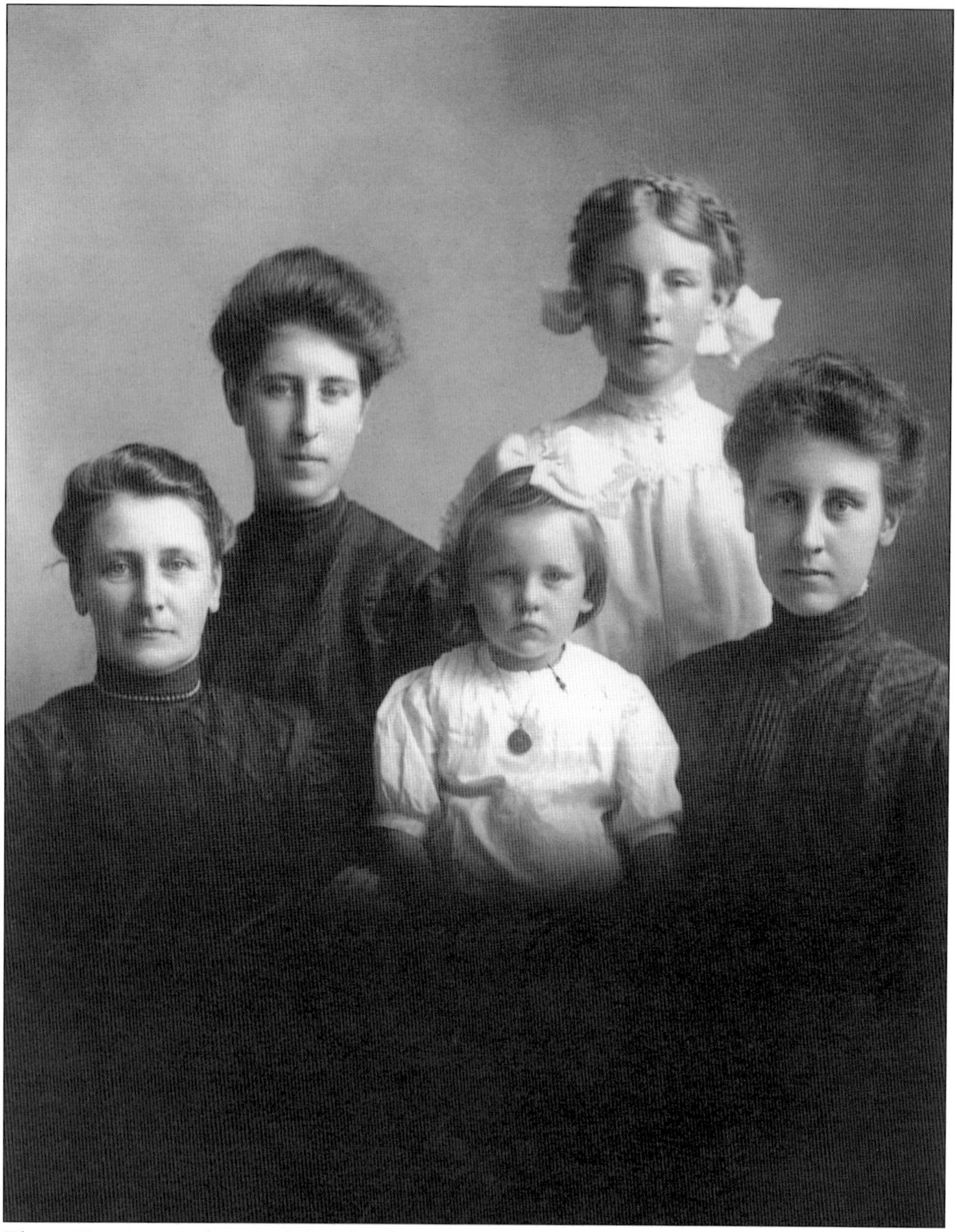

Thone Dieson, seen here with her daughters in 1907, was a community builder and home-lover. Alma Dieson (1885–1979, second row, left) grew up in Dell Rapids, graduating from the high school in 1903 before earning a degree in nursing and going on to a successful career. Emma (1895–1965, second row, right) devoted her entire life to Dell Rapids. After college, she returned home and helped run the family business with her brothers Harry and Ben. Eldri (first row, middle) was the youngest, born in 1905. She never married and worked her entire career for the YWCA in the United States and foreign countries. Georgia (1882–1978, first row, right), the eldest, was born in Minnesota and was the only one of the girls to wed, marrying Martin Hegland in 1911 and giving her parents a grandchild. Thone had a fifth daughter who died in infancy.

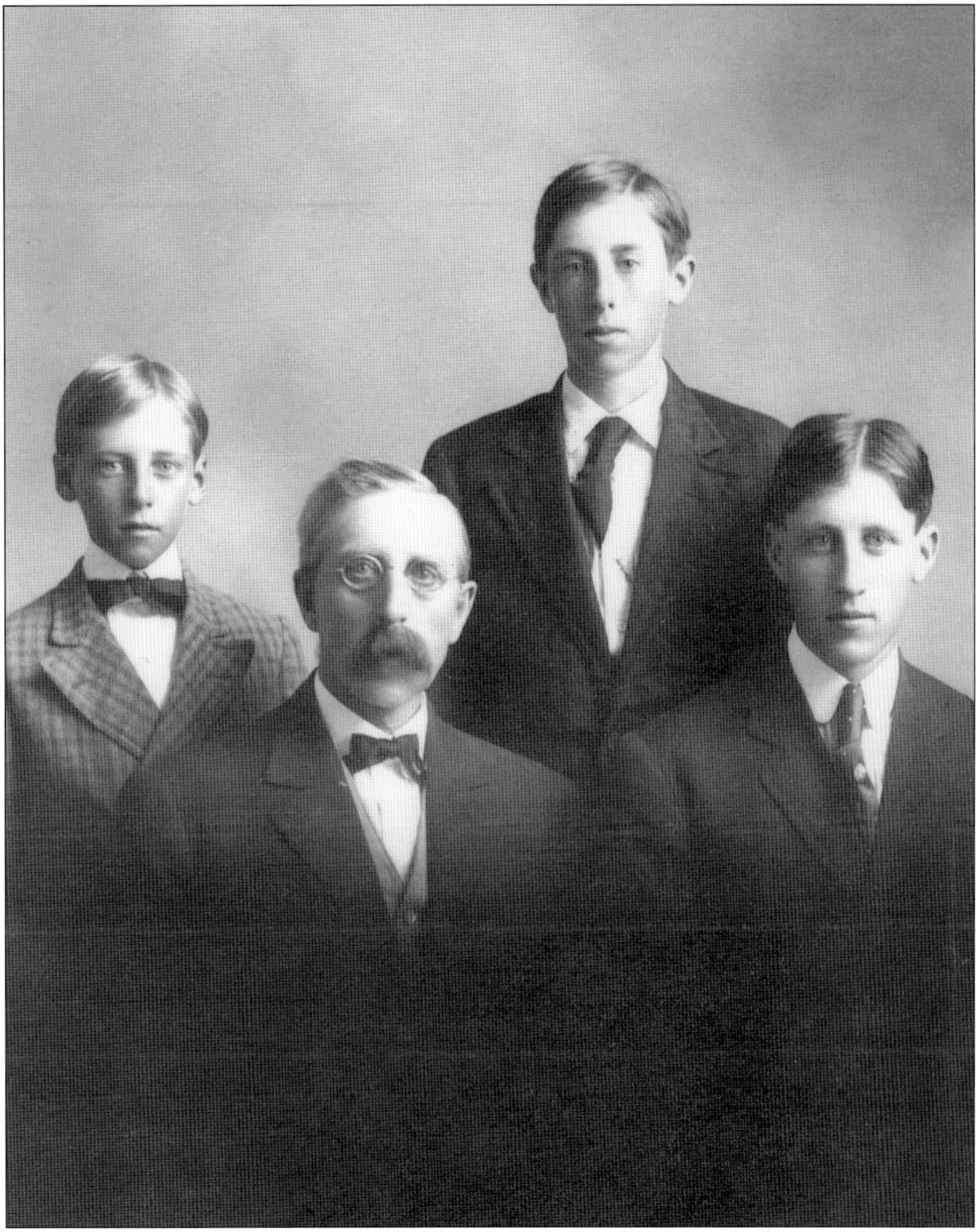

Martin Dieson ran a prosperous business in town, enabling him to provide for his children, all of whom attended college and eventually became successful themselves. After high school, Joe (second row, left), the youngest of the boys, attended the University of South Dakota and eventually held the post of vice consul to Korea for several years before moving to Chicago and becoming an associate with Marshall Field's. He returned home shortly before his death in 1954. Ben (second row, right) was the middle child, born in 1892. After his education at St. Olaf College in Northfield, Minnesota, he returned home in 1915 and joined Dieson's mercantile with his brother Harry and sister Emma. Martin died in 1966, with his first wife preceding him in death. Harry (1887–1979), the eldest son, served in France during World War I, married in 1933, and ran Dieson's mercantile until his retirement in 1957.

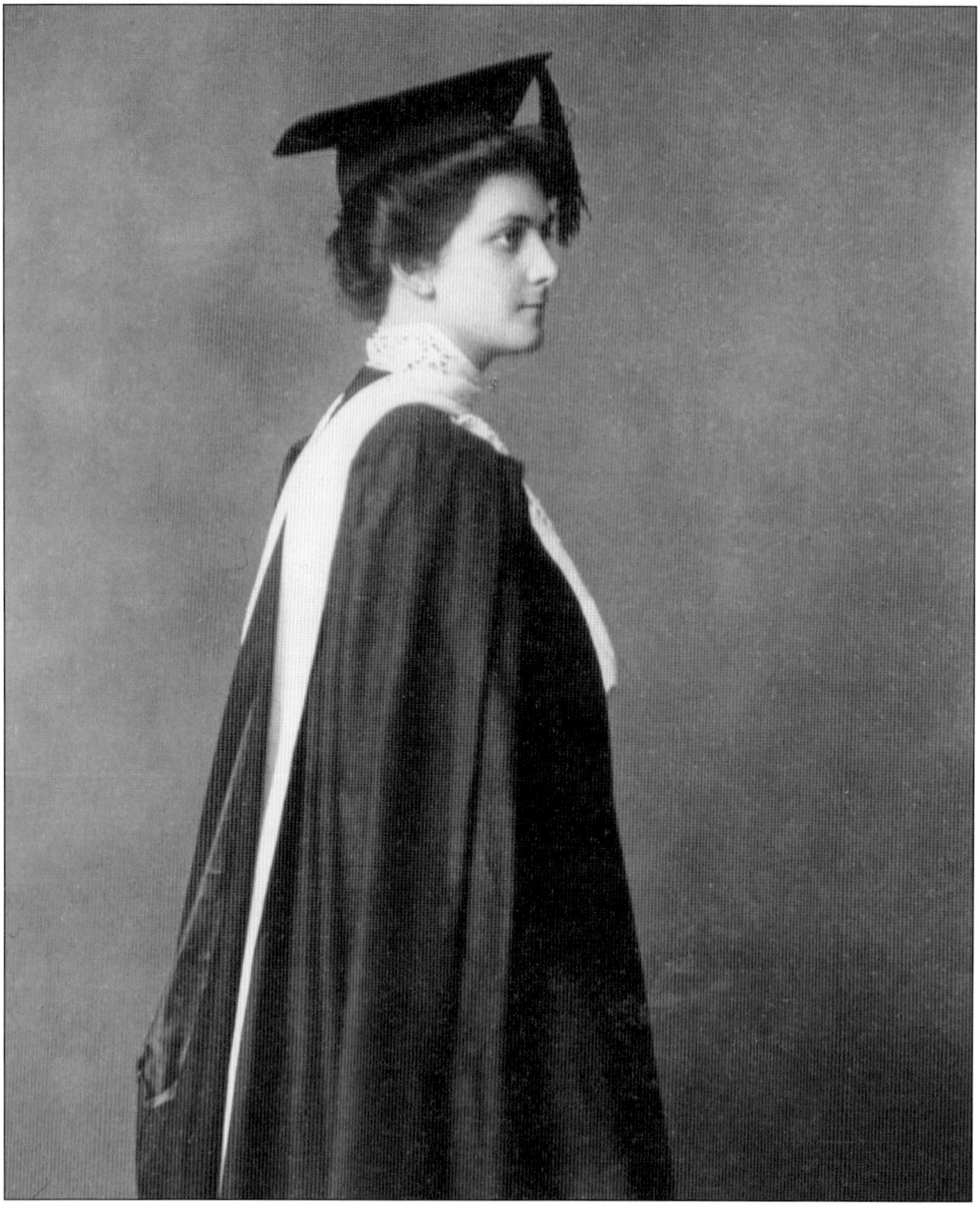

Dr. Charlotte Elliott, a world-renowned plant pathologist, bacteriologist, and botanist, is most remembered for her work with bacterial diseases in cereal crops, particularly corn. She graduated from Dell Rapids High School before continuing on to Stanford University. She went on to study and research at the University of Wisconsin, receiving her PhD as the only woman in the department. Dr. Elliott spent time working with the US Department of Agriculture and made her biggest breakthrough working with bacterial wilt and Stewart's leaf blight on corn. She also worked under Erwin F. Smith, a pioneer in plant pathology. She concluded her research by identifying that a specific corn leaf blight, *Helminthosporium turcicum*, was controlled genetically. She retired from plant pathology in 1946. A woman well ahead of her time, Elliott's work in the field has directly contributed to the success of hybrid corn production.

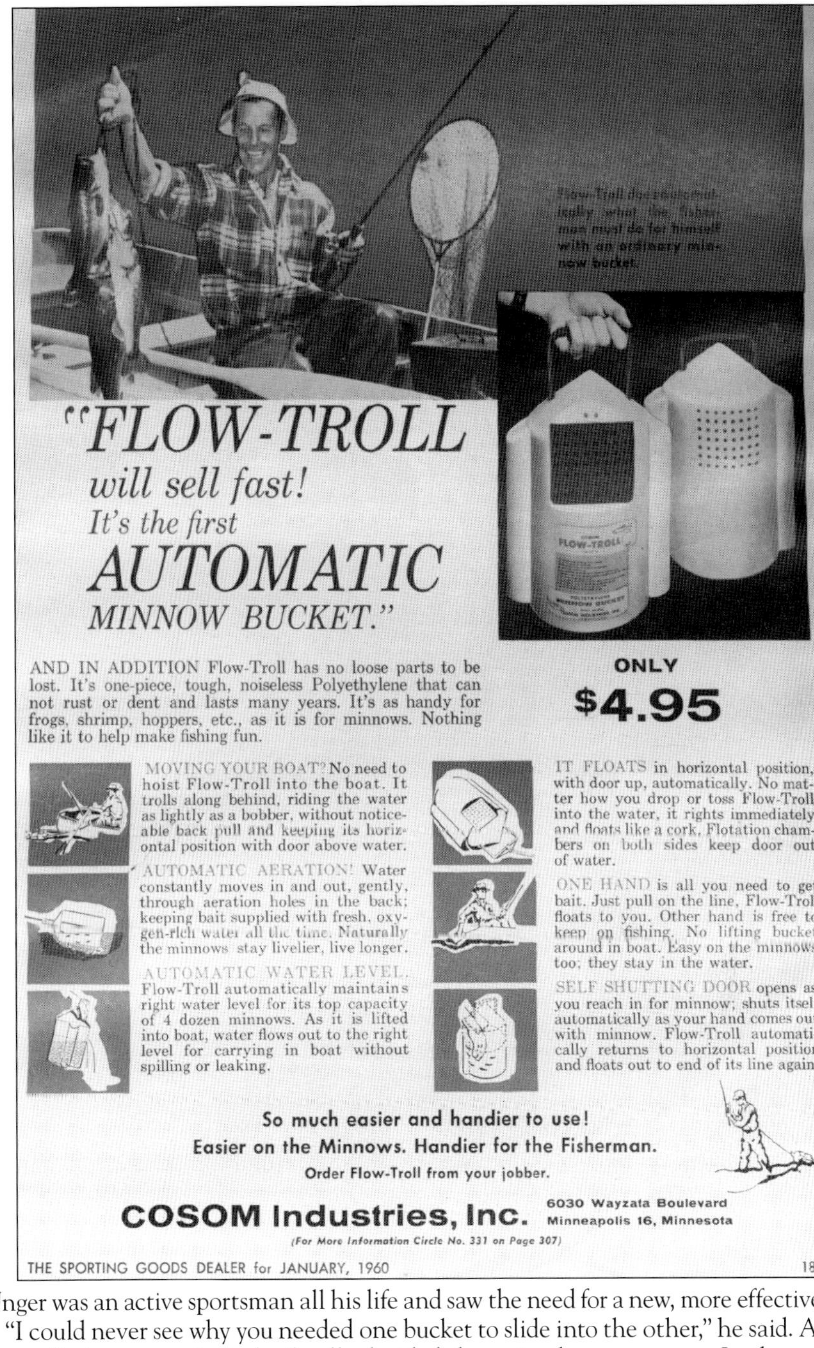

Titus Unger was an active sportsman all his life and saw the need for a new, more effective minnow bucket. "I could never see why you needed one bucket to slide into the other," he said. After years of trying to find a reason for it, he finally decided there simply was not one. In the early 1950s, he began coming up with a way to make a minnow bucket cheaply enough, or else the project would fail. He was told if he could produce the buckets using plastic, they would sell. He teamed up with COSMOS of Minneapolis, and production began. The flow troll minnow bucket sold for $3.95 in 1959, and Unger received 10¢ for every minnow bucket sold until the patent ran out. The flow troll minnow bucket can be found at any sportsman's store across the United States and is the best-selling minnow bucket of its type.

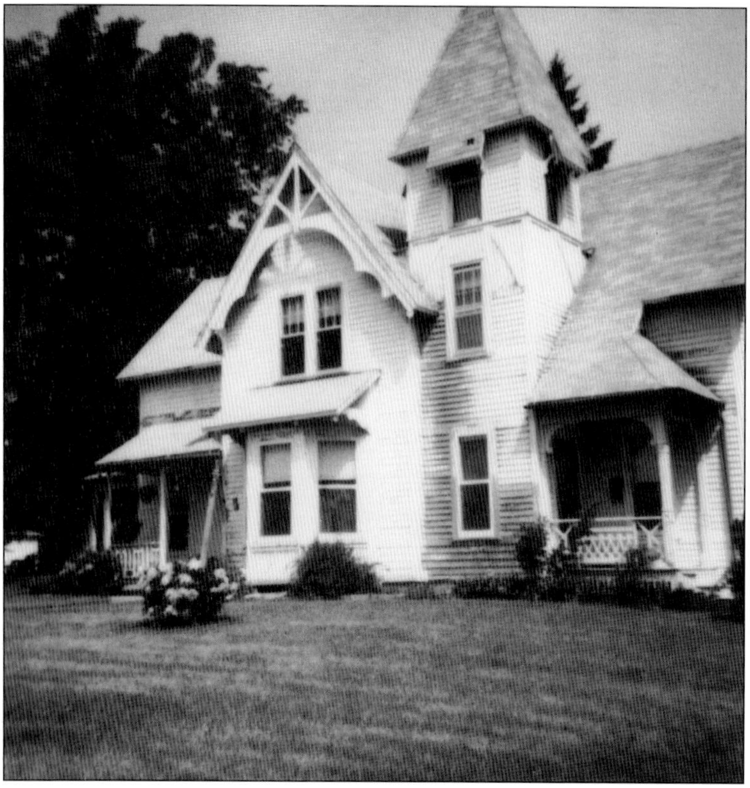

Lucile Fargo grew up in Dell Rapids during its developing years. Fargo moved to Dakota Territory with her family in 1882, eventually living in the back of her father's store. In 1882, a storm rolled through town, demolishing the Congregational church. Fargo and her father salvaged the remains to build their new home.

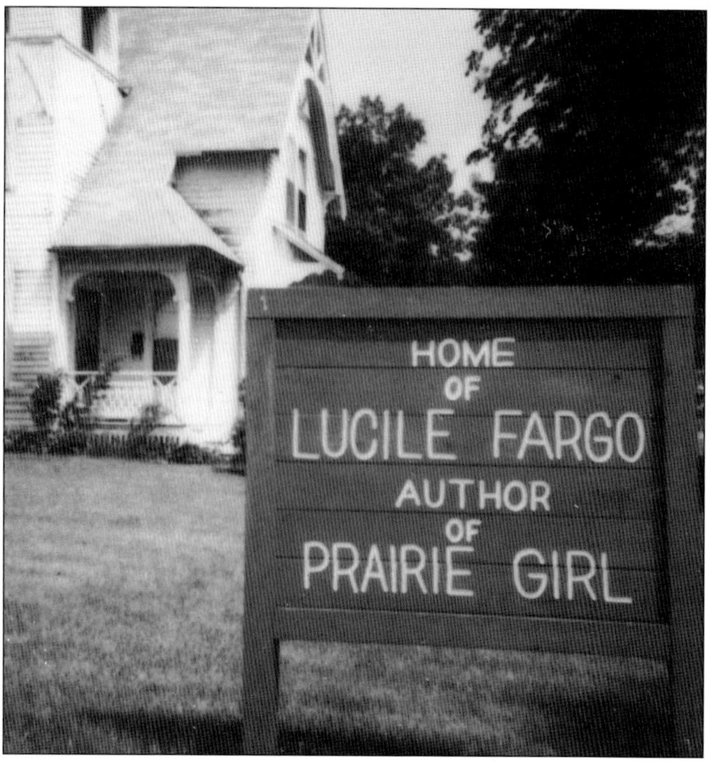

Fargo became a librarian and waited until she was in her 50s before she began to write. She published *Prairie Girl* in 1937, following it up with *Prairie Chautauqua* in 1943. Lucile pictured the pioneer woman as self-sufficient, strong, and independent. She did not like to stay home and knit, opting to spend her time climbing rocks, playing in the river, and getting her hands dirty. Many of her adventures revolve around Dell Rapids—from individuals to popular recreational areas. Fargo passed away in 1962.

Three

MILITARY

With an active American Legion post and auxiliary, Dell Rapids has kept up its traditions of military honors and history. The namesake of the local Legion post, George Fitzgerald, a World War I veteran, inspired generations of members to hold high the honor of serving in the American military. Organized in 1919, the post has expanded through the years to include a Legion Hall, which is still operational, as well as the popular annual tradition of Cootie Days, a carnival put on by the post since 1920 that draws hundreds of visitors to the town. Recognizing the solemnity of Memorial Day, the post also keeps the tradition alive with an annual parade, displaying the colors and ending the morning with a service in the city park. From noted servicemen such as World War I veteran Hans Jorgensen and original post commander John Hermanson to the existing group of veterans, the military has played a prominent role in the leadership and values of the community.

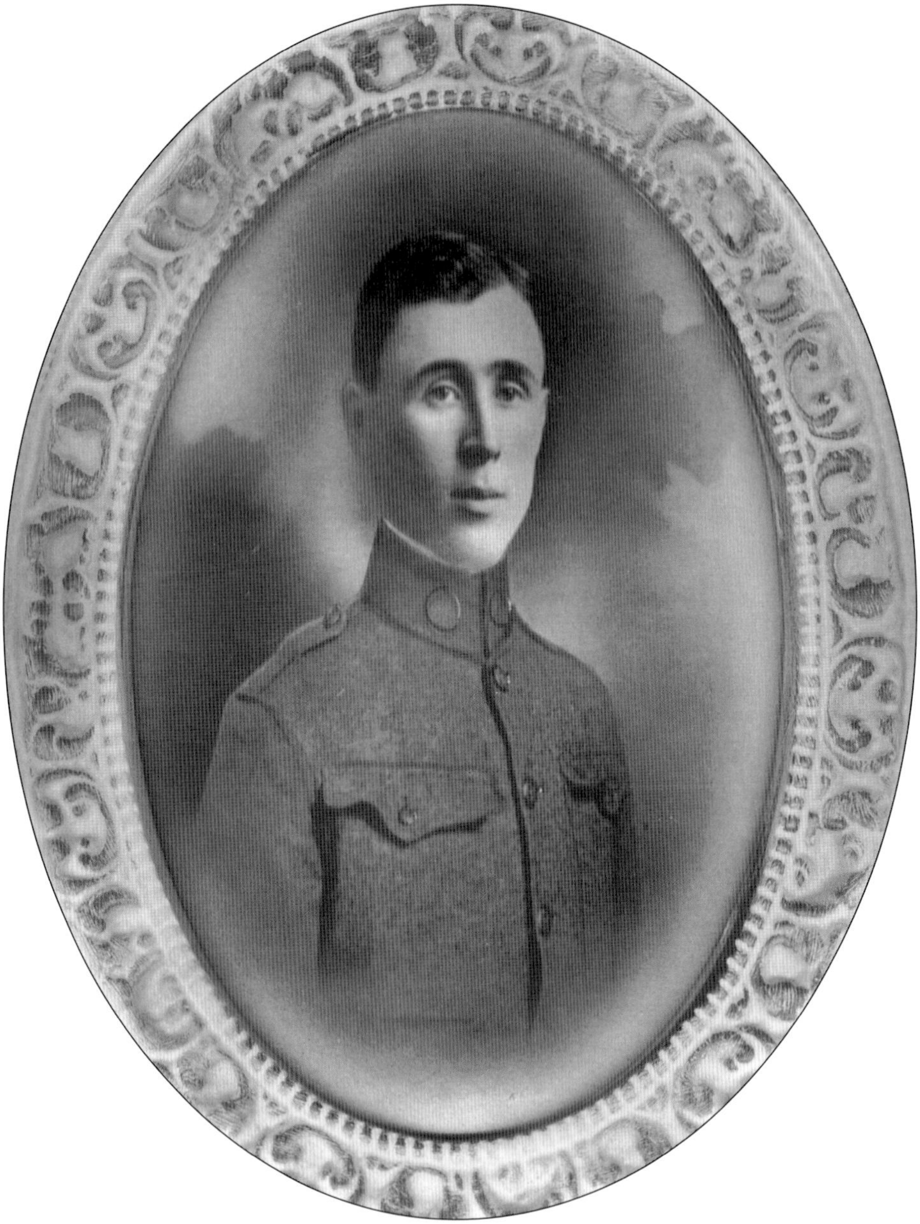

The American Legion in Dell Rapids was named after George Fitzgerald, the first local man to die in World War I. On the morning of September 12, 1918, Fitzgerald was wounded attempting to capture a machine gun nest held by the Germans. For three months, he suffered from the excruciating effects of a shattered hipbone, patiently praying for recovery, but he died on January 8, 1919. Originally interred in a cemetery in France on January 9, he was reinterred after the war in St. Mary Catholic Cemetery in Dell Rapids. On September 13, 1921, Dell Rapids mourned the loss of two more servicemen, David Ferguson and Edson Shreve. Dell Rapids has not mourned a loss of this magnitude since that tearful, somber day. An article in the September 15, 1921, *Dell Rapids Tribune* reads: "Mid lowering skies and a gentle rainfall, as if the very heavens were mourning the fate that befell the Dell Rapids boys who came home to heroes graves." Ferguson, Fitzgerald, and Shreve were reinterred the same day. (Courtesy Dell Rapids American Legion.)

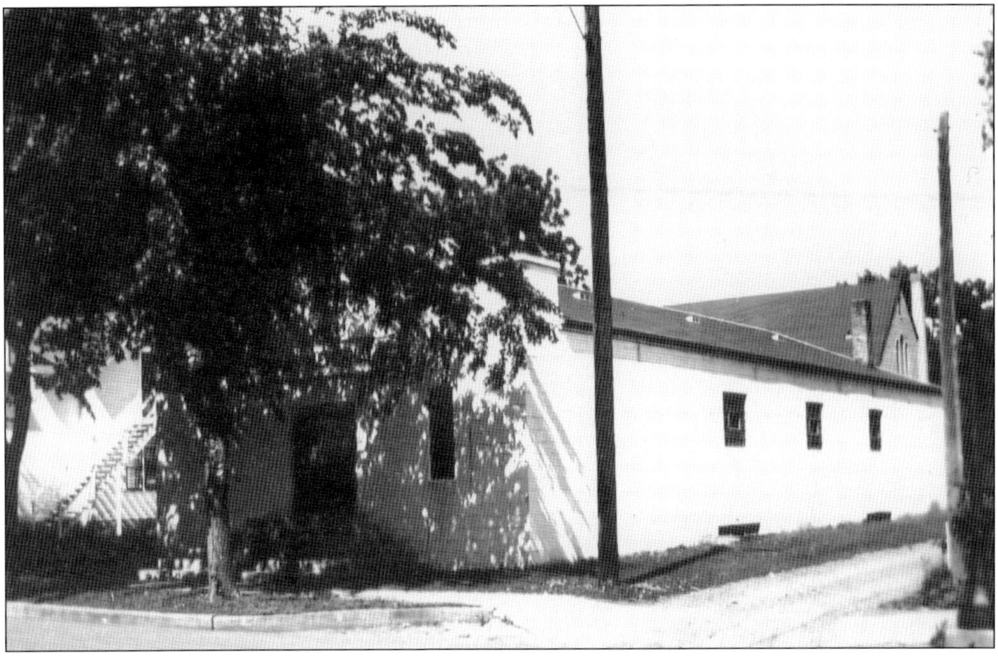

The Dell Rapids American Legion Post No. 65 was organized on November 11, 1919. In 1949, this building was constructed at an approximate cost of $22,000. Prior to the Legion Hall being built, members of the post and auxiliary met north of this location in what was known as the Community Hall. The Legion Hall was a welcome addition to the town, as several community organizations used the building.

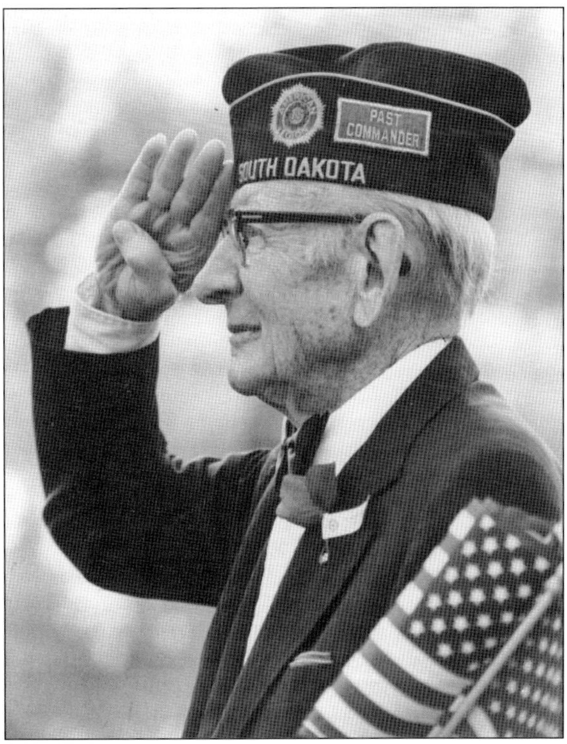

John Hermanson was the first post commander to serve a complete year of service for the Dell Rapids American Legion, in 1919–1920. He was in attendance in Paris, France, when the American Legion Organization was formed following World War I. For many years, Hermanson was responsible for the local Memorial Day services and was a lifelong member of the Legion, receiving a 50-year plaque. (Courtesy Dell Rapids American Legion.)

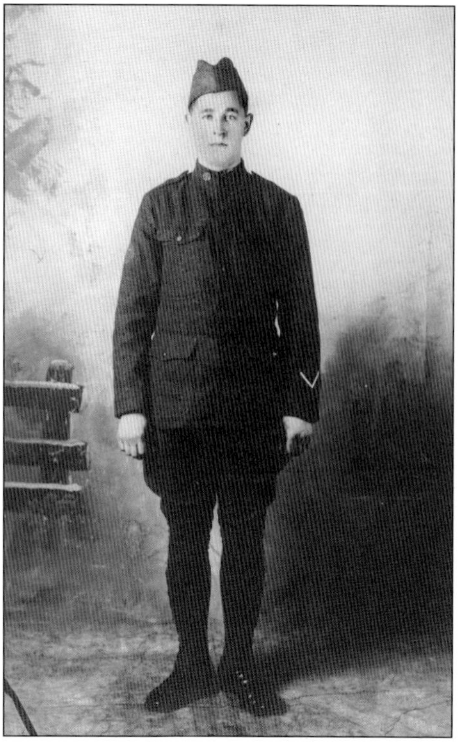

Jorgen "George" Jorgensen was born in Denmark in 1896. At 17, he borrowed enough money to immigrate to America with his sister, Anna, and they arrived in Dell Rapids in April 1913. He worked for area farmers and attended rural school to learn English before leaving for military service in World War I in 1918. In 1919, after he returned home from the war, Jorgensen became a citizen.

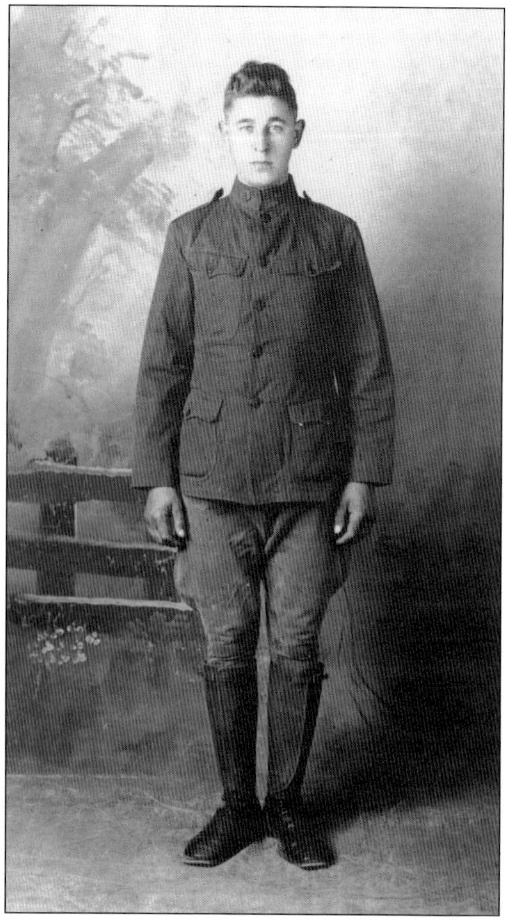

Hans Jorgensen, born in 1894, was orphaned at age two. In 1914, he followed his brother Jorgen and his sister Anna to Dell Rapids. Three years later, not yet a citizen, he and his brother proved their allegiance to the United States by joining the Army in World War I. After the war, Hans returned to the area and remained here until his death in 1972.

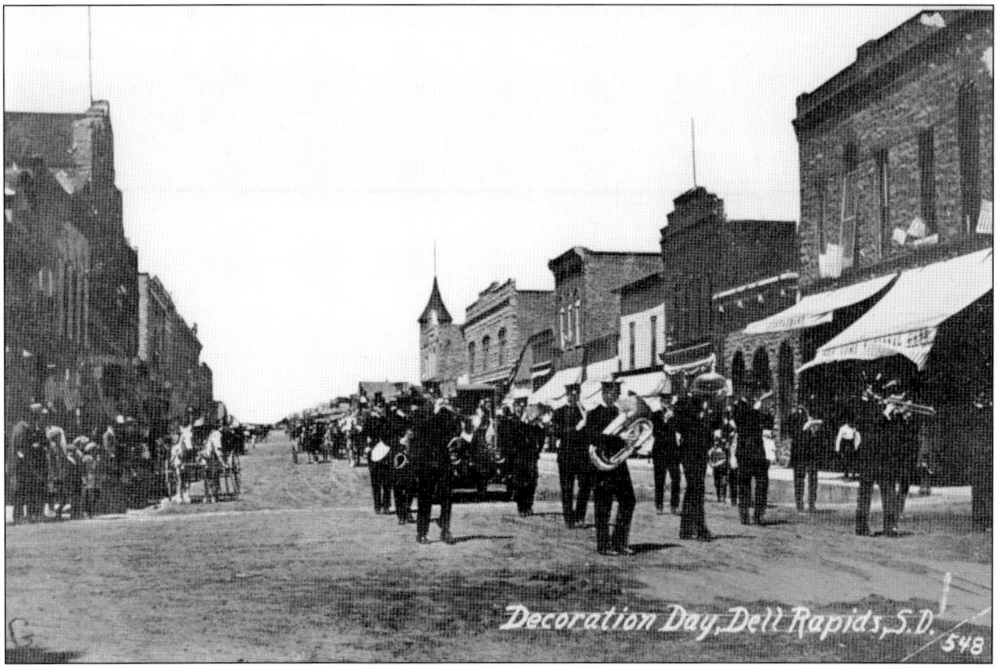

The Dell Rapids Band proudly plays patriotic music during the Decoration Day Parade. Seeing a memorial celebration such as Decoration Day is a common event in town. Main Street provides a perfect location to gather in honor of those who have contributed to or have died in the name of honor and service to the United States.

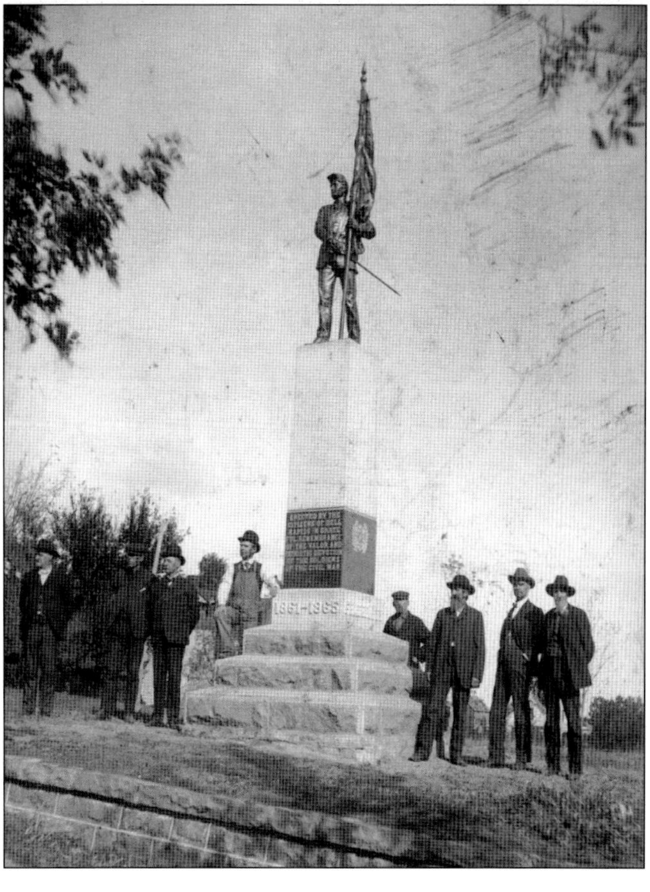

This monument to the veterans of the Civil War is prized by citizens. The old Soldiers Monument was dedicated on July 2, 1908, in remembrance of the "valor and patriotic devotion of the soldiers of the Civil War." Despite severe weather conditions, construction, and the threat of relocation, the Civil War Monument has stood the test of time and remains in its original spot.

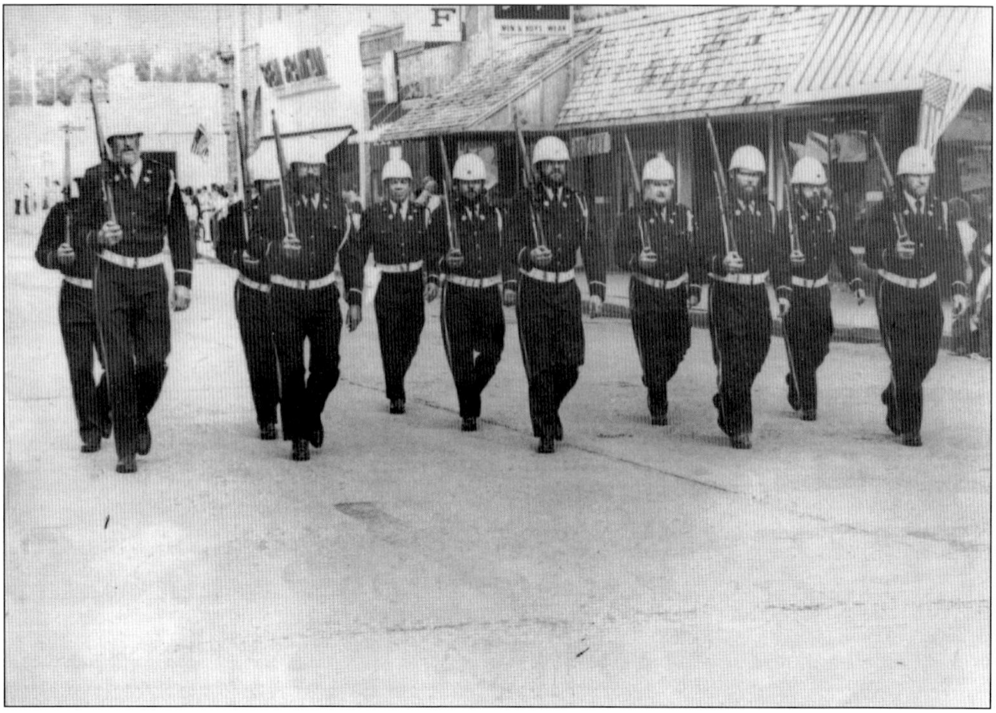

The American Legion is a common sight in Dell Rapids parades, like the 1980 Centennial Parade seen here. One of the centennial events was a beard-growing competition. This heavily bearded bunch includes, from left to right, (first row) Myron Joneson, Dick Mergen, Joe Geraets, David Mousel, and Wayne Burkhart; (second row) Larry Hovde, Greg Hauglid, Roger Park, Mike Weinacht, Bill Zeig, and Gene Marcher. (Courtesy Dell Rapids American Legion.)

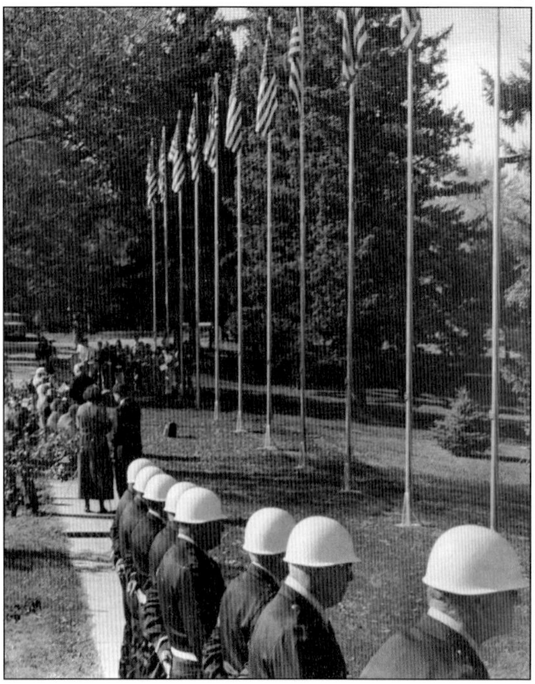

There are 16 flagpoles flying the American flag along the entrance to the Dell Rapids Odd Fellows Home, honoring the 21 people raised in the orphanage who were military veterans. Sgt. Edward Kindred spent his childhood years at the Odd Fellows Orphanage from 1923–1931. Sergeant Kindred's military career was extensive and honorable; to show his dedication to service, he helped spearhead the installation of these flagpoles. (Courtesy Dell Rapids American Legion.)

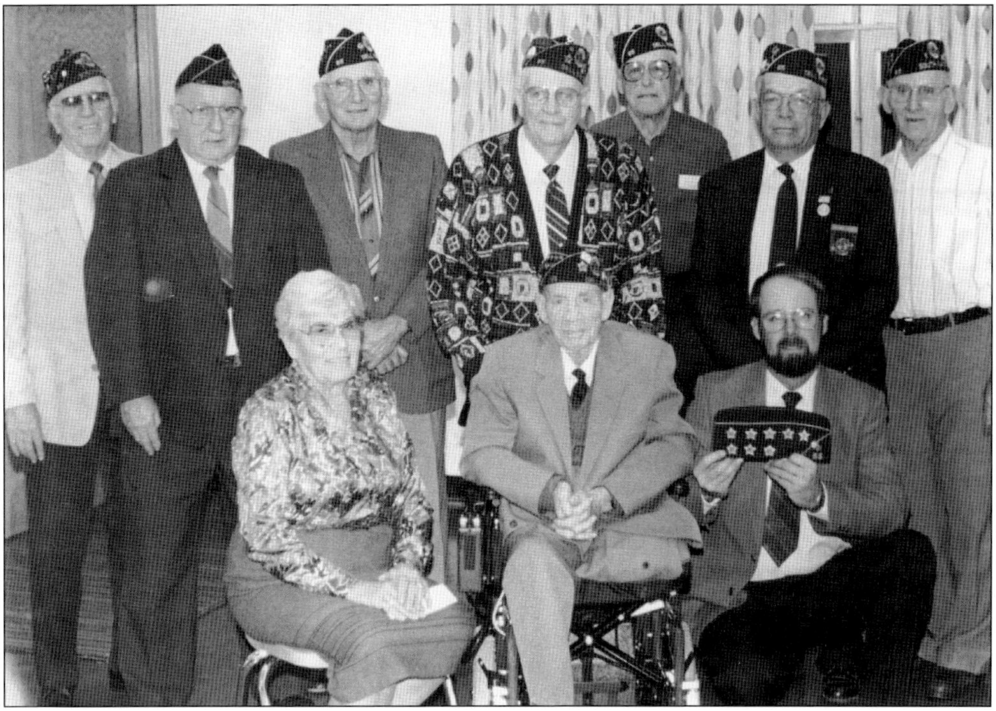

Members of the American Legion have found camaraderie, support, and a feeling of family. These members, who have served their post with honor and loyalty for more than 50 years, are, from left to right, (first row) Mary Schmidt, Gene Marcher, and Daniel Wildermuth (in honor of Arnie Wildermuth); (second row) Gaylord Brown, Dale Dunn, John Nemmers, Harvey Ellefson, John Wenaas, Jerome Posey, and Merlin Schmidt. (Courtesy Dell Rapids American Legion.)

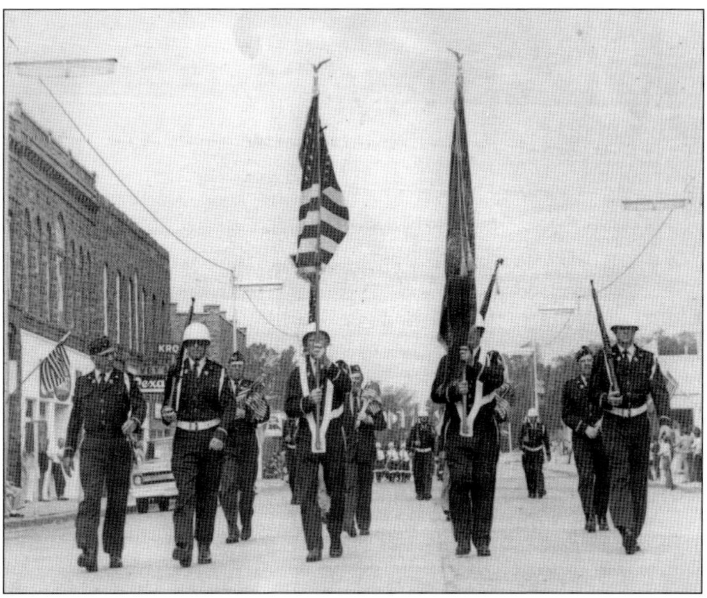

American Legion members, from left to right, (first row) Gay Brown, John Wenaas, Norbert "Stub" Schmidt, unidentified, and Dale Huewe; (second row) Melvin Fiegen, Art Nebben, and Floyd "Bud" Heinemann; and (third row) Joe Geraets and Roger Park lead the parade during the 1980 Centennial Celebration. (Courtesy Dell Rapids American Legion.)

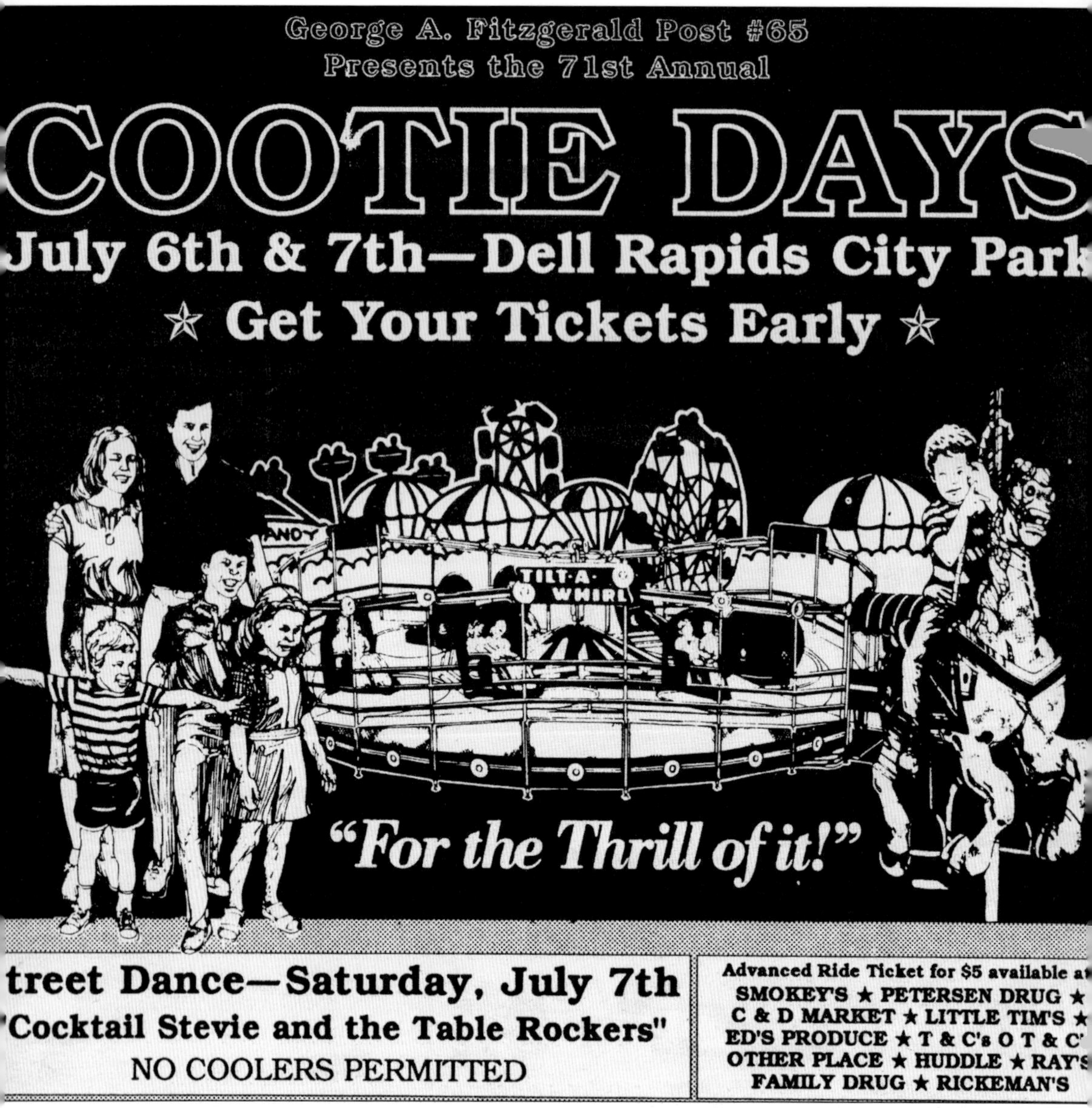

Cootie Days is a popular annual event sponsored by the Dell Rapids George A. Fitzgerald American Legion since 1920, although the official name of Cootie Days was adopted the following year. The deplorable sanitary conditions of war created a problem among many of the returning veterans. Many of the men that came home from the war were often seen scratching from the abundance of lice embedded on their clothes and blankets and in their hair. The constant itching and scratching was unforgettable for those afflicted—so unforgettable that the annual event was named after the pesky critters. The funds raised from Cootie Days sponsored many Legion activities and educational supplies. Amusement rides luring thrill-seekers, bouncy balls for children, and socializing over cotton candy and funnel cakes have all been part of the tradition attracting visitors of all ages.

Four

Town and Business

Dell Rapids has maintained a familiar look and feel since its inception. With a downtown noted for its use of original quartzite from the local rock quarries, the city prides its devotion to the town's identity and historic integrity. The post office has been operational since 1871, keeping Dells folks abreast of the goings-on of the state and country around them. Banks, hotels, and drugstores have operated in the downtown area for more than a century. Social hot spots included the local barbershop and the Dells Theatre, operated by the King family. And with the ongoing central commercial endeavors of small business ownership and agriculture, Dell Rapids continues to expand from its cooperative roots. As techniques and equipment have changed through the years, the trip from the farm to the grain elevator to the local grocery stores has remained a part of daily life.

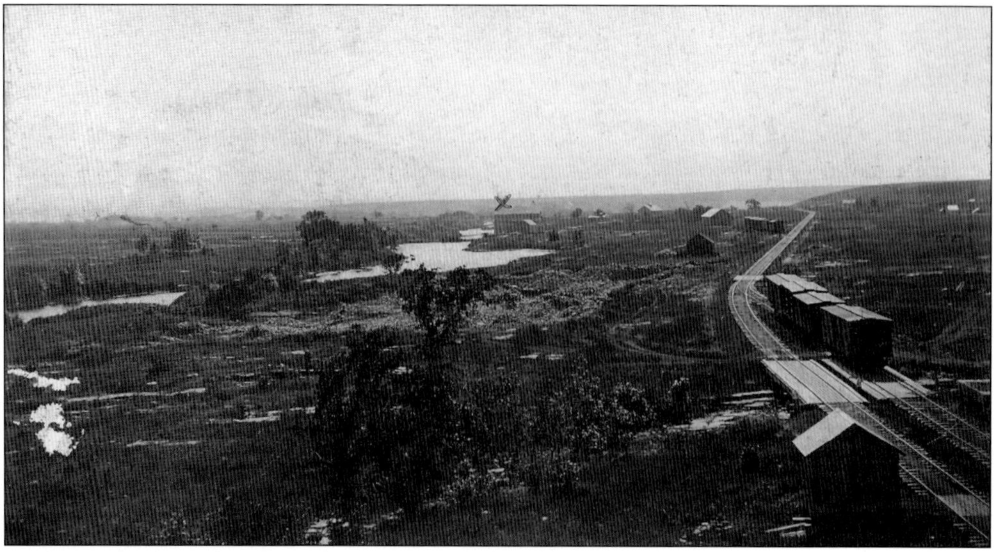

Looking west from the edge of town, one can just barely see the old mill by the dam. On the left is the Big Sioux River. The barrenness of the land is inescapable, but the town has grown considerably since this photograph was taken, with the addition of trees and underbrush and the establishment of homes.

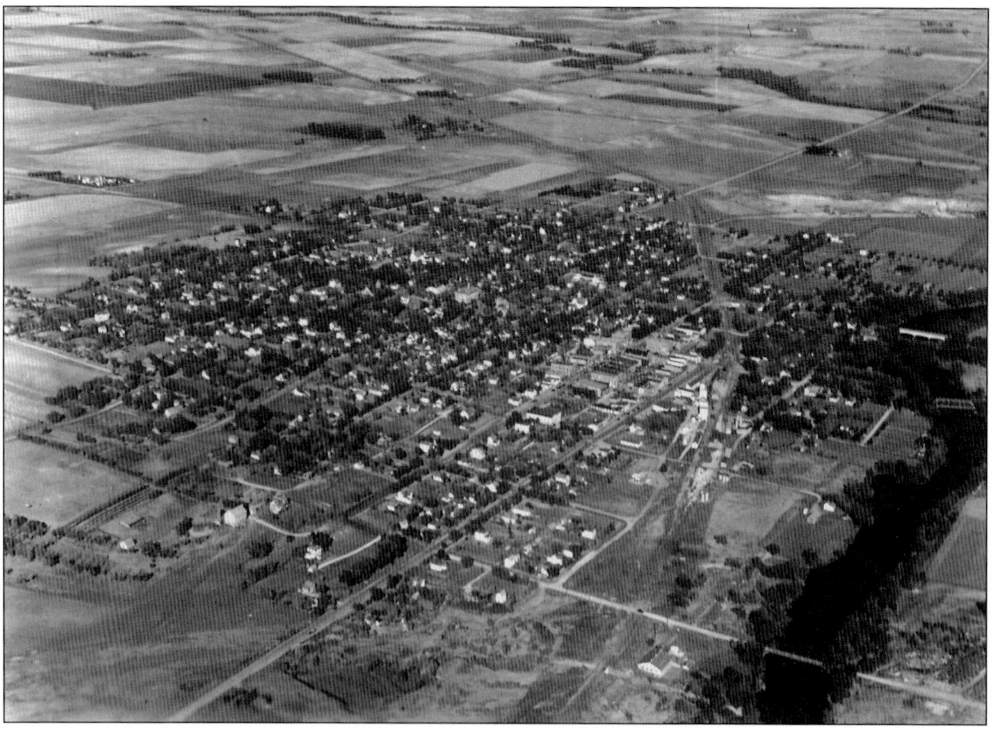

Growth and expansion have played a considerable role in the changes since this aerial photograph was taken. Homes have been built on all sides, expanding the city limits. The quarry has since widened and deepened and the farms on the edge of town have been replaced by businesses and roads. However, downtown businesses, elevator, railroad, and old settlers' bridge all remain in their original buildings, giving the residents a sense of living history.

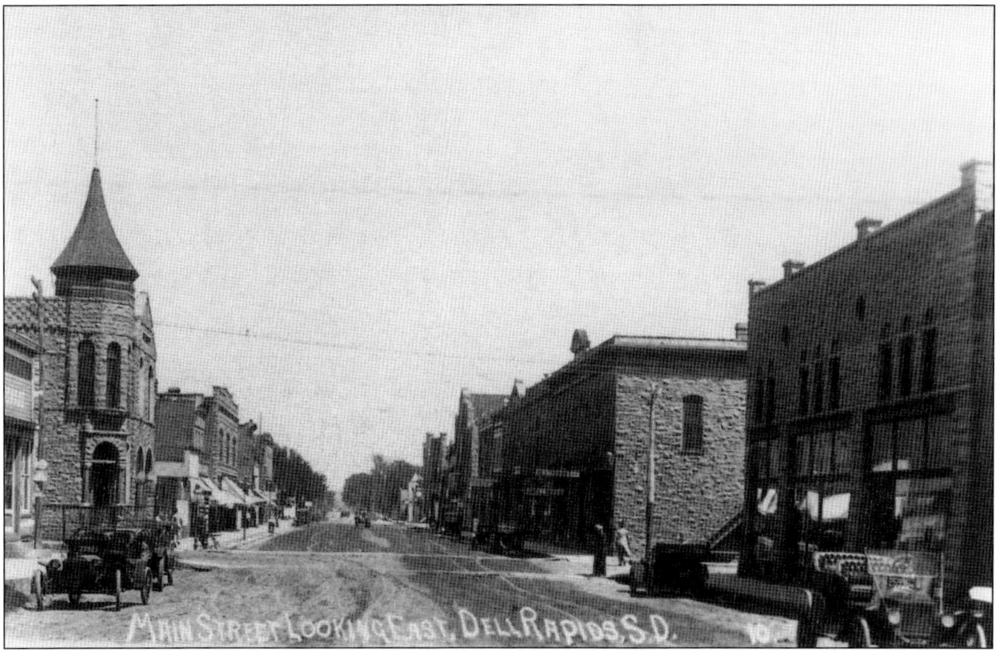

This postcard depicts the early days of Main Street—also called Fourth Street—facing east. Many of these buildings were erected between the late 1880s and the early 1900s, creating a historic downtown district in Dell Rapids. In fact, this entire block is on the National Register of Historic Places.

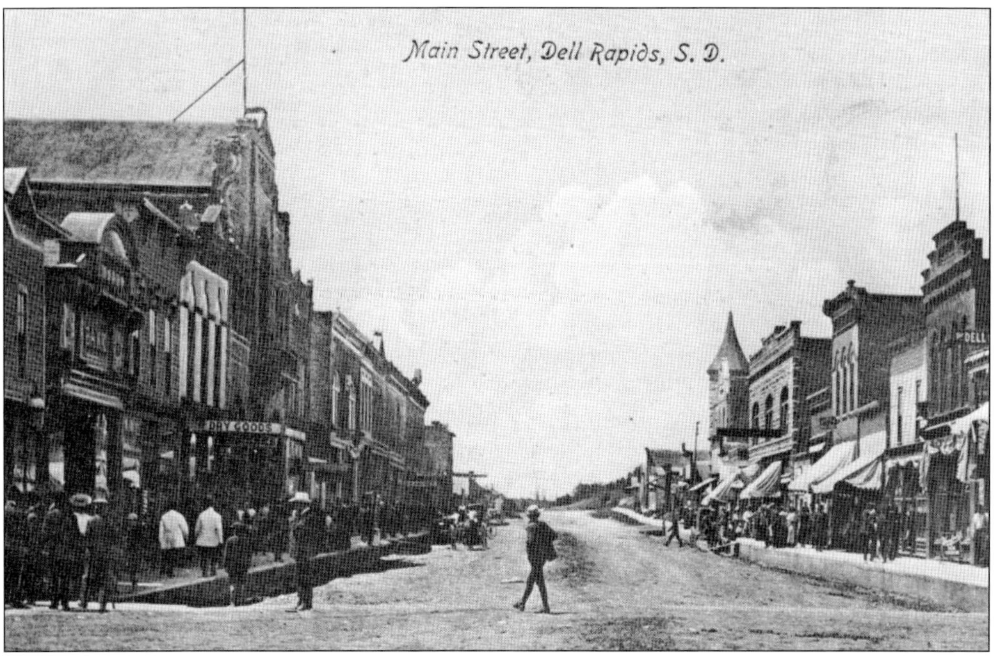

This 1911 postcard, facing west, demonstrates the social and economic value the business district has had on the town. The dirt roads and raised sidewalks were common in small towns during this era, but the quantity of shoppers illustrates that Dell Rapids has always been a thriving community.

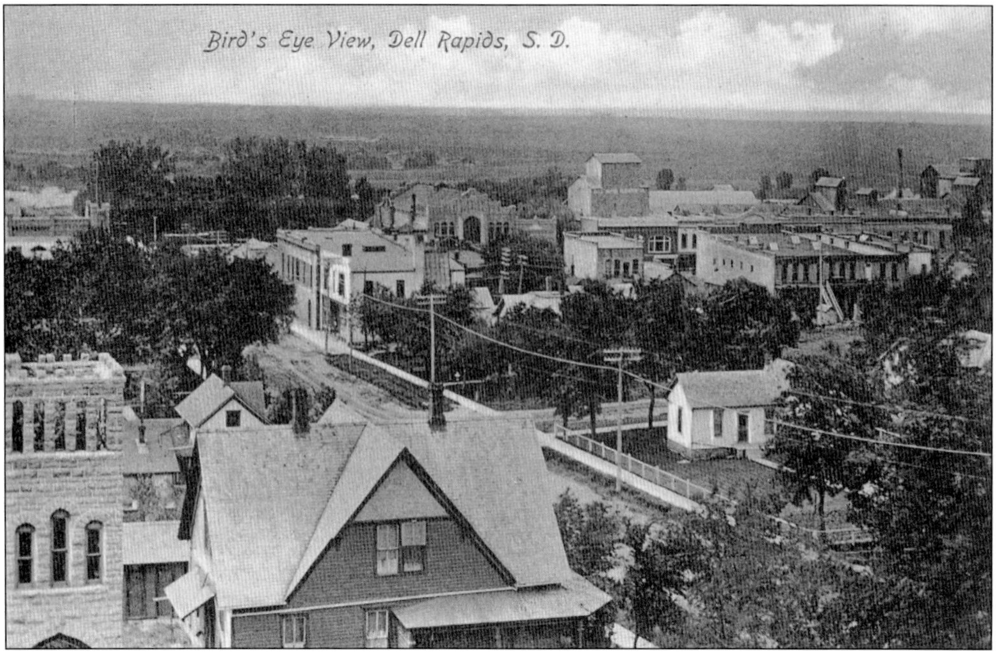

This photograph was taken from atop the old high school building on Sixth Street. Several landmarks are visible, including the old Episcopalian church in the lower left corner; The Grand Opera House, toward the center with the large arched window; and the elevator, just to the right.

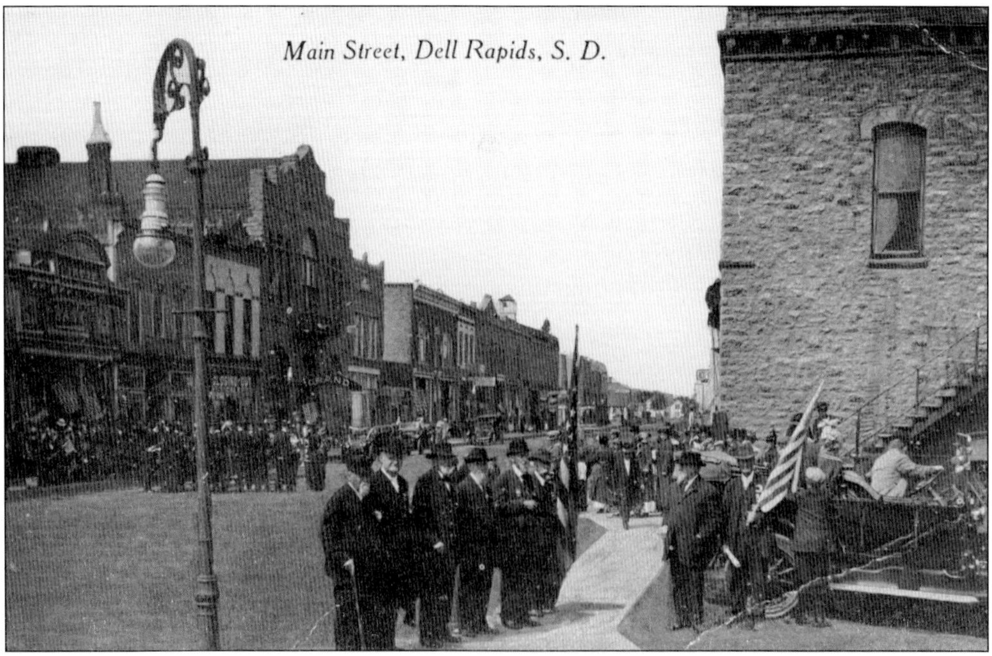

Notable citizens gather for a photograph on Main Street near State Avenue and Fourth Street as the town prepares for a Decoration Day parade. The Grand Opera House and the bank are in the background. The city continues to celebrate Memorial Day, Homecoming, and Quarry Days with parades down this downtown street.

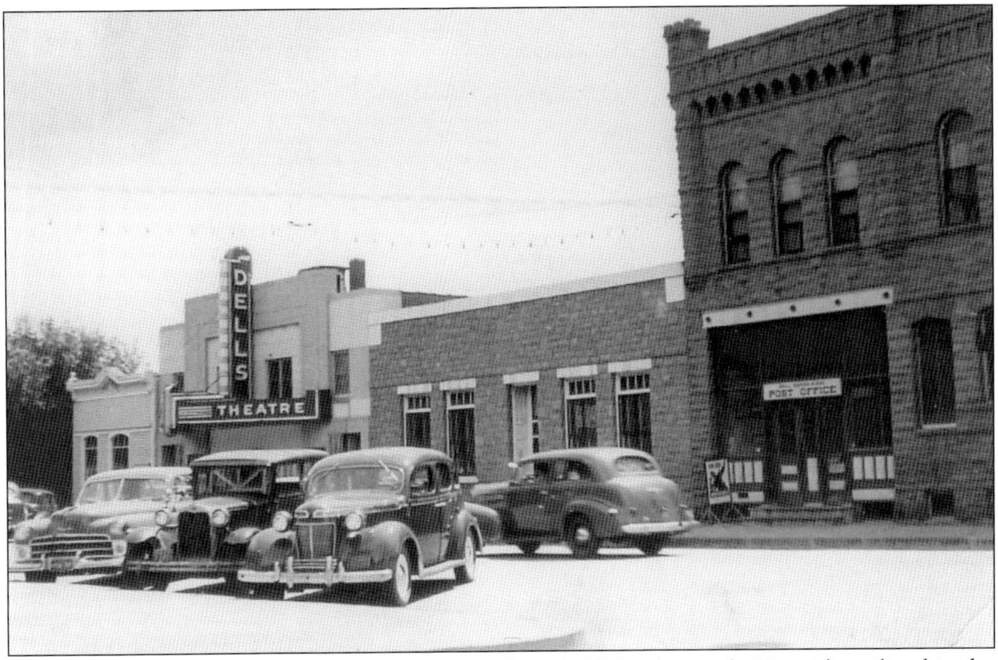

Mail was first delivered to Dell Rapids on December 11, 1871, when only 13 residents lived in the area. Albion Thorne, the first postmaster, kept the town mail in a small black metal box. The post office remained in this building until 1971. Today, the post office delivers to about 2,100 mail addresses.

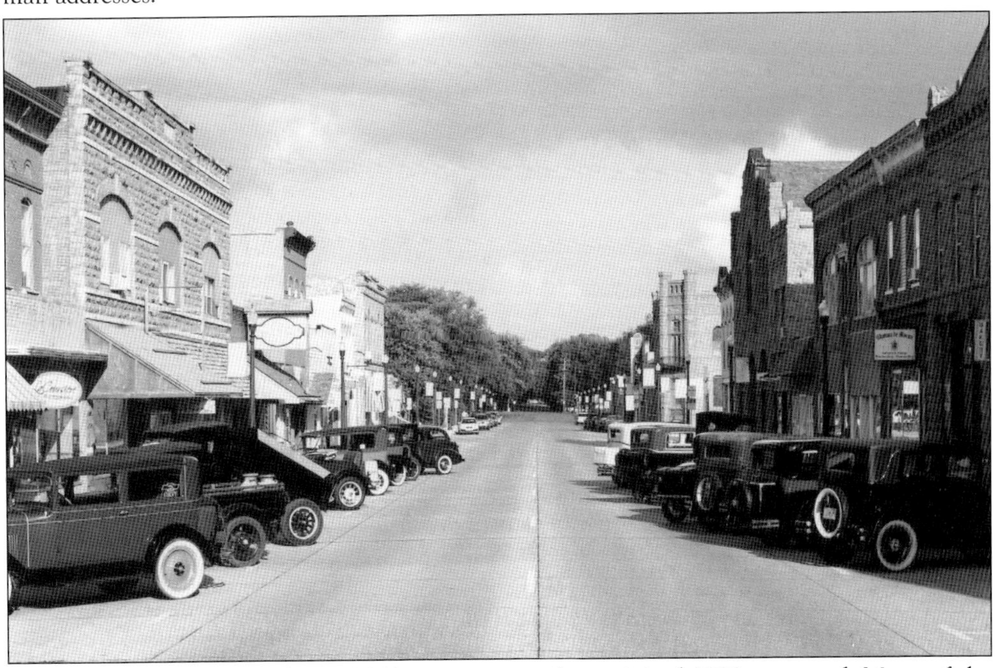

This postcard is a September 9, 2002, re-creation of an original 1930s postcard. Many of the Main Street buildings constructed in the mid-to-late-1880s are still in use today, with storefronts looking much as they did when they were built. Main Street continues to be one of the state's most original and unique business districts.

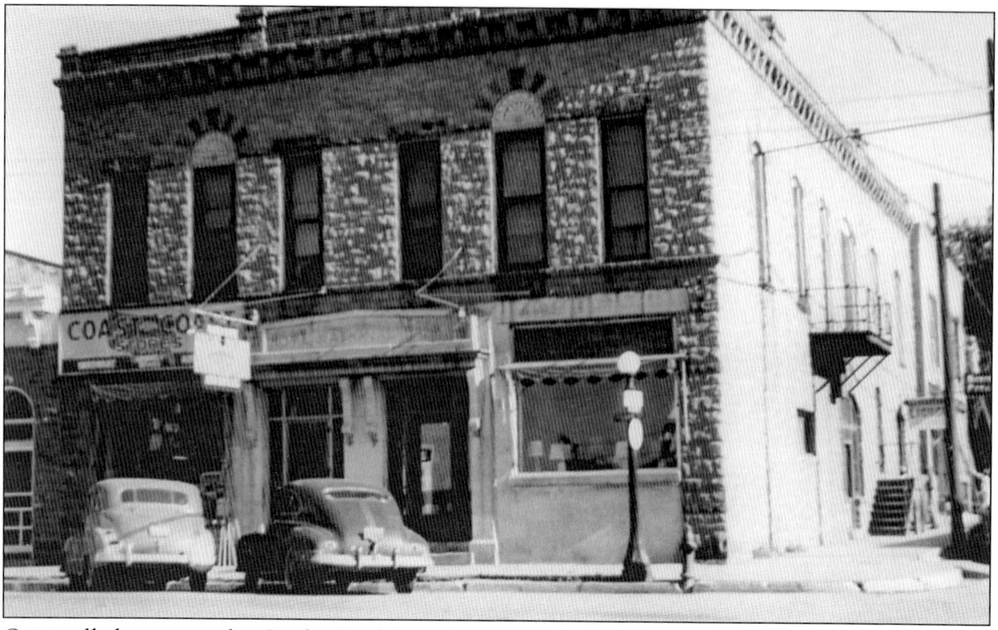

Originally known as the Cooley Building, this structure has received no major alterations since it was built in 1885 and has served as a bank, hotel, harness shop, newspaper, and vision clinic. In the back of the building is an apartment building, built in 1900, which was previously used by the millinery shop and Northern States Power. The front building was constructed with the use of local quartzite.

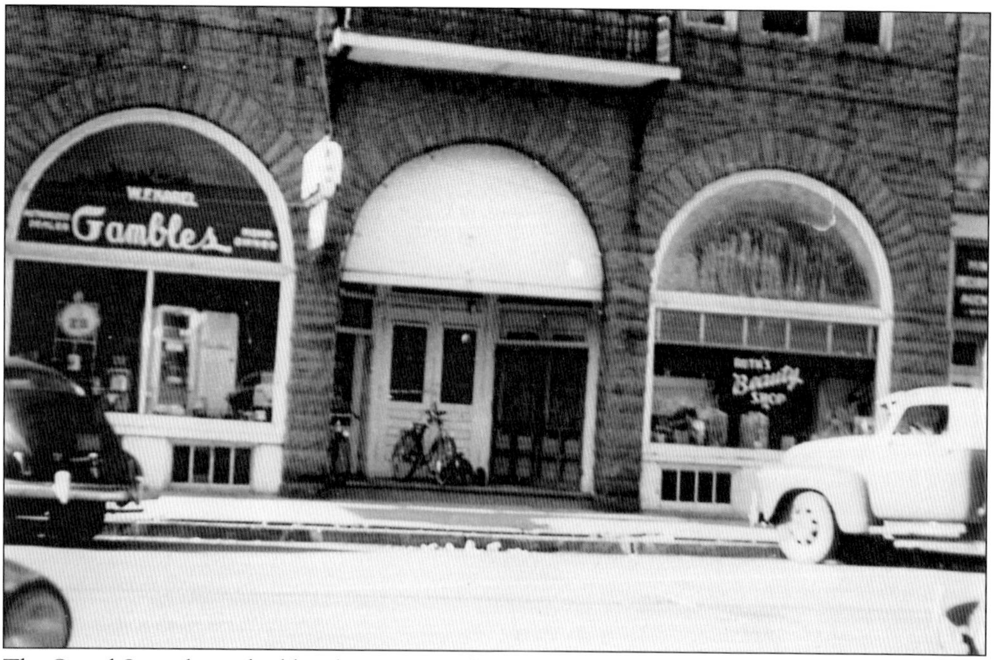

The Grand Opera house building has contained many businesses over the years. In this photograph, one can see Gambles Department Store and Ruth's Beauty Shop, which Ruth Cobb started in 1924. Until a broken arm forced her to quit at the age of 93, Ruth had no plans to retire. At the time of her death, Ruth had run the longest-running business in Dell Rapids.

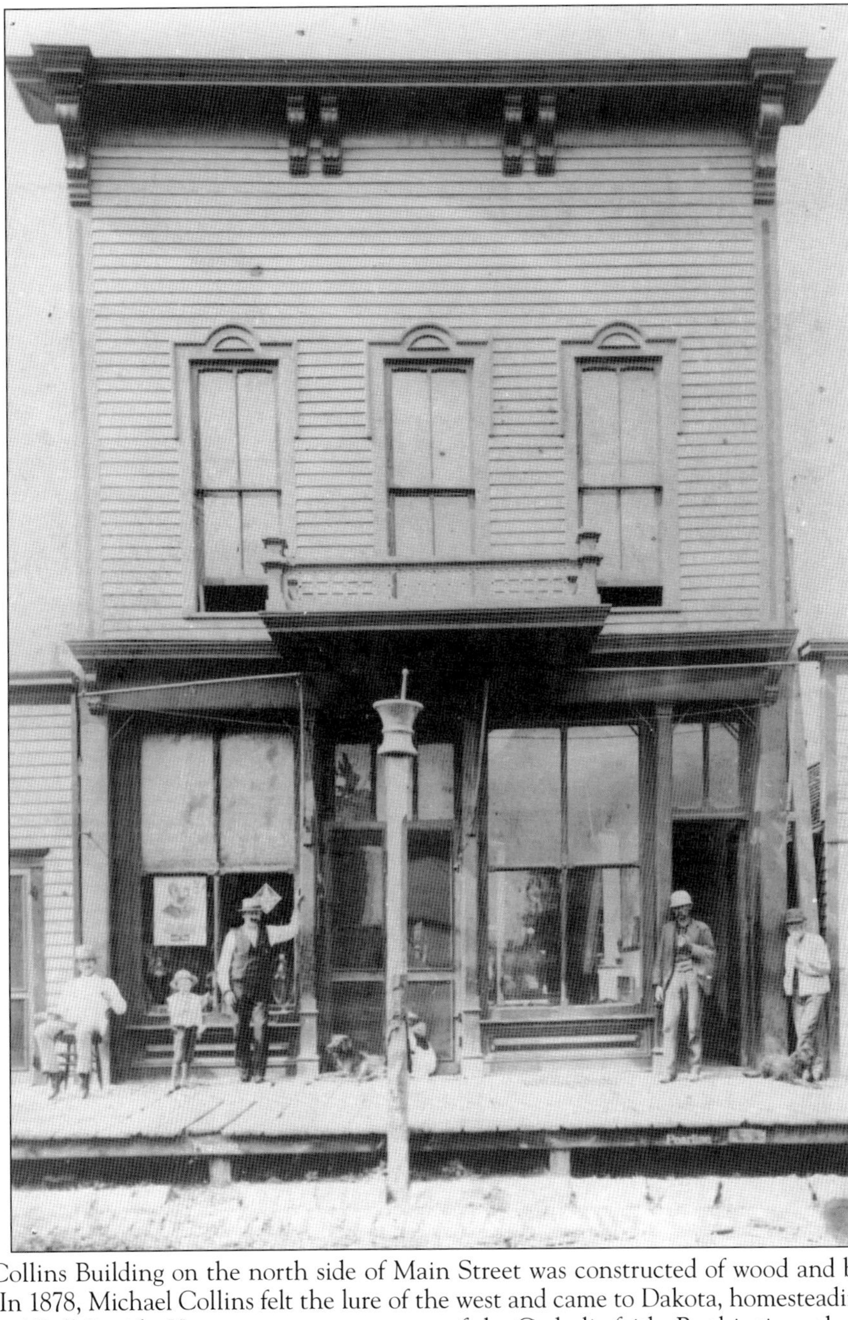

The Collins Building on the north side of Main Street was constructed of wood and brick in 1901. In 1878, Michael Collins felt the lure of the west and came to Dakota, homesteading land north of Dell Rapids. He was a strong supporter of the Catholic faith. By this time, there were too many Catholics to meet in a private home and there was a need for Mass to be celebrated in a public place, so Collins's two-story building was of service for some time. Collins went to Wisconsin in 1880, married his wife, Margaret, and returned to Dell Rapids, where they lived for the remainder of their lives. Besides Collins Drug Store, various businesses such as a harness shop, auto top repair, café, bakery, and menswear shop have all found a home in the Collins Building. In this image, barber Mike Carrigan sits on the far left next to little Joseph Collins and his father, Michael Collins. (Courtesy St. Mary Catholic Church.)

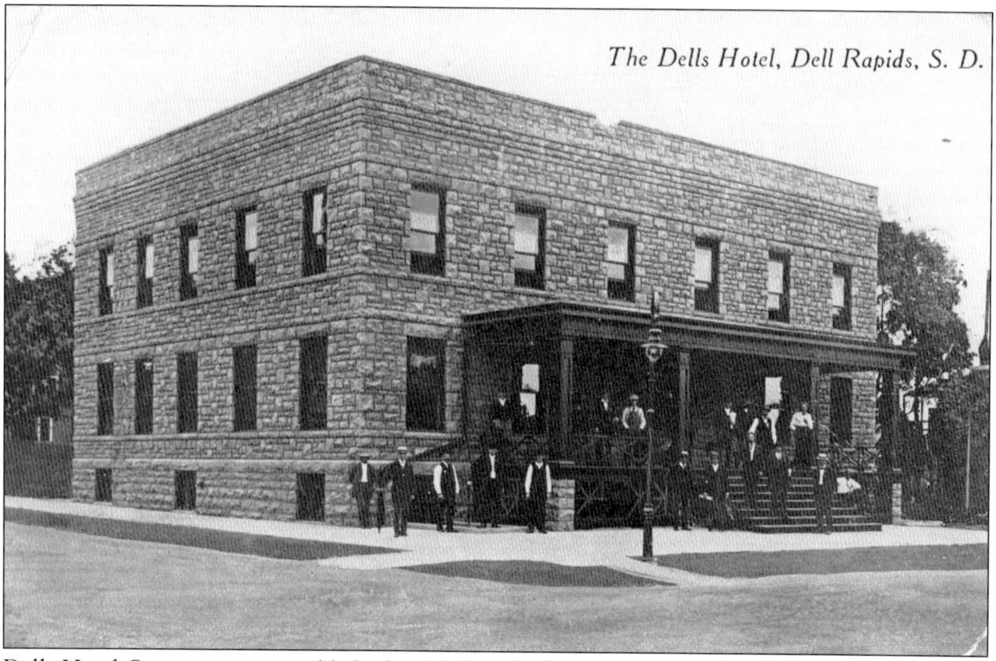

Dells Hotel Company was established in 1907 and a hotel was created with 20 guest rooms and a lobby, office, dining room, and parlors, making it one of the finest in the state. This photograph is believed to have been taken upon the building's completion in 1908, with the shareholders standing in front of the building. (Courtesy Rose Stone Inn.)

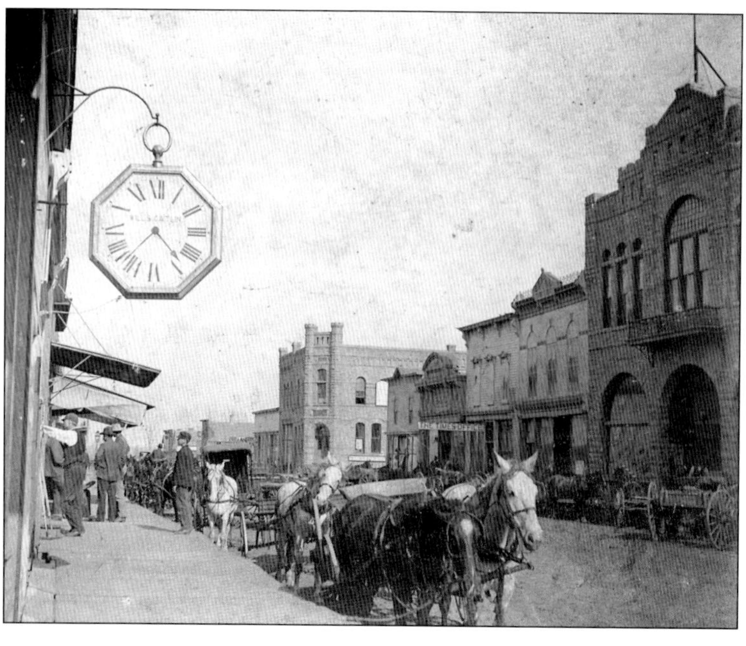

Willard Catlin came to Dell Rapids in 1888 and opened a jewelry store, which he ran until his death in 1928. In addition to his jewelry, he took a course in optical work and later added that line of work in connection with his jewelry business.

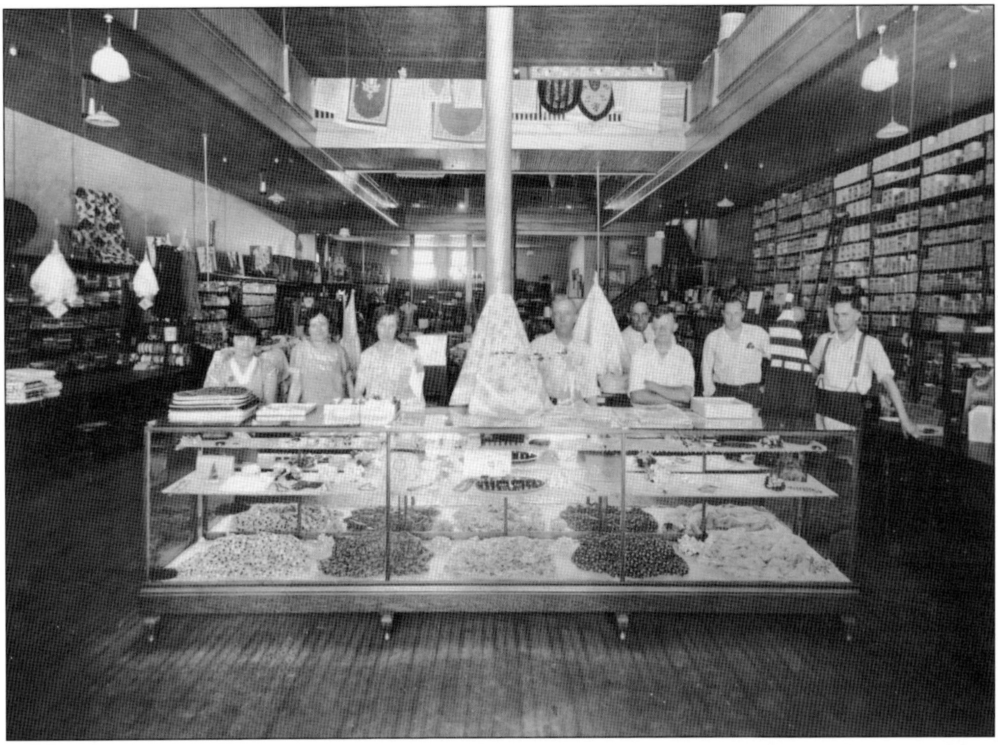

The name Dieson's has become a byword of the buying public in the Dell Rapids area and has been a factor in the growth of the community. Dieson's department store was founded by Martin A. Dieson in 1887 and was a family-run business, with his children Emma, Harry, and Ben in charge of the business after their father's death in 1923.

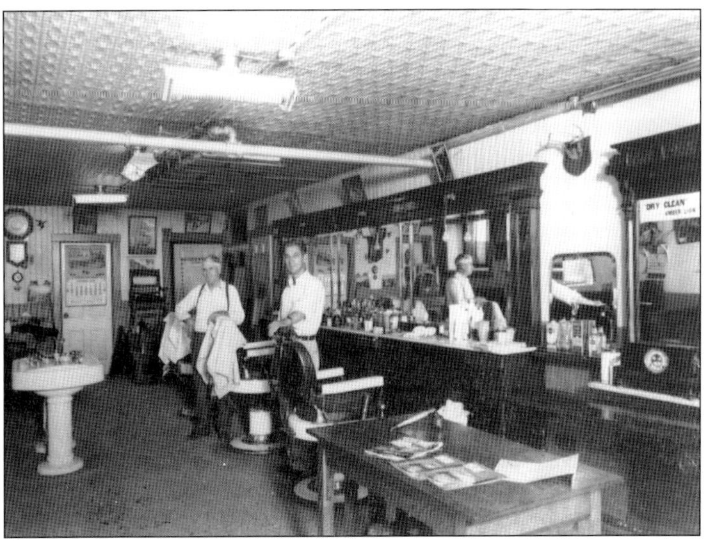

Drummond Barber Shop began in the basement of the Smith Block building in 1915. The shop was a popular spot for the men to exchange the latest news and it rarely closed before 10:00 p.m. or even 12:00 a.m. on a Saturday night. Haircuts, shaves, and clean baths were all 25¢ each. Webster Drummond (left) and his son, Web Jr., take a break from work to pose for this photograph.

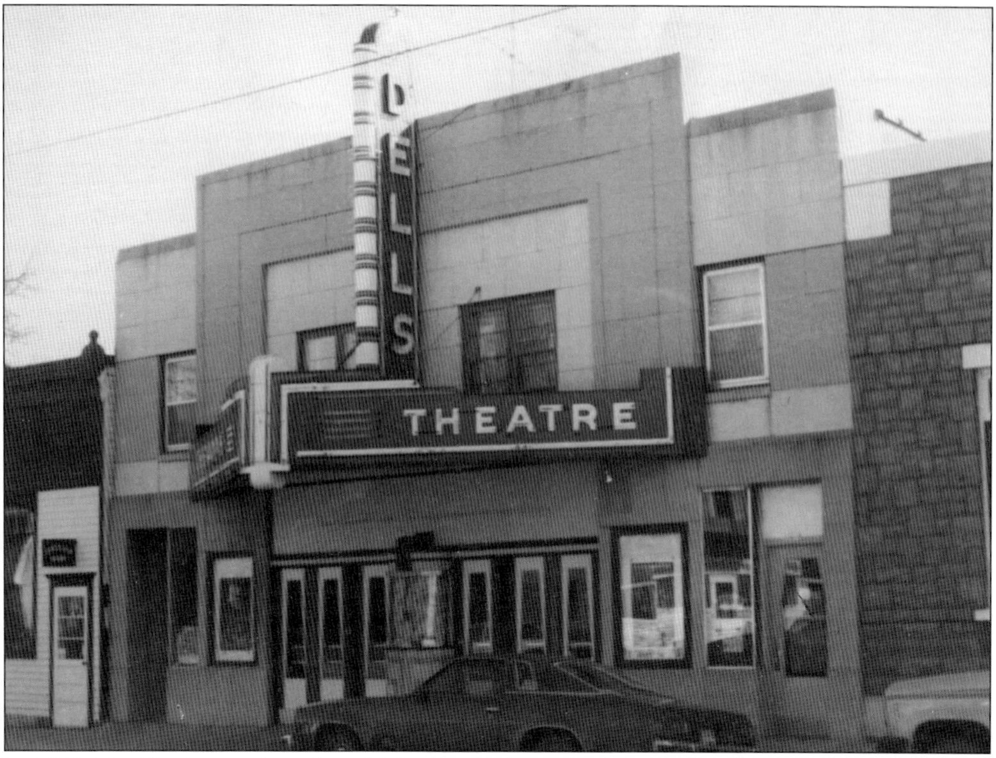

In 1937, John Underwood purchased The Grand from the O'Leary brothers. He immediately saw the need for a new theatre. If all went well, Dell Rapids would be home to the finest theatre in the state. The building was to be 44 feet by 100 feet with a seating capacity of 464. In August 1938, after four months of construction, *Give Me A Tailor*, with Martha Ray and Bob Hope, opened the theatre and was the first showing in South Dakota. The theatre has undergone updates and modernizations, blending the restored original hand-painted stencil wall design and light fixtures with all the benefits of today's technology.

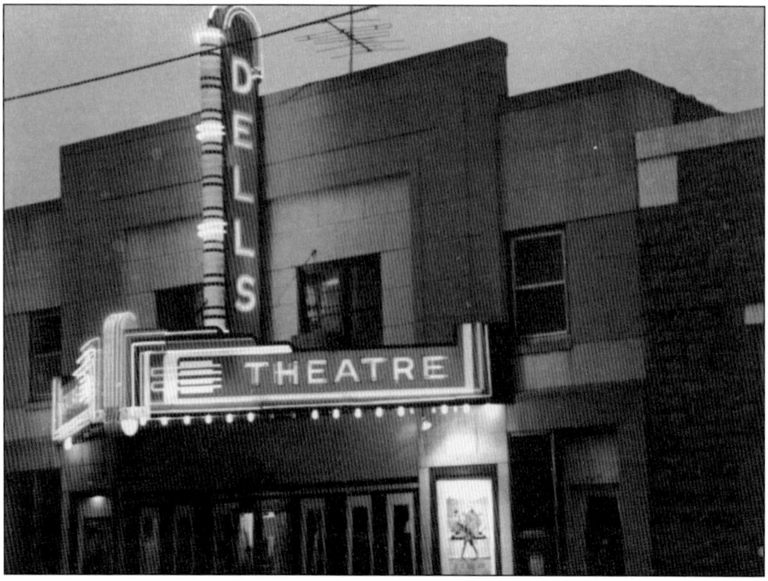

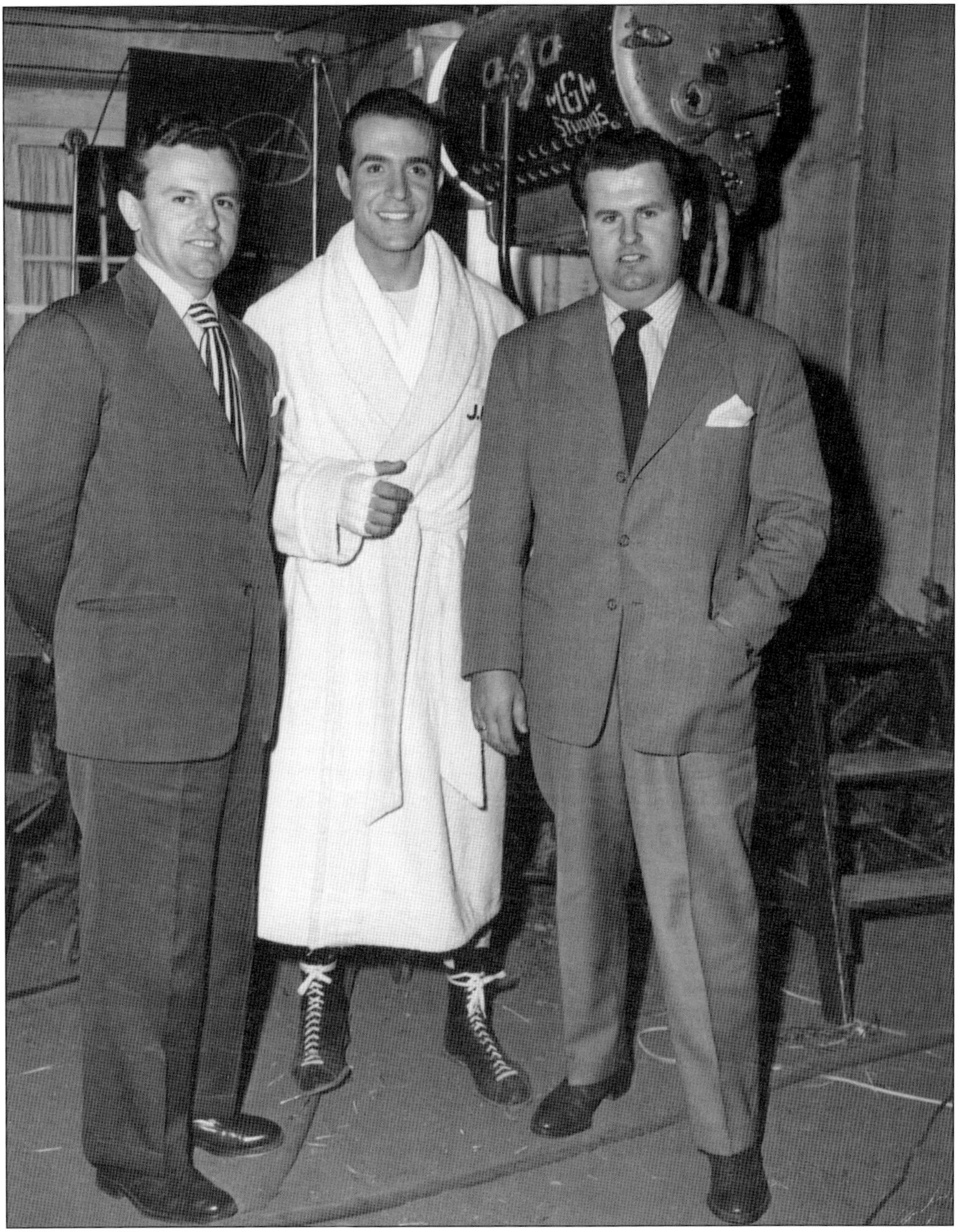

In 1950, Lane King (left), manager of the Dells Theatre, and his brother Justin "Jud" (right), at the time the projectionist at the King Theatre in Adrian, Minnesota, visited some of the moving-picture company lots in Hollywood. On the set of *Right Cross* at the Metro-Goldwyn-Mayer Studios, they pose for this photograph with Ricardo Montalban. The cast also included June Allyson, Dick Powell, Lionel Barrymore, and Marilyn Monroe, who had a bit part but is not listed in the credits. Lane and his brother were no strangers to the theater business. Their father, Perry King, purchased the Dells Theatre in 1942. After serving in the Navy during World War II, Jud operated the theater with Lane. The business changed over the years, but it was the people that kept their interest. Jud's career in the theater business ended when he died in 1997.

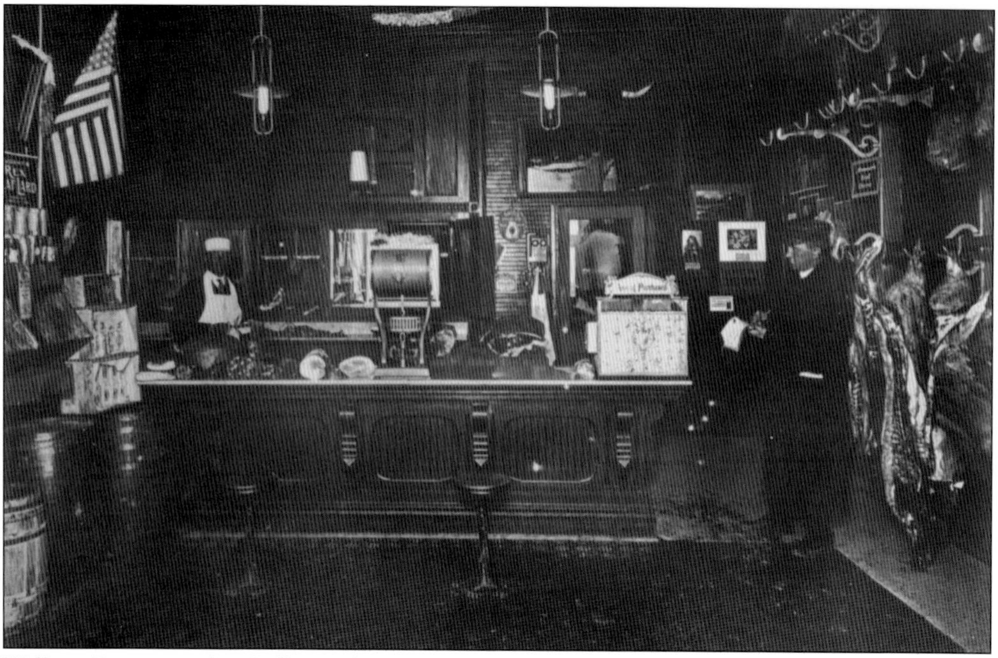

William Beto moved to Dell Rapids in 1904 and was a longtime businessman in town, operating Beto's Meat Market, and, in later years, a locker plant. He was known for his honesty and integrity in business. This building has been a meat market of some kind since it was built in 1903.

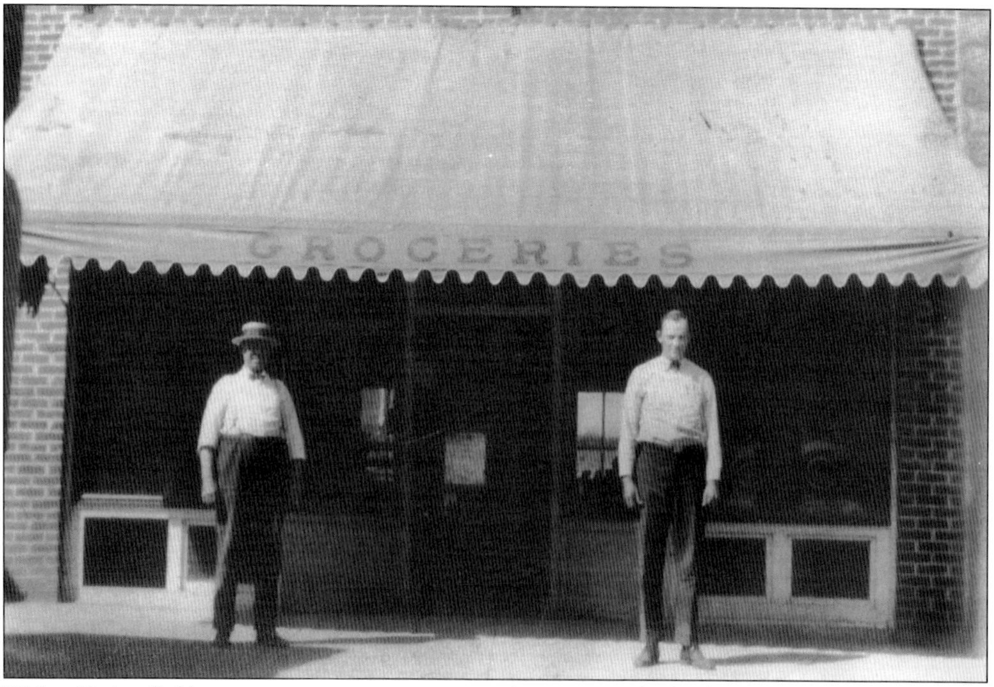

Walter Briley (left) was no stranger to running a business, as he had run a hardware store with his father, William. By 1920, Walter and his brother Frank built and operated a grocery store just across the street from Rimes' General Store. Eventually, Walter's son Norris (right) joined the business. Norris carried on the tradition and opened his own business in Sioux Falls.

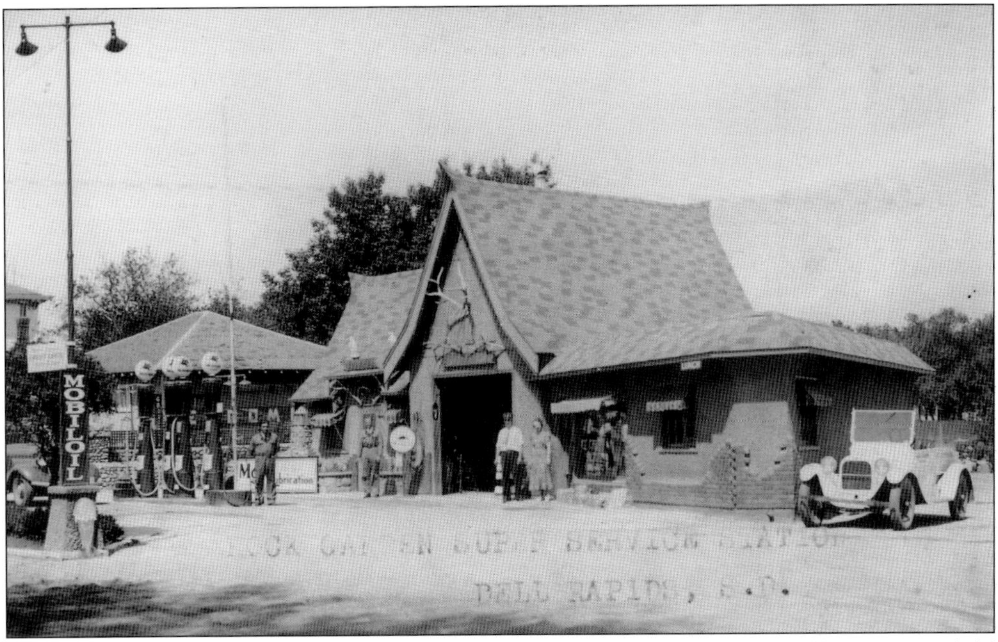

In the 1930s, Gus Langeberg operated a White Eagle filling station on Highway 77—now Garfield Avenue—and transformed the north side of the property into an exhibit replicating the Black Hills of South Dakota. It is estimated that more than 1,000 people per week stopped to see his work. The building has since been renovated to accommodate Schwebach Realty and Insurance, but the outside architecture of the building has been kept intact. (Courtesy Tom Schwebach.)

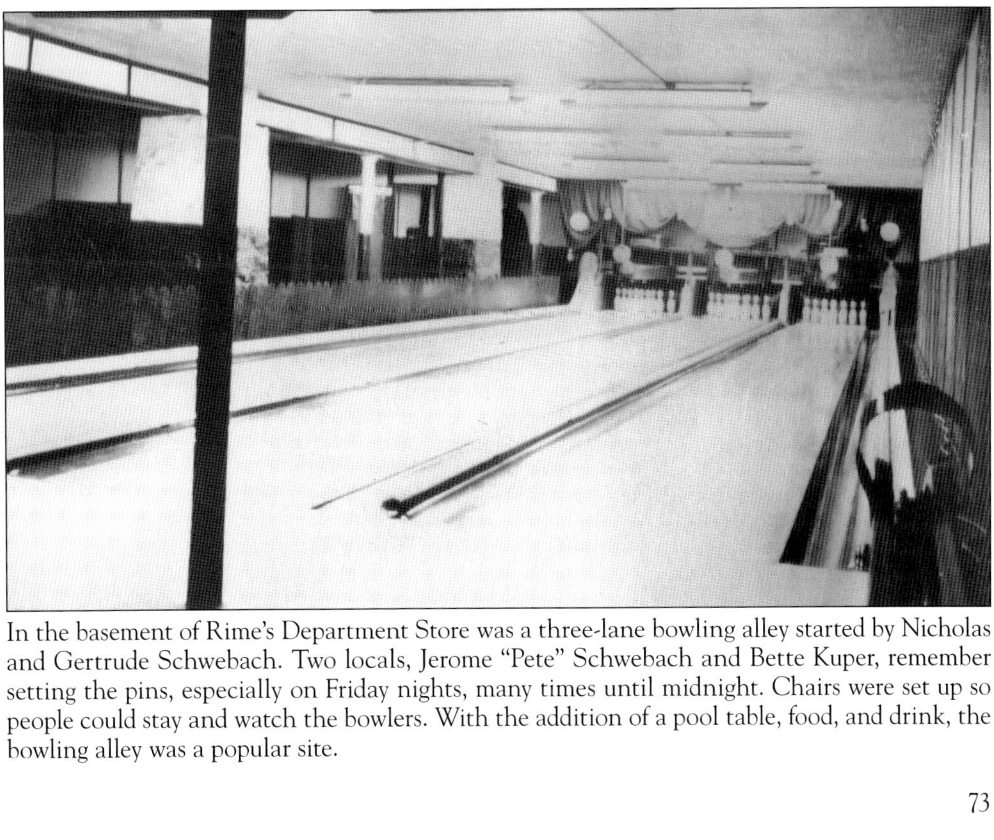

In the basement of Rime's Department Store was a three-lane bowling alley started by Nicholas and Gertrude Schwebach. Two locals, Jerome "Pete" Schwebach and Bette Kuper, remember setting the pins, especially on Friday nights, many times until midnight. Chairs were set up so people could stay and watch the bowlers. With the addition of a pool table, food, and drink, the bowling alley was a popular site.

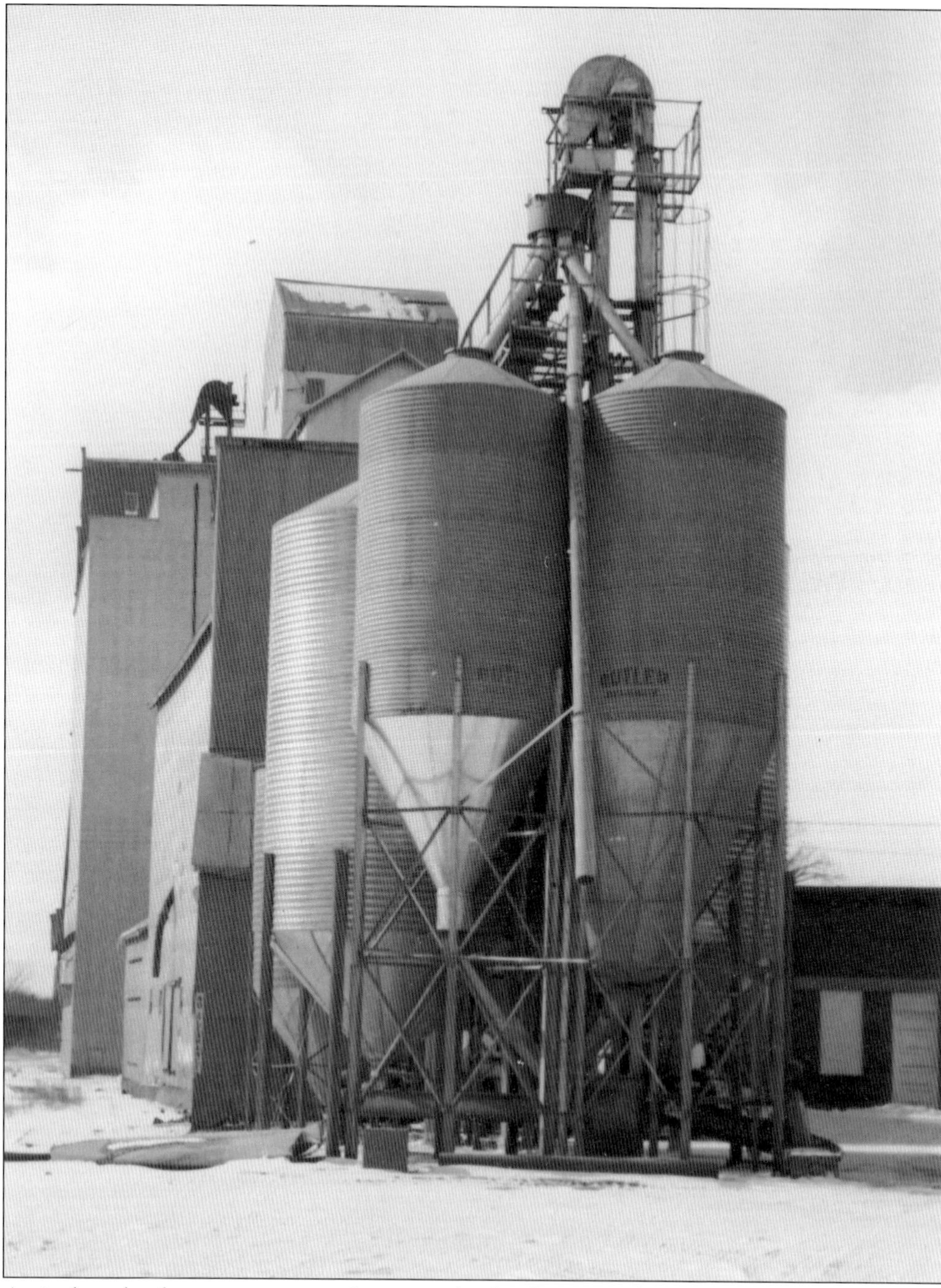

Agriculture has been a major contribution to the development of South Dakota and particularly to Dell Rapids. Since the early pioneers of the area arrived, farming has been a way of life. The top commodities in the area have been corn, soybeans, wheat, cattle, and hogs. Early residents harvested their crops using a team of horses; today, larger and more expensive equipment, such as combines, make it an easier, quicker, and more efficient endeavor. These advancements have allowed the farm sizes to increase and, unlike the early days, the majority of the livestock production—particularly cattle and chickens—is no longer for personal, in-home use.

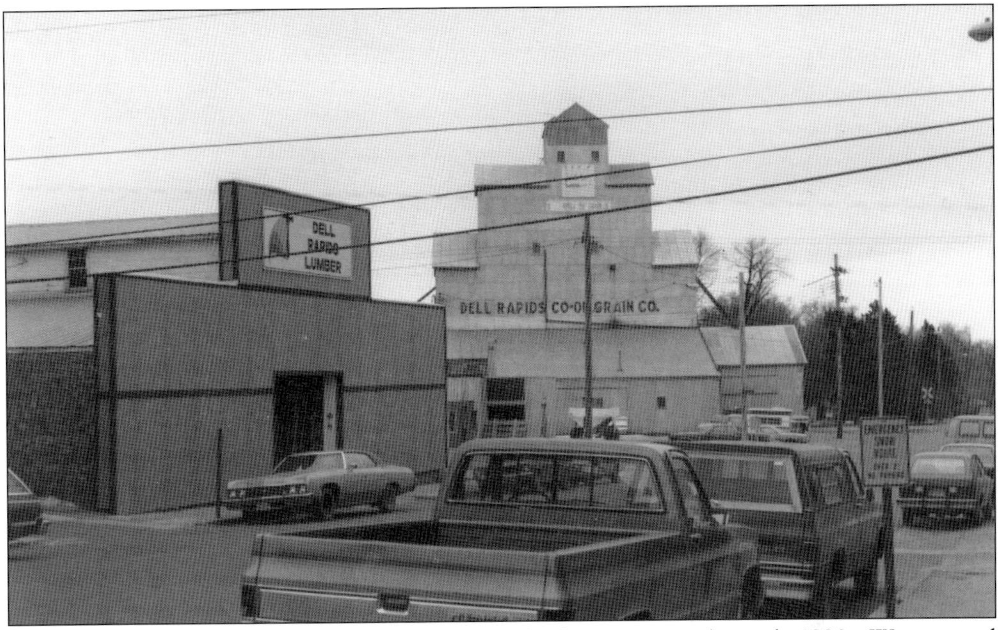

The local grain elevator has served as a hot spot for farmers since the early 1880s. Wagons and trucks still line up outside the structure to unload their yield. W.L. Briley and Chris Williams served as managers during daytime hours and the town's sources for feed included Main Street businesses owned by E.J. Elliot and Charles Blow.

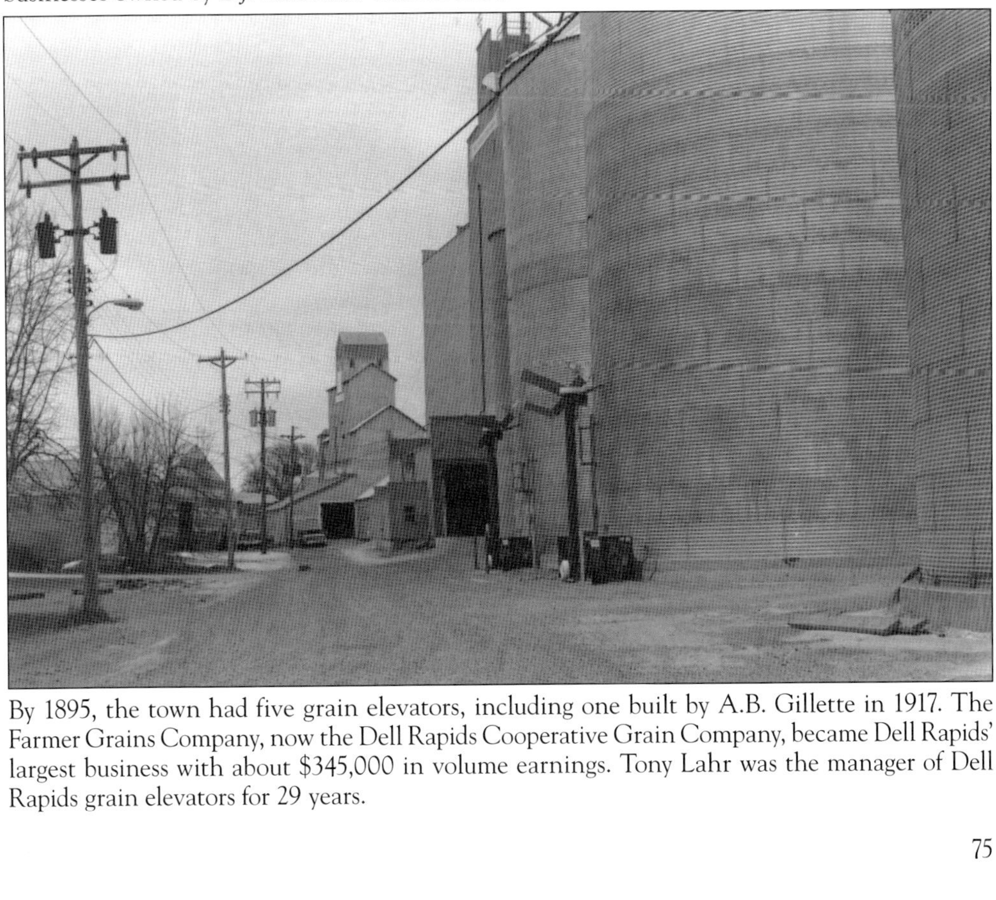

By 1895, the town had five grain elevators, including one built by A.B. Gillette in 1917. The Farmer Grains Company, now the Dell Rapids Cooperative Grain Company, became Dell Rapids' largest business with about $345,000 in volume earnings. Tony Lahr was the manager of Dell Rapids grain elevators for 29 years.

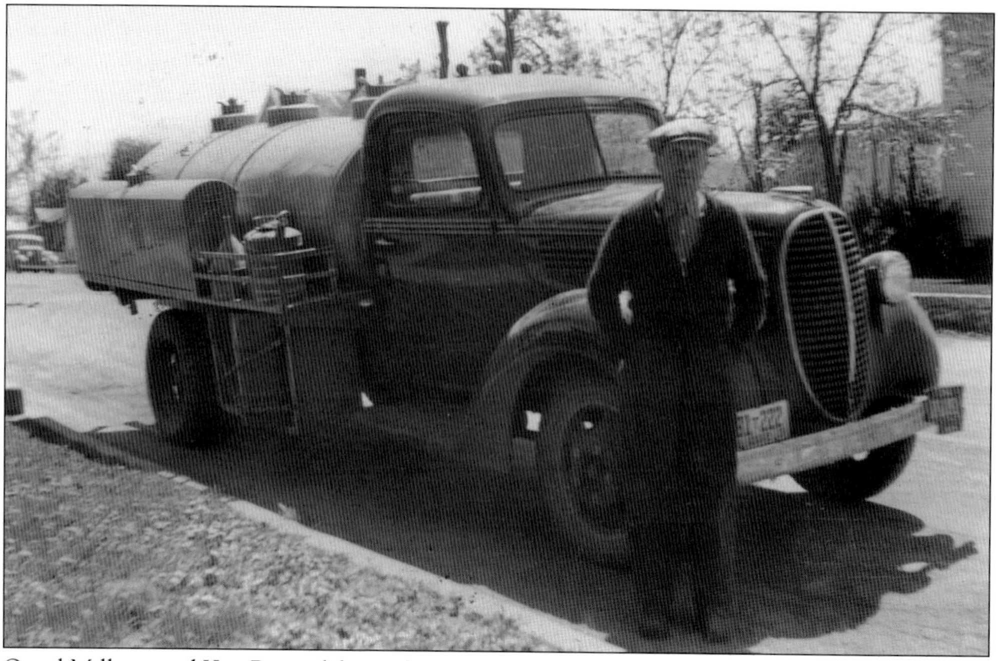

Orval Millette and Ken Boyer delivered groceries to many of the homes in Dell Rapids. In 1936, a Chevrolet panel truck was purchased with money received from the government as a bonus to World War I veterans. There was one delivery a day Monday through Friday and two deliveries on Saturdays. Clyde Cooper stands in front of a fuel delivery truck. (Courtesy Michelle Haggar.)

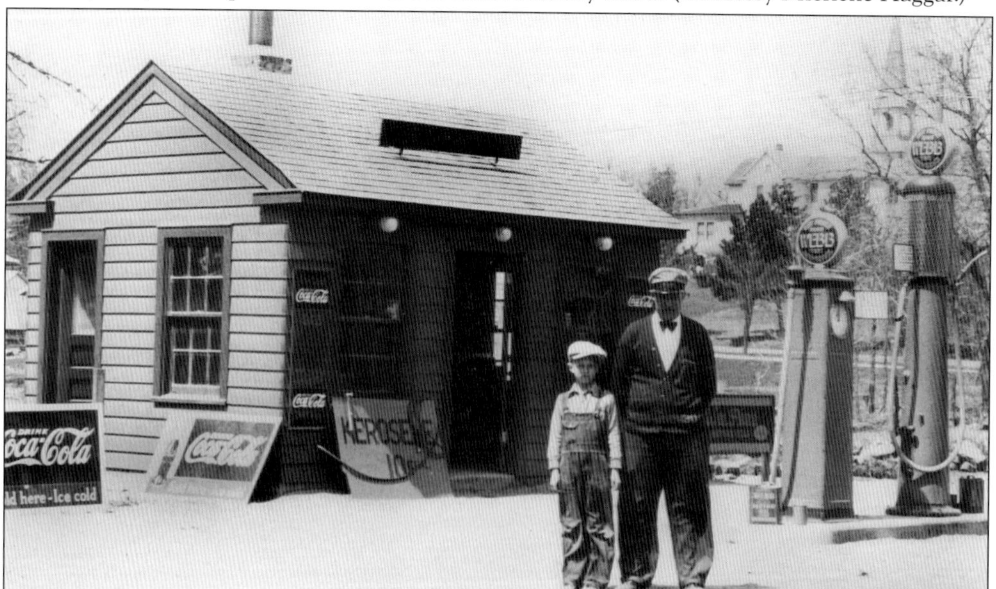

This gas station was owned by Clyde and Harold Boyer, and it remained almost unchanged from 1934 to 1977, when the Boyers retired. Gasoline was once 20¢ per gallons, and oil was 15¢ a quart. Many locals remember stopping in for candy and pop and during elementary school recess, and there were occasional accidents when a ball would roll down the street, giving children an opportunity to stop in the station. Kenneth Boyer is pictured with his uncle Harold. (Courtesy Michelle Haggar.)

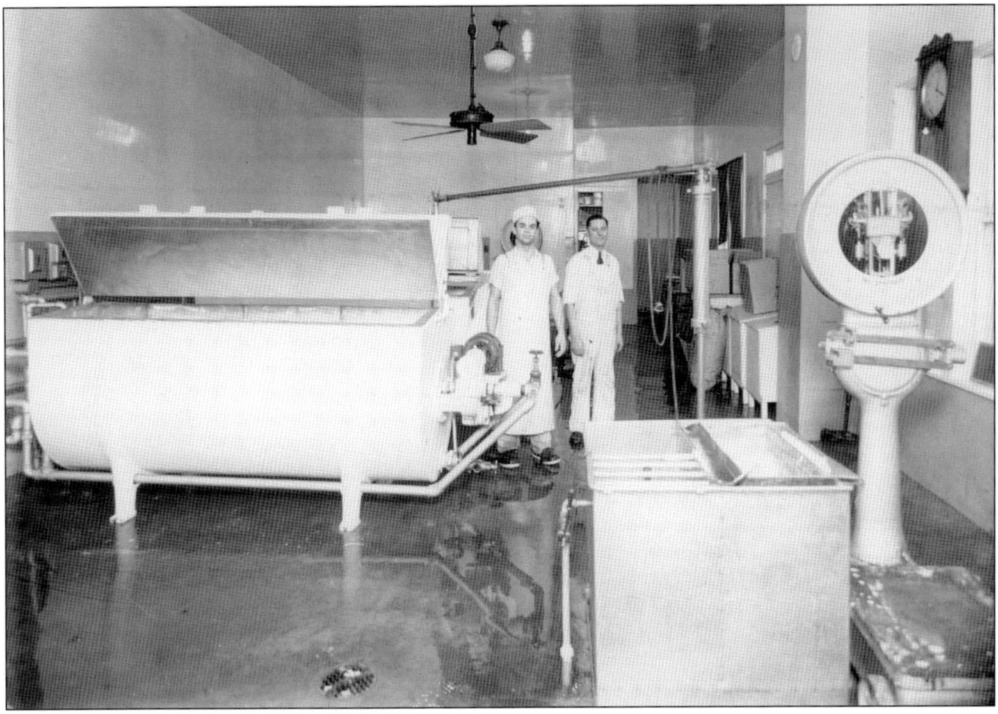

The Dell Rapids Creamery was the first in the Sioux Valley, in 1882. Butter was shipped as far away as New York and in January 1895, the creamery was cited as a model establishment by the Farmers' Institute. A farmers' cooperative creamery operated until the late 1940s and the building was later turned into a publishing business. Melford Blegstad (left) was the butter maker in 1941.

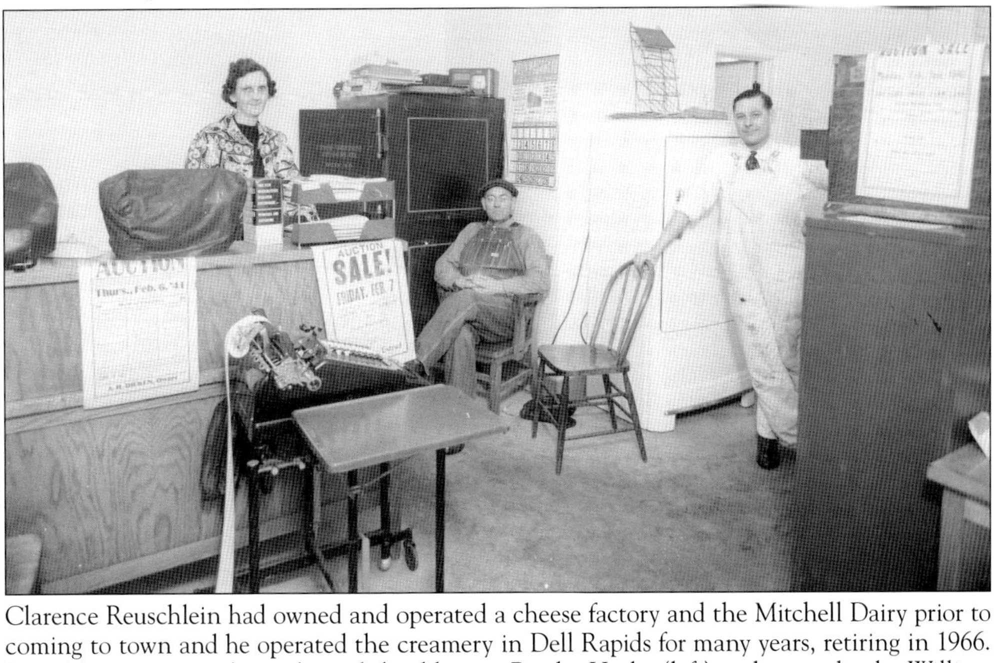

Clarence Reuschlein had owned and operated a cheese factory and the Mitchell Dairy prior to coming to town and he operated the creamery in Dell Rapids for many years, retiring in 1966. Reuschlein is pictured at right with bookkeeper Bertha Husby (left) and cream hauler William Munk (center). The building was later sold to Smith Publishing.

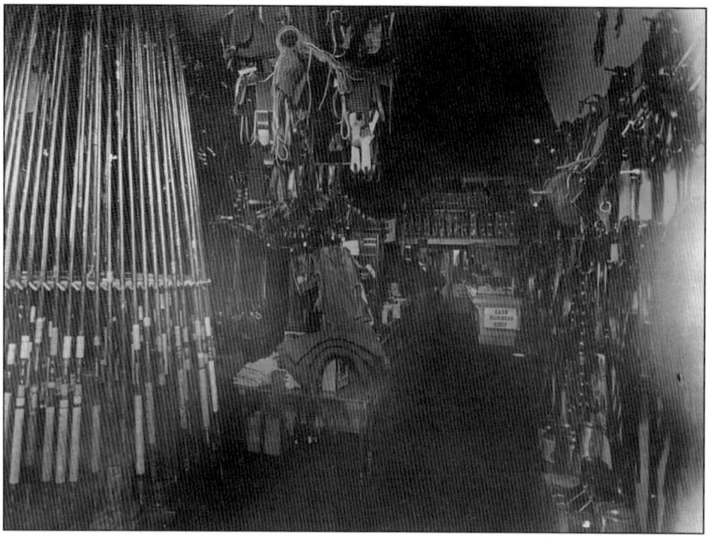

By 1880, two harness shops had been established in town, one of which was owned by James Nisbet, an early pioneer of the community. Fred Barbour, after completing a four-year course, came to Dell Rapids and purchased the business from Nisbet. Sigfrid Swanson (center) worked for both Nisbet and Barbour until 1918, when he went into business for himself.

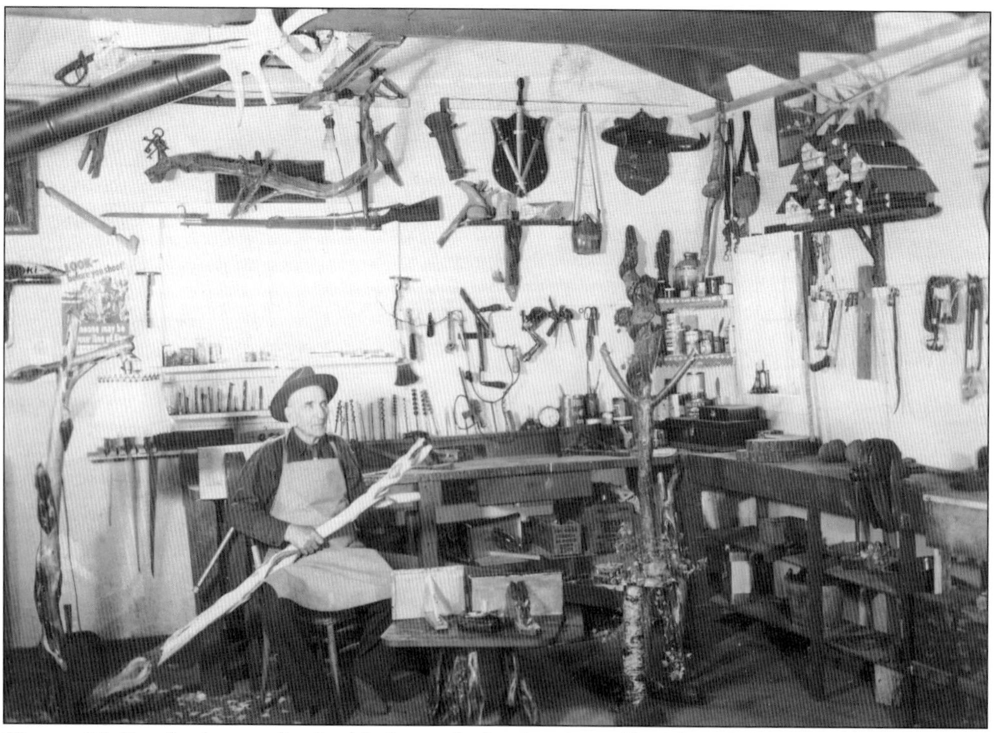

Chester Mallory had wanted to build a home for his family and had found the perfect lot. However, several businessmen also wanted the lot, so without wasting time, he made the necessary trip to complete the deal. Upon his return, the businessmen were already busy on the lot, but Chester's purchase was legal so he got his land. He built the entire home, by himself, with one arm.

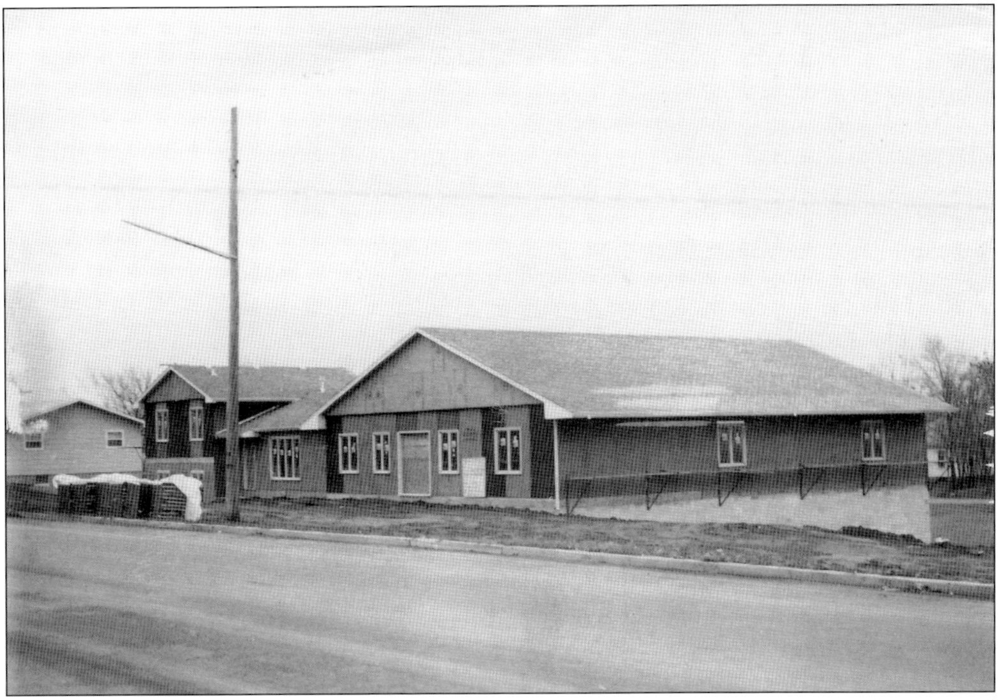

Local funeral homes have played an important role in society by documenting history and consoling families. In 1969, a new facility was built with all the modern conveniences to fit the needs of the community. After partner John Hermanson retired, James Kahler became the sole owner. Kahler Funeral Home has been a family-run business since.

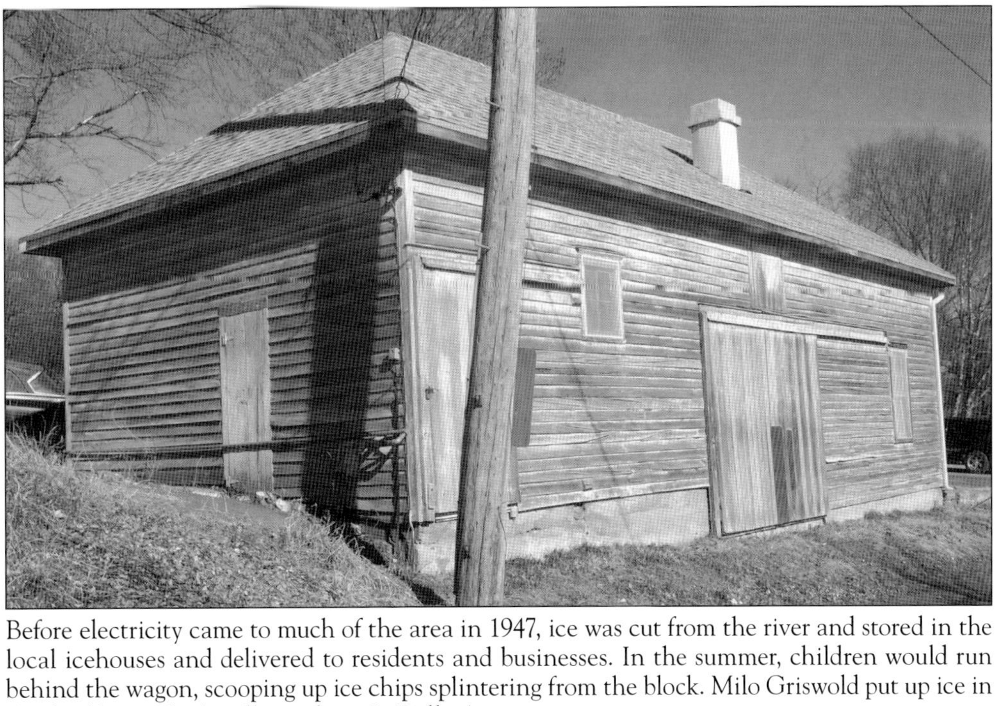

Before electricity came to much of the area in 1947, ice was cut from the river and stored in the local icehouses and delivered to residents and businesses. In the summer, children would run behind the wagon, scooping up ice chips splintering from the block. Milo Griswold put up ice in this building, which still stands on LaDelle Avenue.

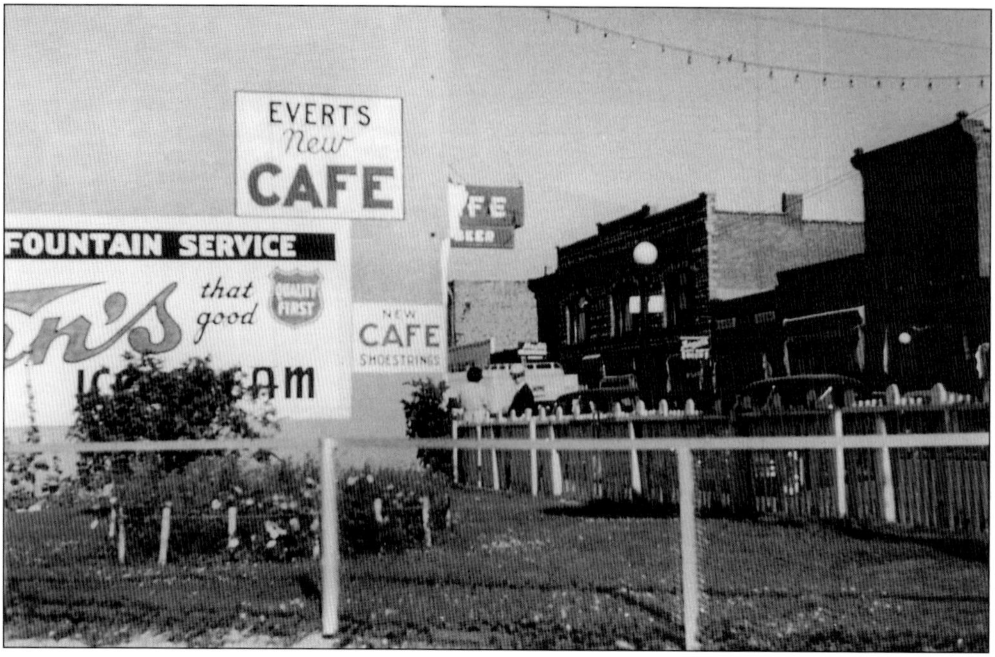

The southwest corner of Fourth Street and Orleans Avenue has seen many changes since the establishment of the town. Early on, the corner was home to three businesses, including Uline's Bank and General Store. It was later transformed into a gas and service station where Luray "Chink" Irwin sold popcorn on Saturday nights.

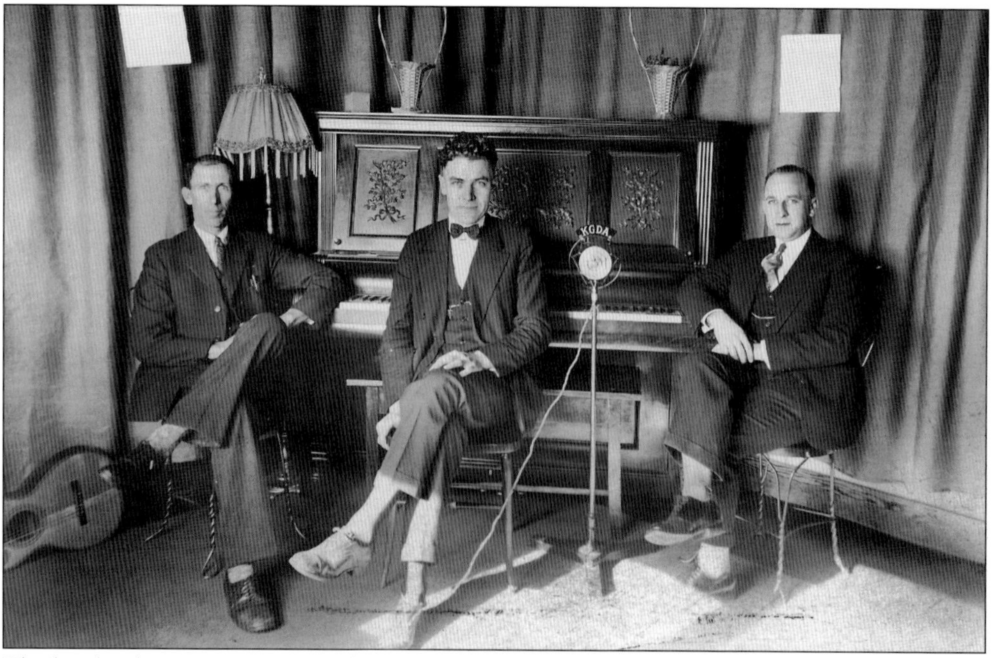

The local radio station was owned and operated by Jim Nelson (left) from 1925 to 1930, in the early days of radio. Area talent and piano pupils of Edna Kraus and Ada Putnam took turns playing on air throughout the week. The station, located on Third Street, had the call letters KGDA—"Kind Greetings Dells Announcing." The two other men are unidentified.

Five

CHURCHES

The community has always placed a central focus on the importance of faith, religion, and the church. The town has a prominent Catholic church and school, St. Mary, which continues to operate with a flow of students and congregation members. It also boasts what is considered the oldest still-standing building in Dell Rapids, the First Baptist Church. Pastors, priests, and ministers have kept the townspeople close to their faith since the settlers first arrived. Traditions can be traced back and tied to notable people of the cloth, such as St. Mary's Father Boley, Rev. C.C. Moe at the Lutheran church, and the Rev. E Aelits of the Reformed church, which he helped organize in the early 1900s. Much of the early growth of the town can be attributed to the organization of churches, a focus of pioneers who sought places of worship to call home.

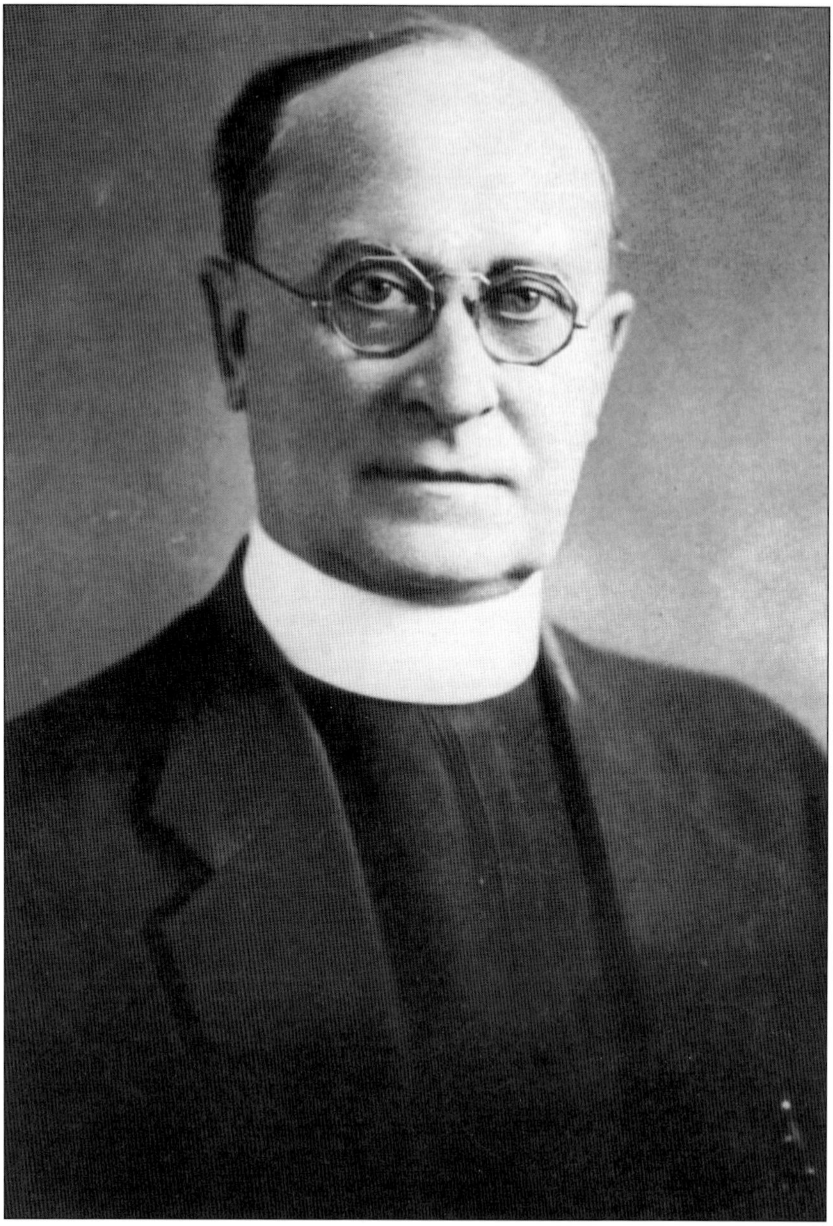

Father Charles Chrysostom Boley was born in 1874 to Joseph and Cecilia (Hertzog) Boley. He was educated at St. Francis College in Loretto, Pennsylvania, at St. Charles Seminary in Baltimore, Maryland, and at St. Bonaventure College in New York. He was ordained December 22, 1901. In 1906, Father Boley came to St. Mary Catholic Church to lead the parish and stayed for the next 32 years. In addition to the parish in Dell Rapids, he served the missions of Garretson, Huntimer, and Colman. Father Boley won the hearts of many in town quickly, often participating in town events. On any Sunday, Father Boley could be found at the baseball diamond; he was a professional umpire, and his decisions were seldom opposed. He was a forward thinker, enlarging the parish house and urging the building of the school, foreseeing the growth in the parish. Father Boley remained dedicated to St. Mary parish until his death on January 5, 1937. (Courtesy St. Mary Catholic Church.)

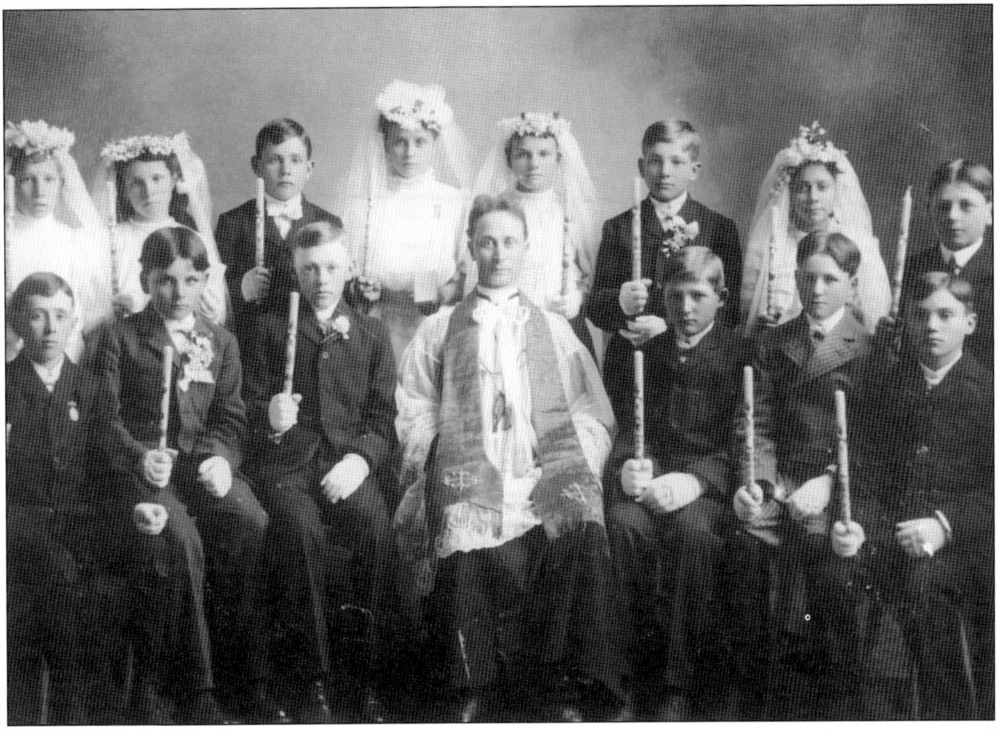

The original 12 families of 1898 had increased to 80 by 1910. On June 9, 1907, 14 children participated in the first Solemn Communion including, from left to right, (first row) George Fitzgerald, Tony Cronin, Arthur Linahan, Father Boley, Frank Bricher, Henry Collins, and Robert Staudenraus; (second row) Ellen Lovelette, Marie Fitzgerald, Pat Devine, Lena Schrier, Lily Staudenraus, Edward Eulberg, Regina Evans, and Ray Wise. (Courtesy St. Mary Catholic Church.)

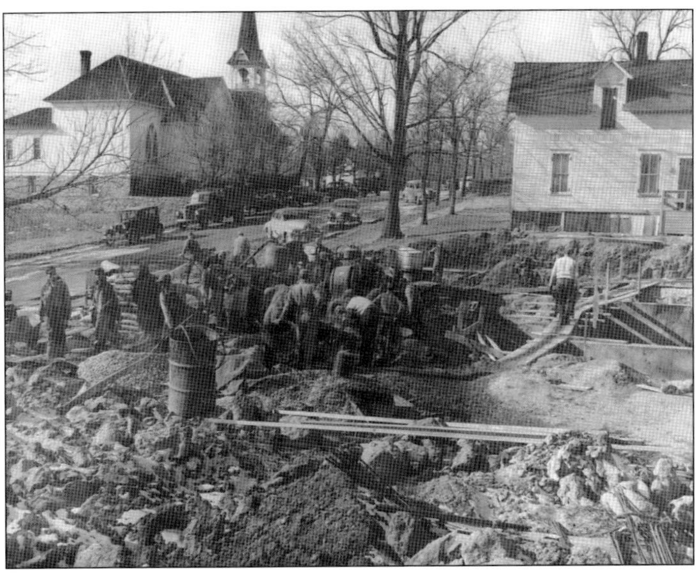

For many early settlers, a place to worship was just as important as food and shelter. Susie Cotter told her husband, "If we don't get a church here, we are going back to Iowa." Her faith and determination, like that of many others, helped build the first church. Crew members began construction on the new Catholic church beneath the shadows of the original church and rectory. (Courtesy St. Mary Catholic Church.)

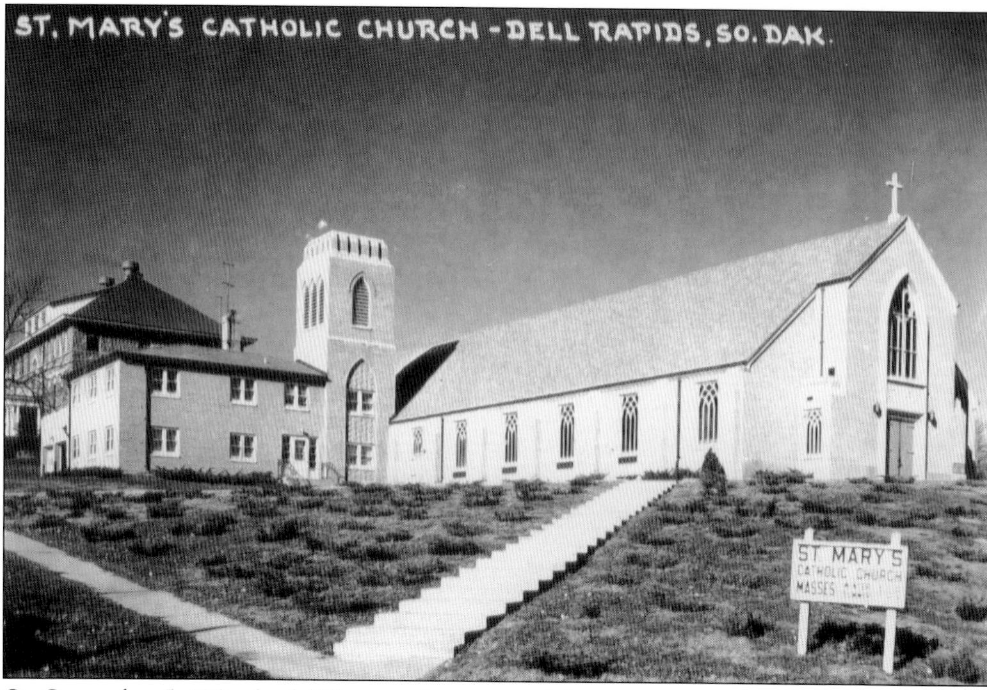

On September 5, 1951, the fulfillment of prayers and devotion occurred with the dedication of the new church and rectory, costing an estimated $225,000. Visiting priests celebrated the first Mass together with Revs. Joseph Nemmers, Charles Nemmers, and Joseph Nemmers from St. Mary parish. The next generation of faith had begun with the same loyalty as before. (Courtesy St. Mary Catholic Church.)

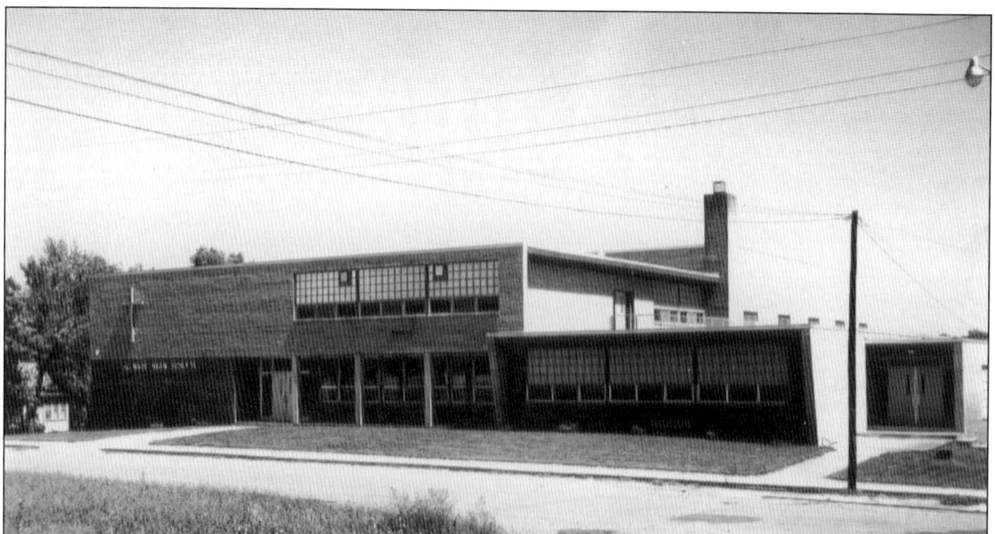

In 1957, Father Meyer said, "Now is the time to do something about this challenging situation. At present there are 226 students in grade school and 80 students in the high school." The first class to graduate from the new St. Mary Catholic High School was in 1958. St. Mary Catholic school system is the only K–12 single-parish-supported school in the state. (Courtesy St. Mary Catholic Church.)

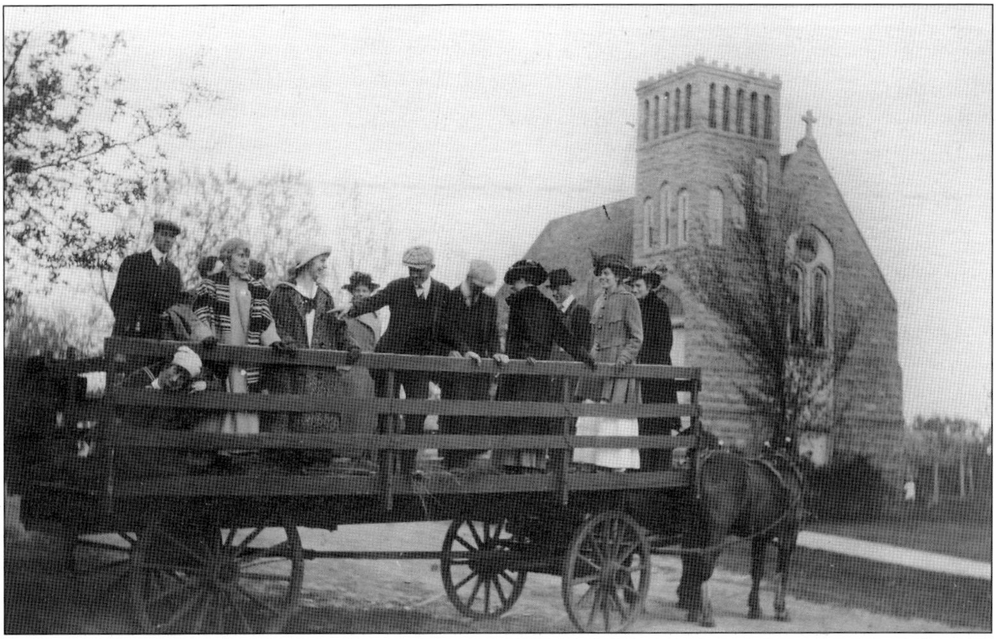

The youth of Dell Rapids gather on a wagon ride for a field trip. The Civil War memorial statue and several churches were once considered a central location in town. This photograph was taken facing southeast, with the Episcopal church in the background.

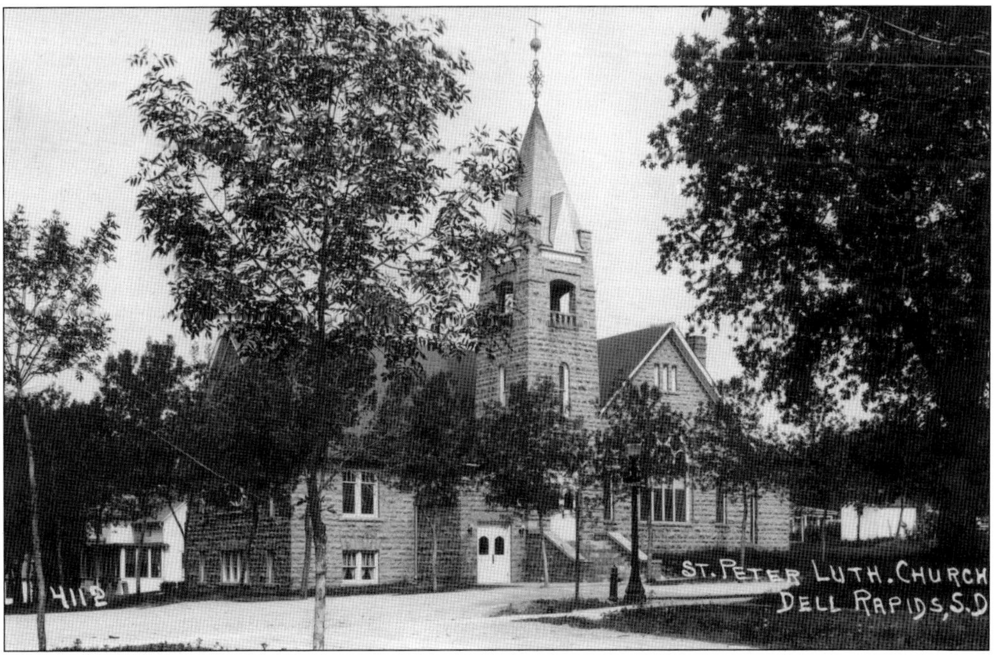

The Lutheran faith was well established in the area before 1874, but St. Peter Lutheran Congregation was organized in 1887, and the first church was built in 1902. On March 29, 1918, the Stordahl and St. Peter's Lutheran congregations in Dell Rapids were combined, and it was decided that St. Peter's Church should be used for worship. (Courtesy Dell Rapids Lutheran Church.)

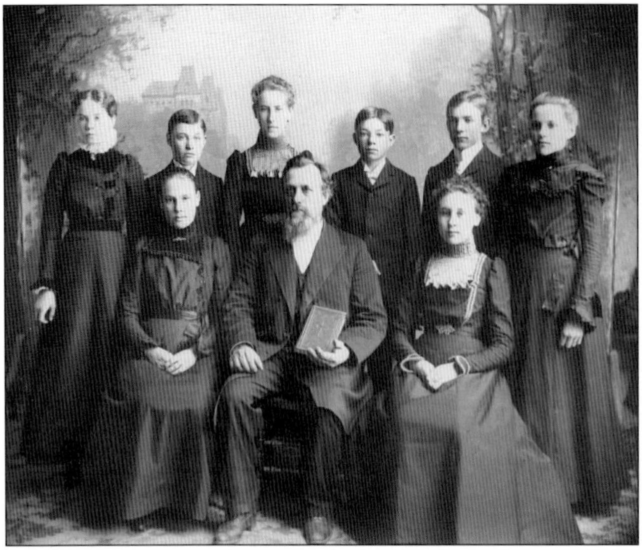

Confirmation is a public profession of faith prepared for by long and careful instruction. In 1893, the confirmation class consisted of one individual, Marin Luther Johnson. In 1900, under the guidance of Rev. C.C. Moe (seated, center), these children were confirmed. They are, from left to right, (seated) Ingeborg Aslakson and Georgina Dieson; (standing) Petra Karsrud, Andrew Stordahl, Alma Dieson, Gilbert Berge, Peter Brende, and Emma Nelson. (Courtesy Dell Rapids Lutheran Church.)

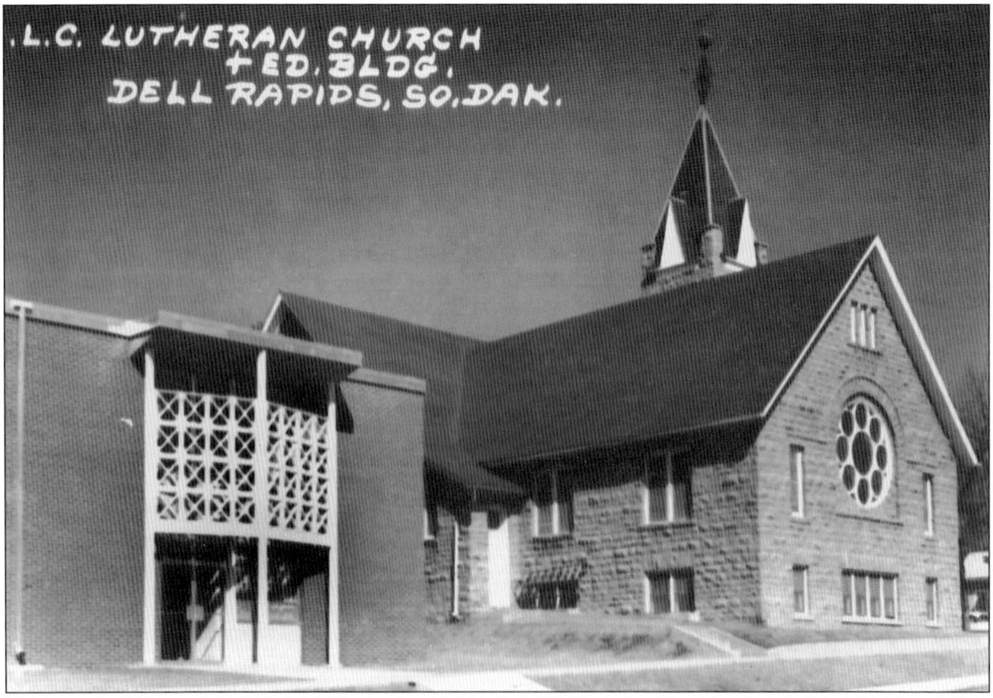

The Ray Wood property was purchased in 1959 and construction of the Lutheran church education unit began in 1960, with a ground-breaking on September 16. The unit was completed in 1961 and dedicated on January 25, 1962, at a cost of $172,000. The educational unit was declared debt-free in 1974. The burning of the mortgage took place during the Centennial Celebrations. (Courtesy Dell Rapids Lutheran Church.)

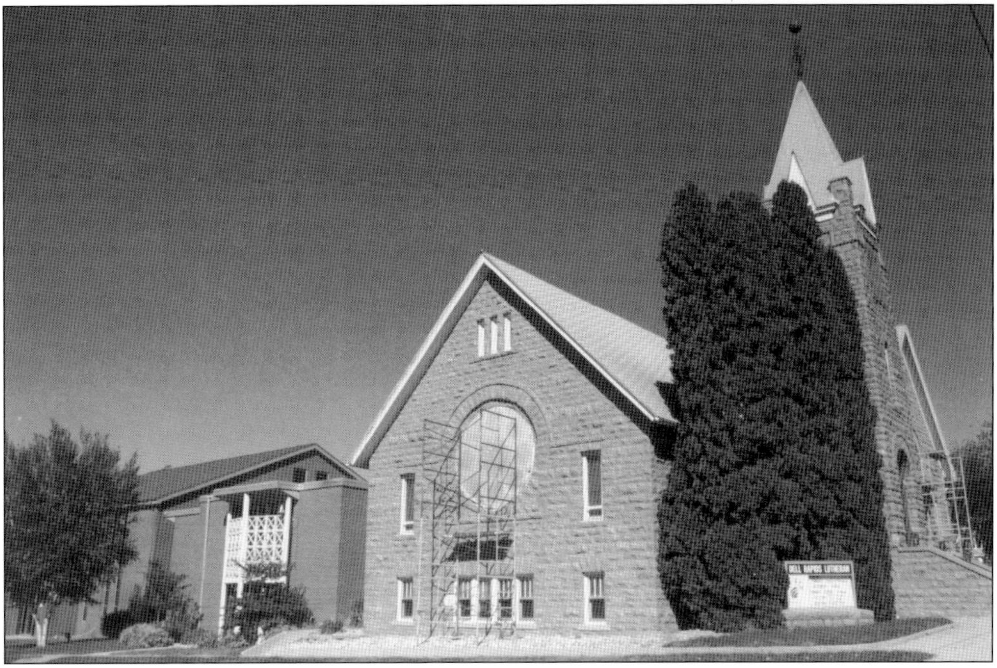

In 1874, St. Peter's Lutheran Church (later Dell Rapids Lutheran Church) was built by the Paulson brothers with the use of local quartzite. The theme chosen for the centennial celebration in 1974 was "Built on a Rock," in keeping with Matthew 16:18, in which Jesus says that "on this rock I will build my church." The original St. Peter's Church is in the National Register of Historic Places. (Courtesy Dell Rapids Lutheran Church.)

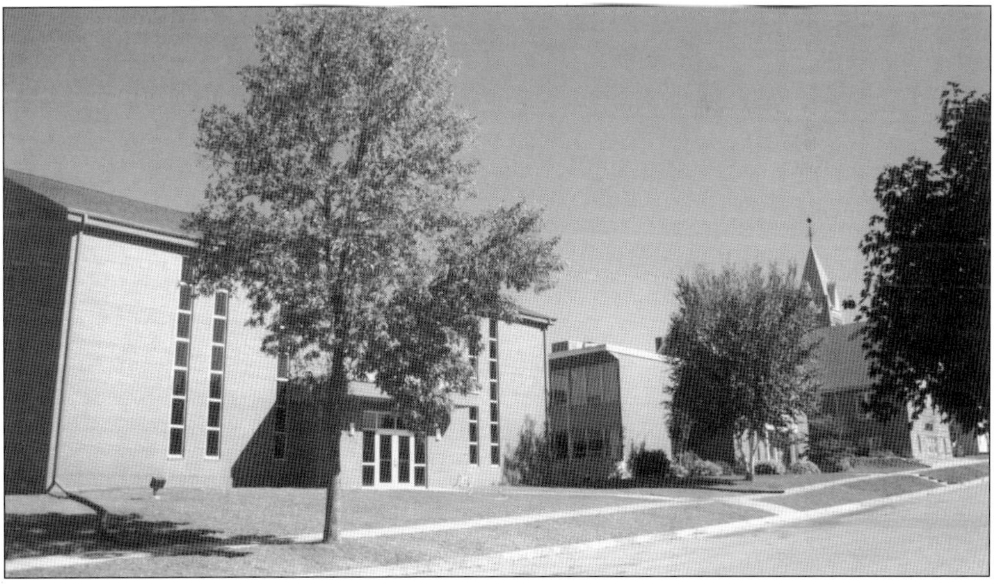

The local Lutheran church grew with the addition of a basement in 1923, five art windows in the sanctuary in 1938, and a pipe organ in 1947. Pastors such as Ole Odland, Elroy Skaar, and Mark Docken have all come and gone. With a new expansion dedicated on Easter Sunday 2003, the Lutheran faith shows no signs of diminishing in Dell Rapids. (Courtesy Dell Rapids Lutheran Church.)

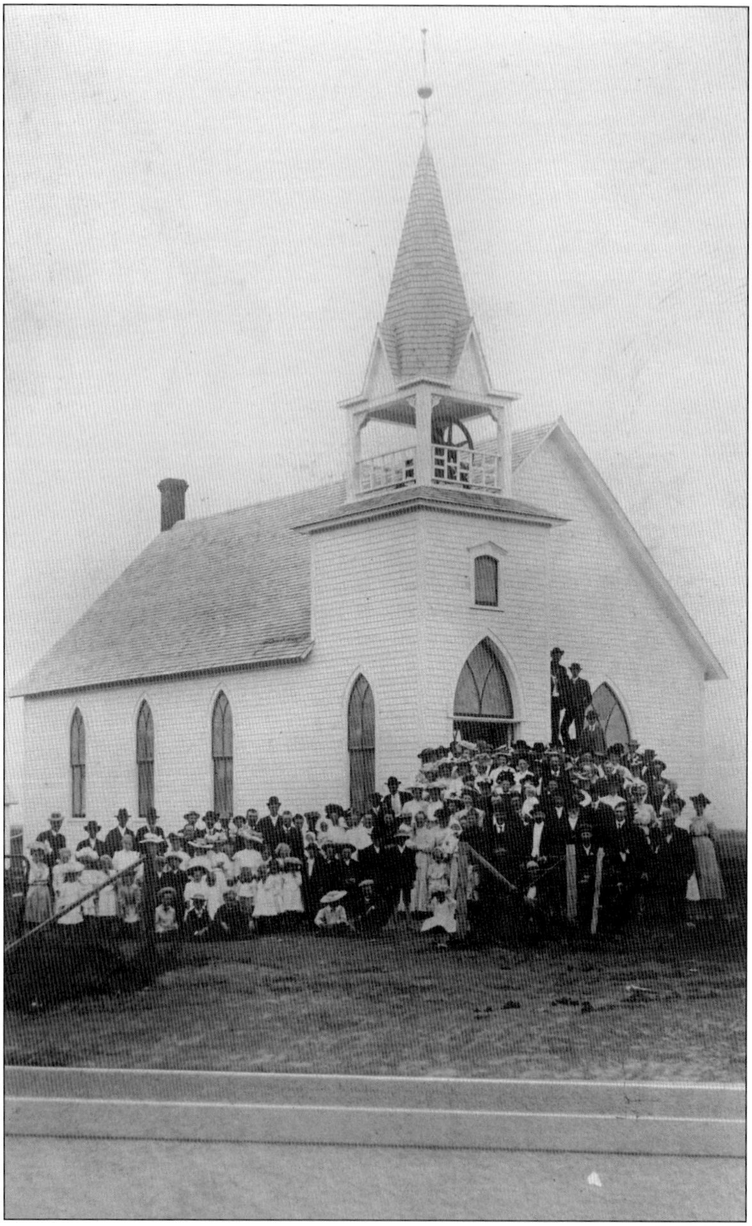

In 1899, the Lewis Rave family moved from German Valley, Illinois, to a farm northeast of Dell Rapids. Their correspondence with friends and neighbors back home regarding fertile land and an abundance of harvest drew plenty of German settlers to the area. Families from Illinois and Iowa with names like Rave, Heeren, Bokker, Janssen, Sieps, Roskam, Heymeyer, Hollstein, Kruse, and Leuning all came in hopes of a new life. Their struggles would not be easy or short in duration and their convictions and determination were tested. In 1901, the 12 original families held prayer meetings in private homes and in the nearby "Hart Schoolhouse." In 1902, the Rev. Zindler, who came once a month from Sibley, Iowa, to look after the spiritual welfare of the small group, came to Dell Rapids. Under the leadership of the Rev. E. Aeilts, the group petitioned to organize a church in the spring of 1905. The name Logan Reformed Church was adopted as the area was called "Logan Valley." (Courtesy Dell Rapids Reformed Church.)

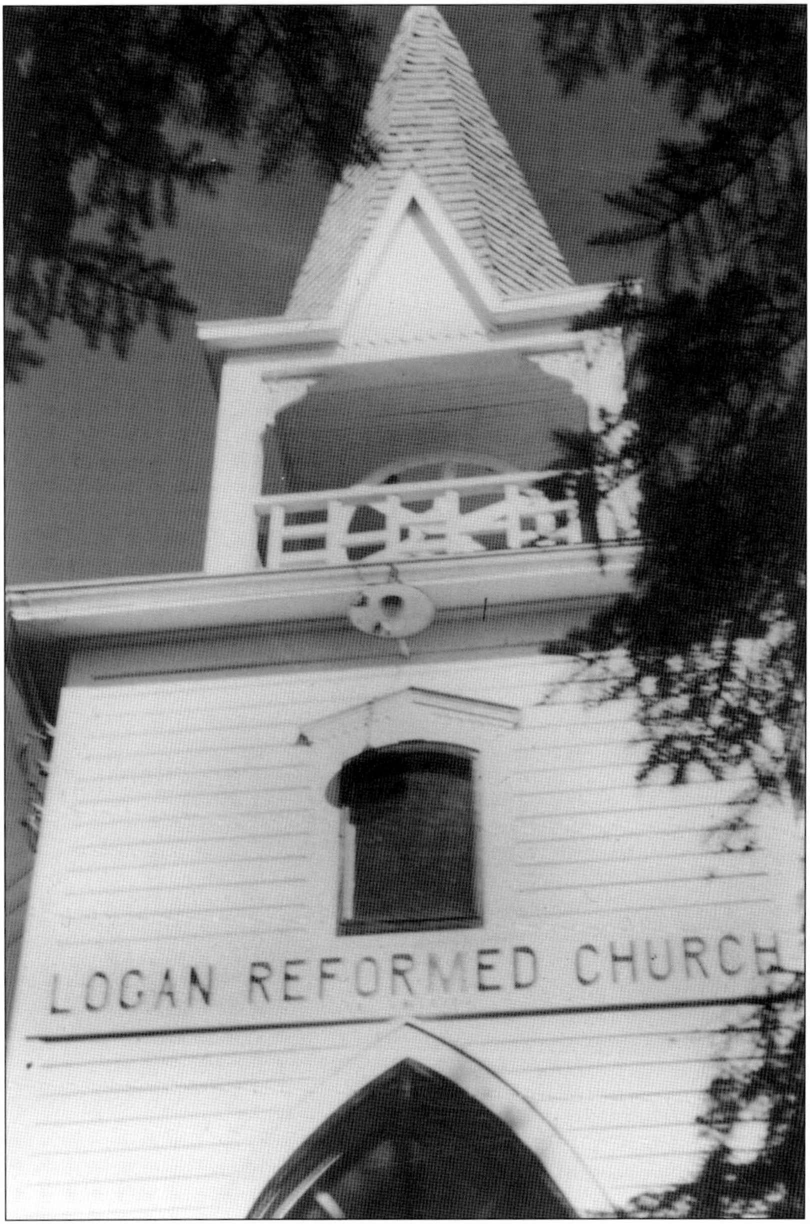

The first official consistory meeting was held June 12, 1905. John Heeren was elected president. At a meeting in 1906, it was decided that the trustees would look for a suitable five-acre tract of land on which to erect a church building and parsonage, as well as a cemetery site. Of the three possible options, the land owned by M.W. Grieff was chosen for the church and cemetery. Records show that Mrs. Frauke Fischer, who died on March 26, 1908, was the first individual buried in the Logan Reformed Cemetery. During a congregational meeting on July 30, 1907, it was unanimously decided to build a church. After three years of planning and building, the church was ready for dedication by midsummer 1908. The total cost of the church was $3,162.45, with much of the labor willingly donated. The building and land would serve the needs of the congregation for many years, until 1967, when the congregation bid farewell to the old and celebrated the new. (Courtesy Dell Rapids Reformed Church.)

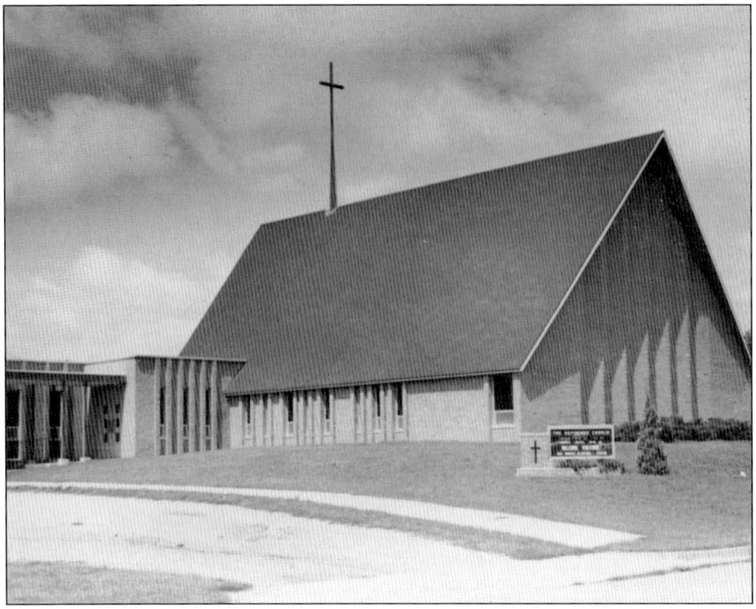

In 1963, after much soul searching and prayers, it was decided to relocate the church. Land was purchased in Dell Rapids, and, in 1966, plans for the new building were approved. The name was changed to the Reformed Church since the name "Logan" had been taken from the township where it was formerly located. (Courtesy Dell Rapids Reformed Church.)

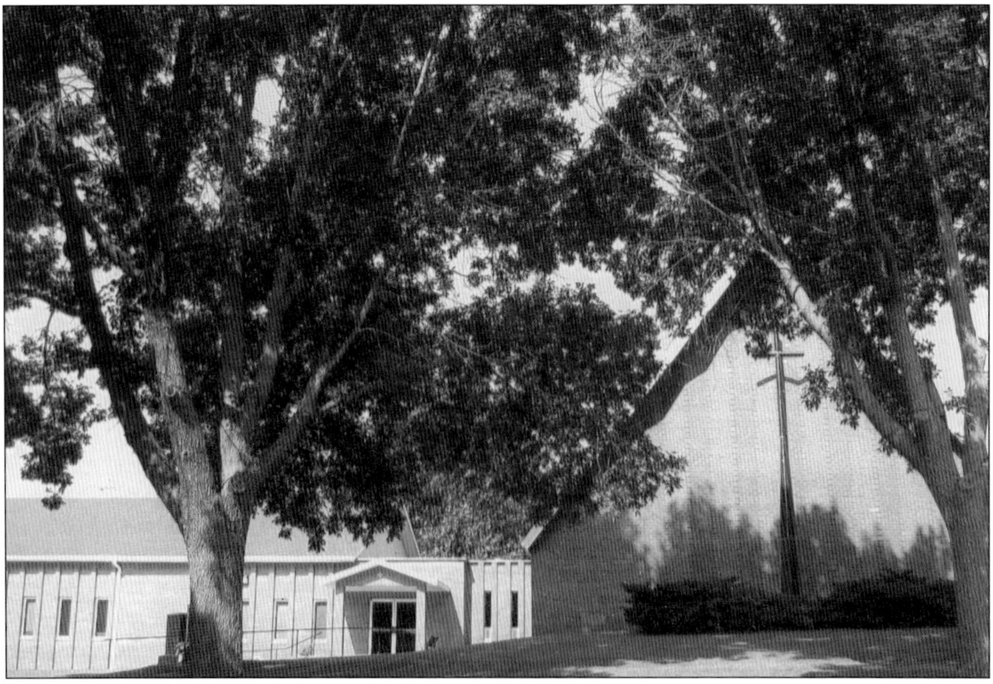

On September 3, 1967, the first worship service in the new church was held. Dedication services were held on October 8, and an open house two days later. The old church was dismantled, and the material from it and the former parsonage and garage were sold at auction. On October 10, 1976, only nine years after dedication, the church building was debt-free. (Courtesy Dell Rapids Reformed Church.)

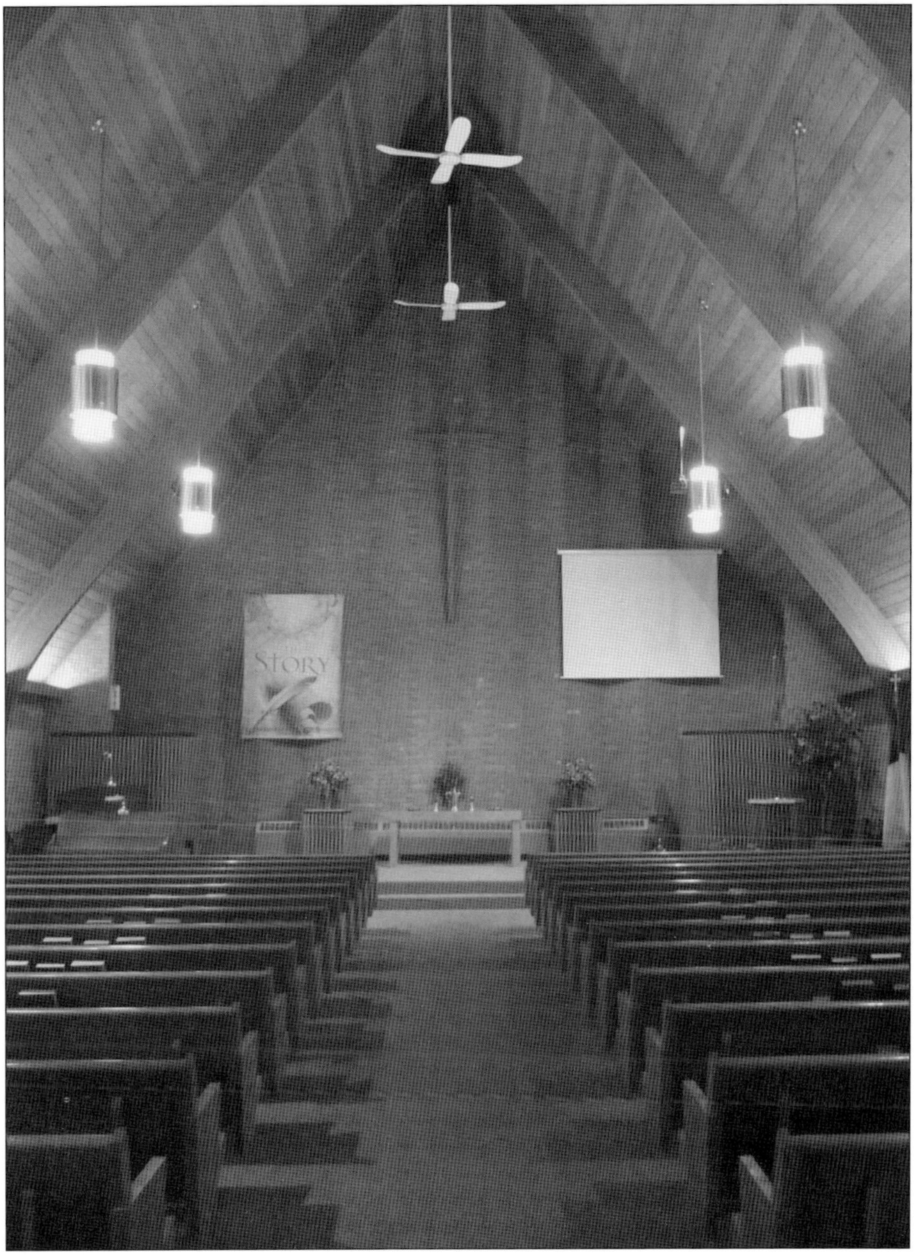

The chancel area of the new church was "designed to speak." Four items of significance are displayed, signifying the confidence in Christ as savior and lord. The Bible is partially visible, and the shelf on which it rests is clearly seen. The pulpit is to emphasize the word of God. The table in the middle suggests fellowship with Christ and his people. Another sacrament, Holy Baptism, is signified with the font. The baptismal font reminds the congregation that their relationship with Christ means the death of sin by opening the way to the freedom and responsibility of holy living. The naked cross is a symbol telling the congregation that Christ went beyond death to the resurrected life. The organ or choir is part of the people's response to God. The total sanctuary is designed to easily accommodate 240 for meaningful worship. The function of the remainder of the building is for education and fellowship. (Courtesy Dell Rapids Reformed Church.)

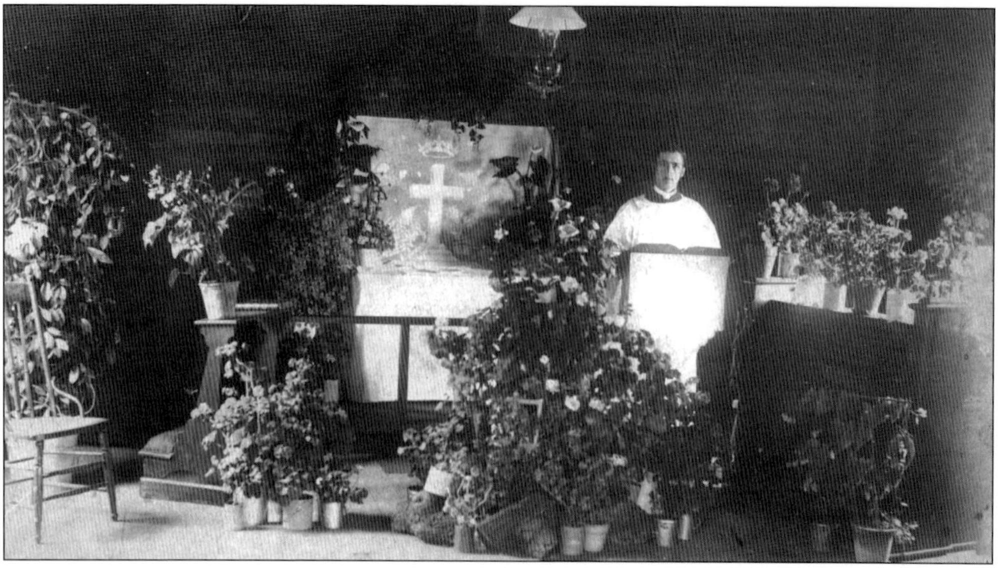

The idea of establishing an Episcopal church in town was first introduced in 1879. Services were held at irregular intervals by ministers from out of town until T. Howell Richards (above), a lay leader, came to take charge of the mission. Richards was ordained deacon in 1884. Under his leadership, membership increased and the work of the church progressed. Richards left the parish and the ministry in 1897.

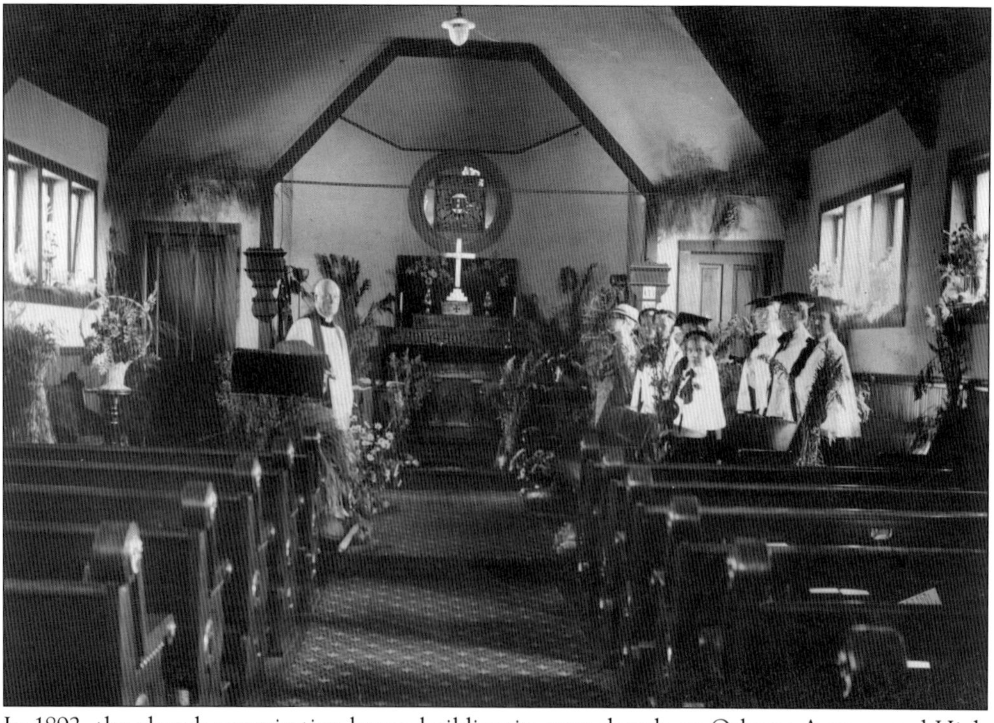

In 1892, the church organization began building its new church on Orleans Avenue and High Street (Sixth Street), a granite stone structure of English-style architecture. It was completed the following year, and, on a Sunday in June 1893, all the members dedicated the "Church of Living Water." In 1984, the church was deconsecrated and sold to a private resident.

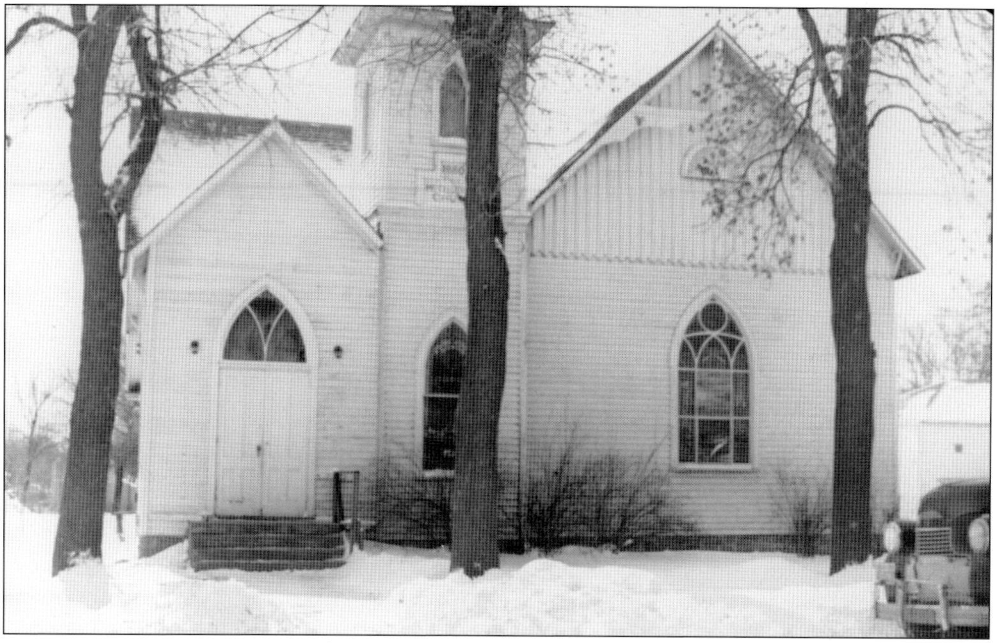

In 1879, land was purchased for $20 on the corner of State Avenue and Third Street to build a new Methodist church. The railroad later cut the lots in two, compelling the Methodist congregation to look for new land. This photograph of the church on Fifth Street was taken on March 12, 1950, before the building was razed to make way for a new church. (Courtesy Dell Rapids United Methodist Church.)

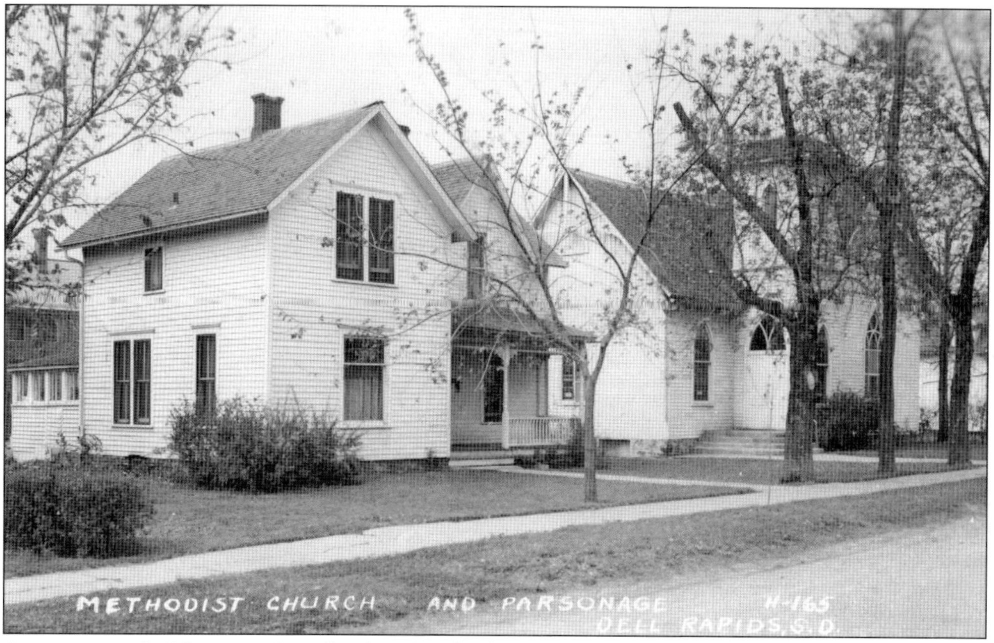

Approximately 20 years after the first Methodist sermon had been preached in the area, the Methodist Episcopal Church was officially organized in Dell Rapids on July 26, 1880. In 1881, a lot for the church was purchased for $395. In 1884, another lot was purchased for $135 for the parsonage. (Courtesy Dell Rapids United Methodist Church.)

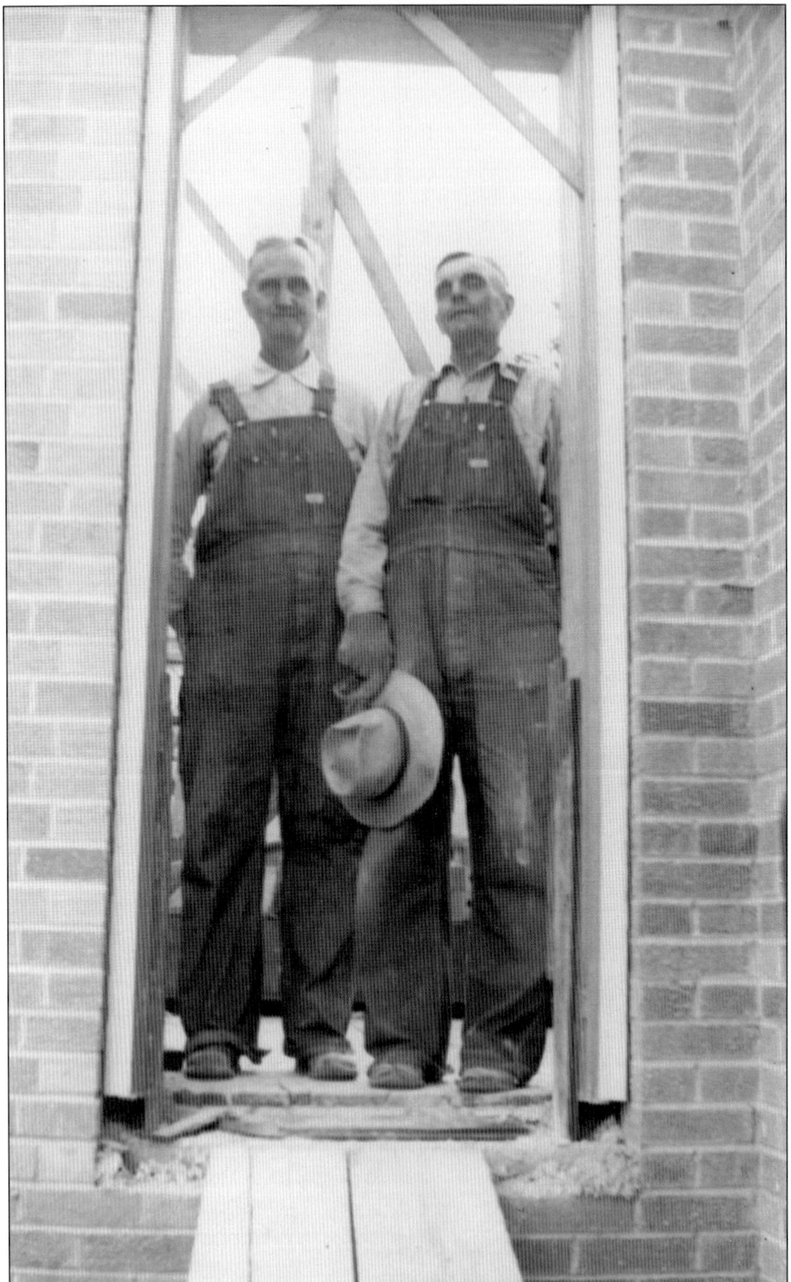

When Rev. Harlan H. Arms arrived in Dell Rapids in 1948, the need to provide adequate space for the growing congregation was apparent. On March 13, 1950, the men of the church started tearing down the old building, and hours of volunteer labor were donated for both the wrecking of the old and constructing of the new church. Two retired members, George Ellis (left) and Ernest Kasten, took a hand from start to finish, working side by side, day after day with Reverend Arms. Ground-breaking services were held on April 2, 1950, and during the ceremony, Bruce Hart presented the spade to the pastor. Neil Jensen stood nearby and represented the future generation of the church. (Courtesy Dell Rapids United Methodist Church.)

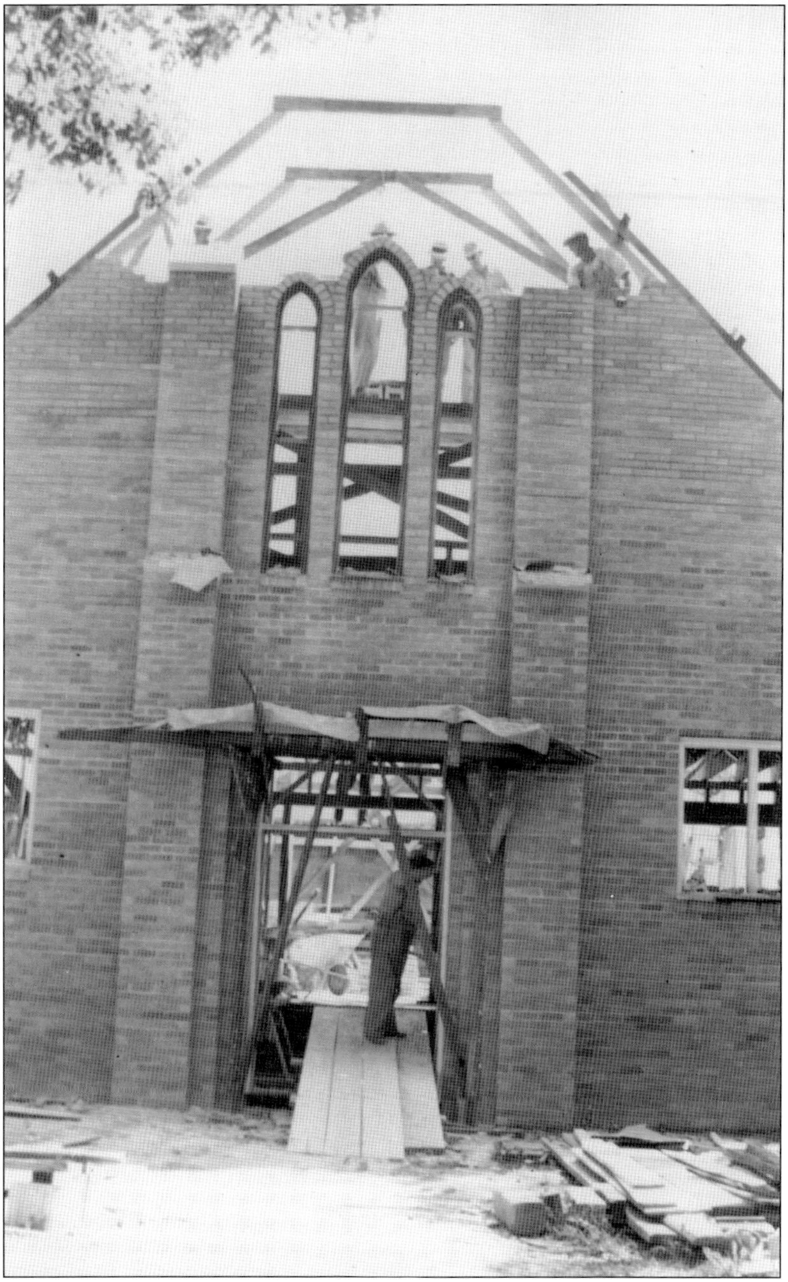

Even though Rev. Harlan H. Arms was retired, he consented to come back because of the dire need for a resident pastor. The next three years were fruitful and important ones in the history of the Methodist church. Reverend Arms had the personality, leadership ability, and construction knowledge necessary to bring the church's building program to a head and carry out a successful finish of the new church. The total cost of the new church had been affixed at approximately $46,000. A gift of $2,500 was made by the Board of Missions, and a loan of $10,500 was secured locally. By June 1, 1952, the debt had been reduced to $7,500, and early in 1955, the entire debt was wiped out. During the building time of the new church, worship services and church school were held in the nearby Legion Memorial Hall. (Courtesy Dell Rapids United Methodist Church.)

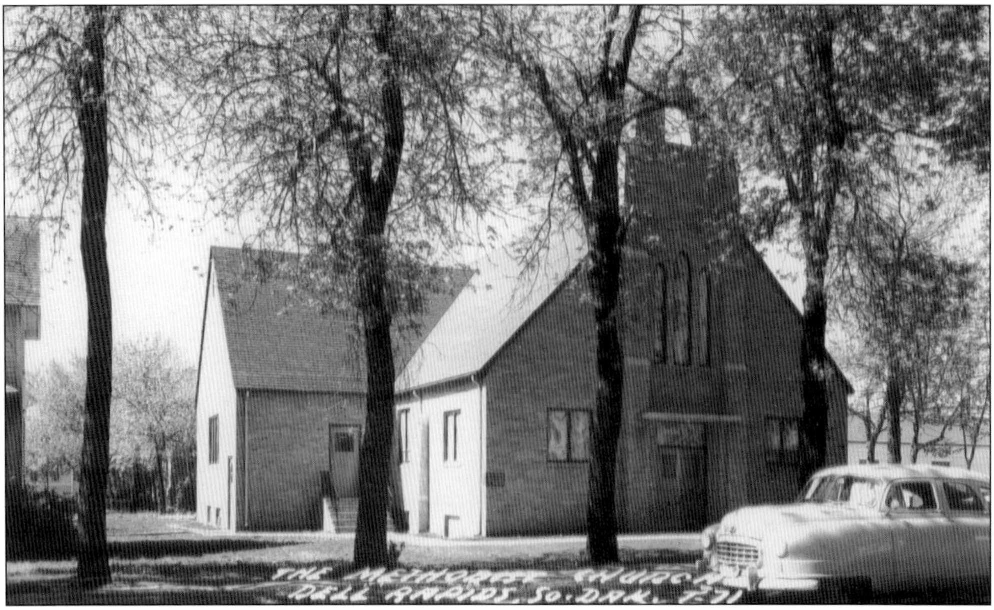

The Methodist church has had many changes over the last decade. Originally called the Methodist Episcopal Church in 1880, it is now called the United Methodist Church of Dell Rapids. With the addition of several Presbyterians, the membership has continued to grow and necessitated expansion, with more construction and outreach. (Courtesy Dell Rapids United Methodist Church.)

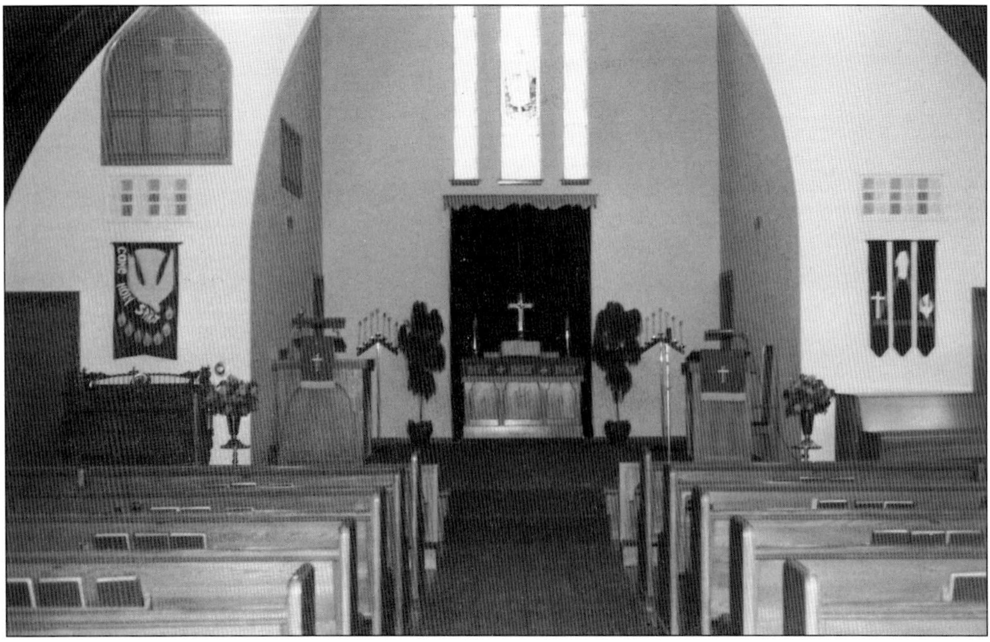

These stained-glass windows were installed on the south side of the Methodist church in memory of Robert Christensen. The center window has the symbol of the Latin cross, while the west panel has the symbol of the burning torch, symbolizing the witnessing of Christians. The east window depicts the Censer, which is symbolic of prayer. In 2005, the church celebrated 125 years. (Courtesy Dell Rapids United Methodist Church.)

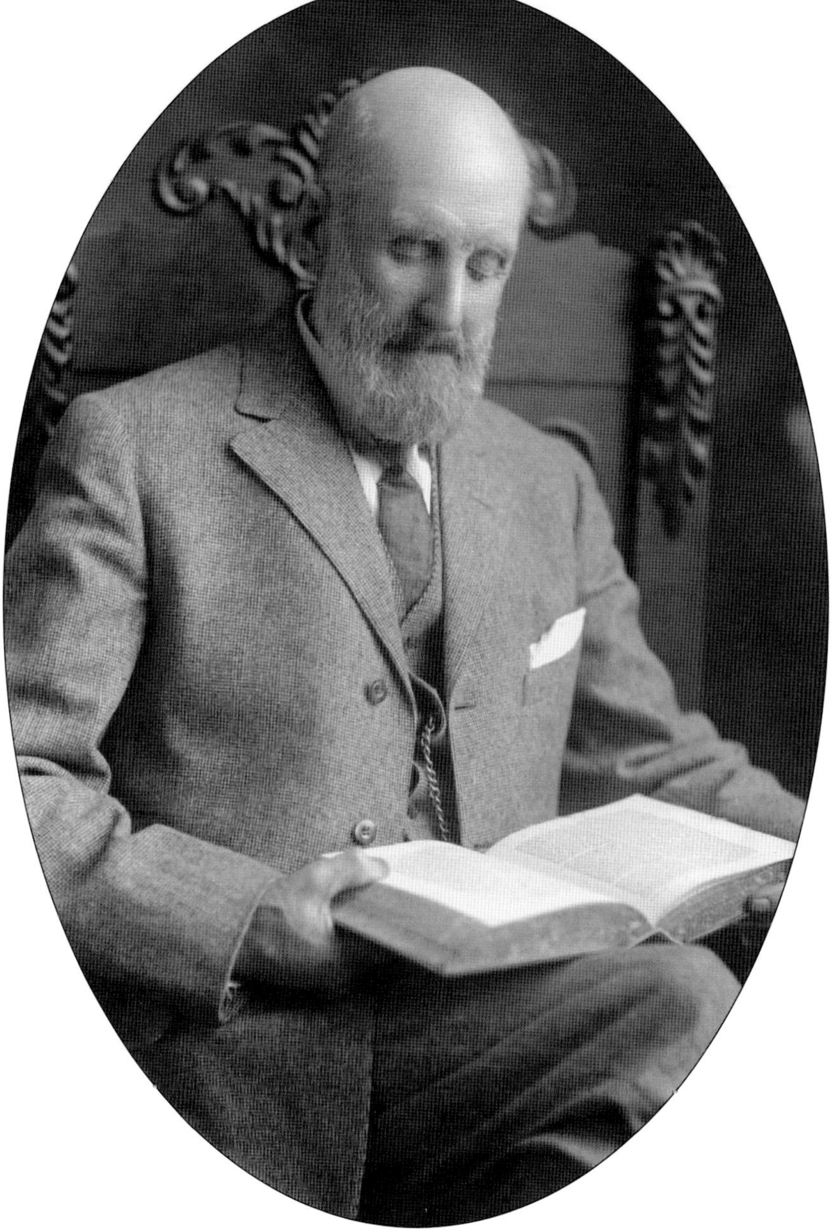

Rev. William T. Hill was the first resident minister in Dell Rapids. On June 7, 1873, a group of pioneers came by covered wagon from Wisconsin. Among them were Reverend Hill and his wife, Elizabeth. He was a Civil War veteran and was postmaster for Confederate prisoners at Fort Douglas in Chicago while in the service. Reverend Hill filed on Soldiers Homestead east of town. He remained the Baptist minister for five years, serving Dell Rapids and several area churches and receiving a salary of $100 a year, if funding was available. The little Baptist church was the northernmost mission in Dakota at that time, except for the Presbyterian Indian Mission in Flandreau. Reverend Hill left Dell Rapids in 1881 and returned to Illinois, where his wife died. He then returned to his farm in Dell Rapids and married Hannah Walker, lived on the farm for a few years, and later moved into town. The Hills were active in the community until his death in 1916.

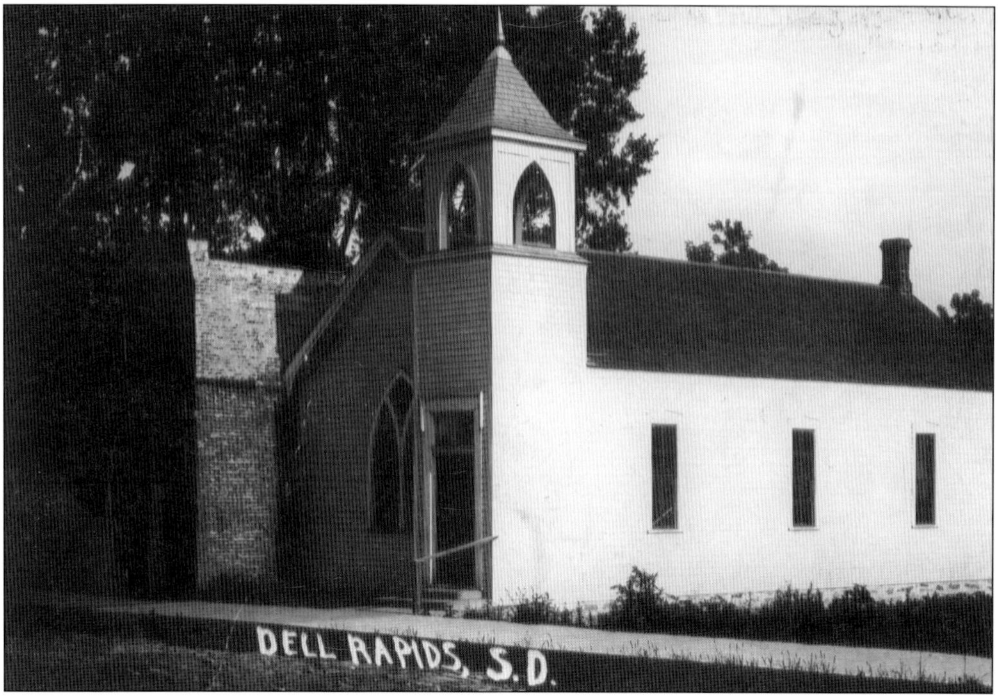

In 1872, a group of Baptists met in the Peter Morse home and organized a church with 16 charter members. They met in private homes and the newly built schoolhouse. As the town grew, so did the Baptist church membership. The first service in the new building was held on July 18, 1880, and planks were used as seating. The building was eventually sold to Danish Baptist. (Courtesy Dell Rapids Baptist Church.)

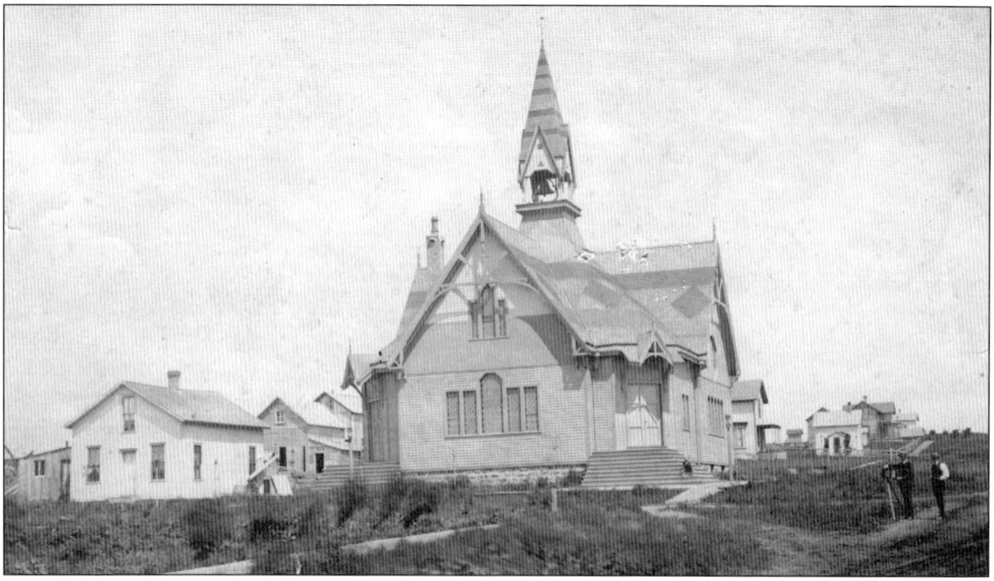

The Baptist denomination grew rapidly, and within a few short years, the congregation had outgrown its original building. On June 8, 1884, the Baptists held a dedication ceremony for their new home. This early view of the church is a reminder of the lack of trees and roads. This is the oldest public building in Dell Rapids and is still in use. (Courtesy Dell Rapids Baptist Church.)

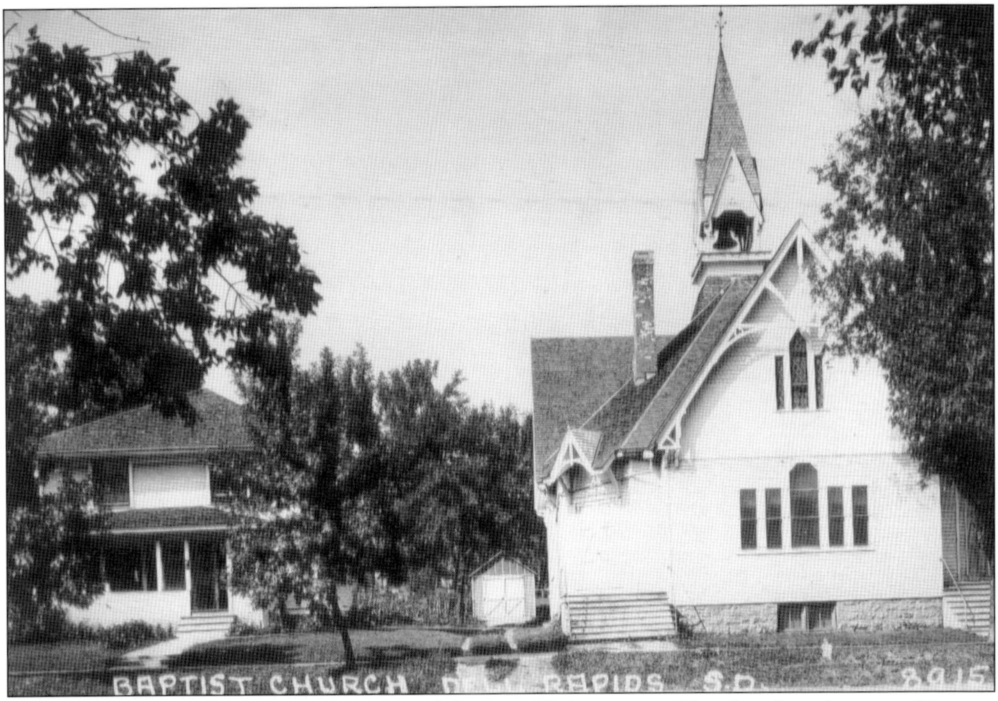

In 1903, the first parsonage was purchased for Rev. J.F. Bryant and his family to live in—31 years after the church was organized. Before Reverend Bryant, who lived there from 1903 to 1907, pastors had lived in rented houses, but in 1903, the church bought the property to the west from Michael Collins for $1,300. (Courtesy Dell Rapids Baptist Church.)

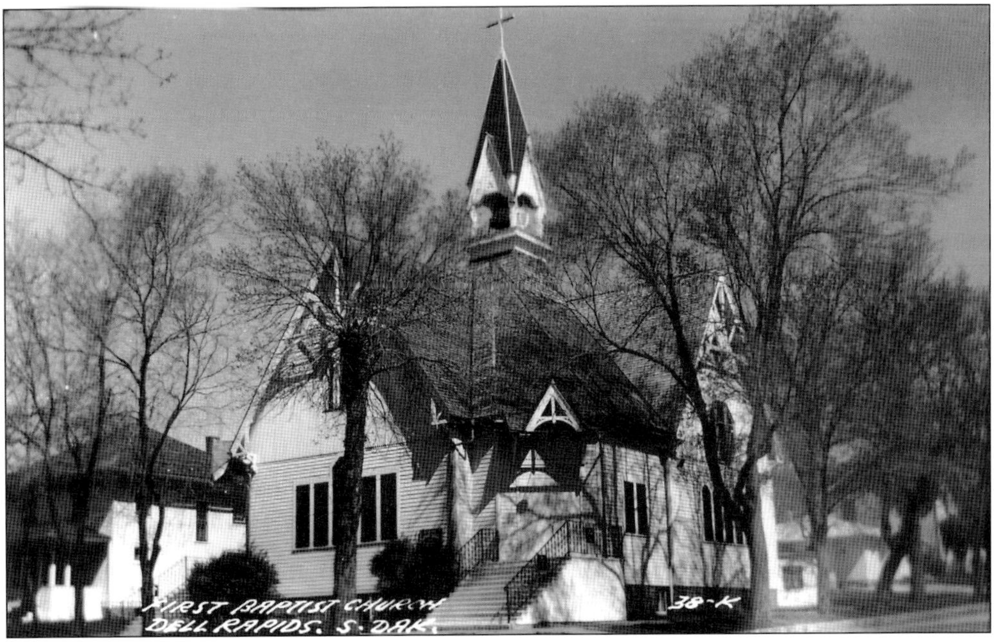

The First Baptist Church is still the largest building of its kind in town. In 1884, when a windstorm blew down the school, classes were held in the Baptist church until a new school building could be constructed. (Courtesy Dell Rapids Baptist Church.)

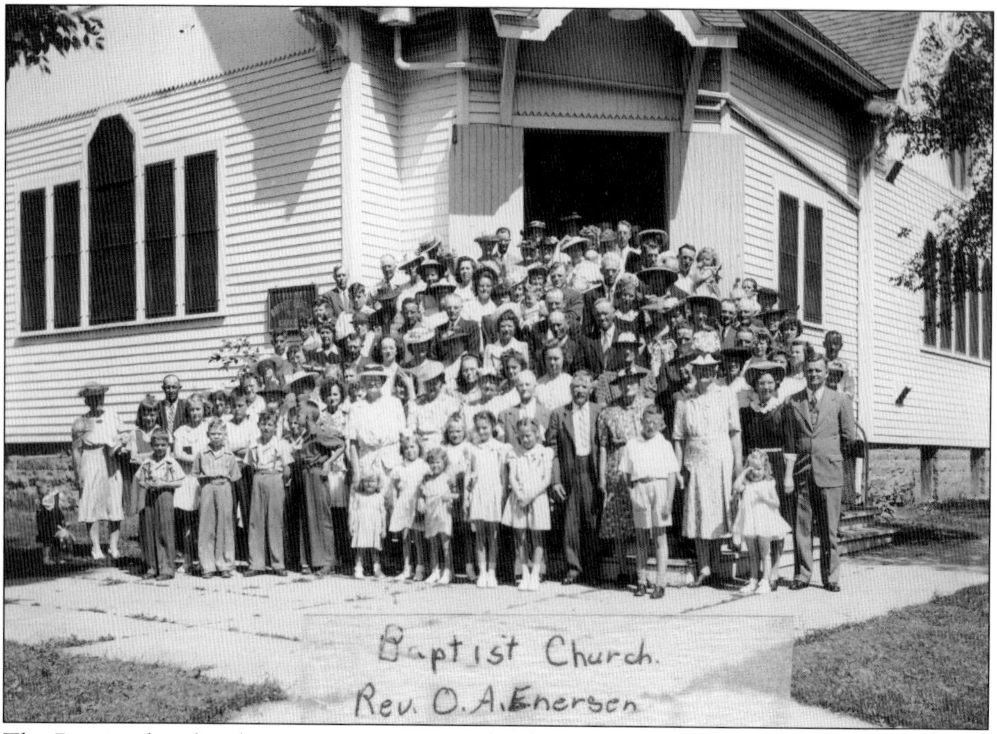

The Baptist church, whose congregants pose for this group photograph, has celebrated many accomplishments and anniversaries throughout its rich history. In 1972, the congregation celebrated its 100th anniversary. Many have traveled from far and near to celebrate the foundation of their faith with fond memories. In 2012, the church will have been established in South Dakota for 140 years.

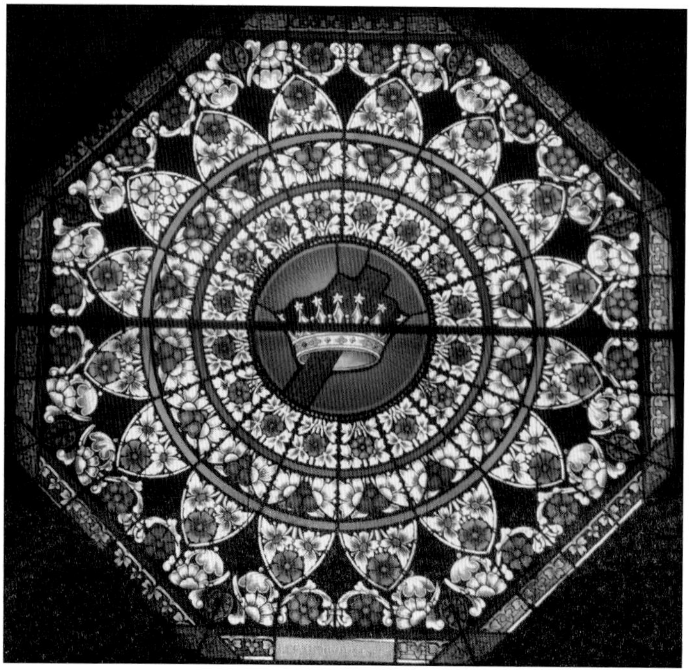

In 1883, Reverend Williams, a missionary from Nellore, India, lived in Dell Rapids for about a year. Reverend Williams wrote to the missionaries at Nellore telling them about the Baptist church. Those missionaries and the Telugu Christians took up an offering to help build the church. Reverend S.G. Adams used this special offering to help pay for the beautiful, octagonal, stained-glass window on the west side of the building.

Six

Public School

Home to two major school systems, Dell Rapids has kept up both its public and private institutions through decades of progress. From its erection in 1885, the public school has seen many physical changes through years, including the addition of a high school in 1886, the building of a new school in the early 1900s, the move to a new high school in 1970, and the construction and occupation of a new, state-of-the-art elementary building in 2011–2012. Originally housed in the old Dieson home, kindergarteners now enjoy their own wing of the current elementary school. Once held in the Veterans Memorial Hall, teams now enjoy multiple gymnasium facilities around town. Since 1938, when Ethel Sagmoe was crowned the inaugural homecoming queen, the homecoming parade and coronation are still well attended, community-wide events.

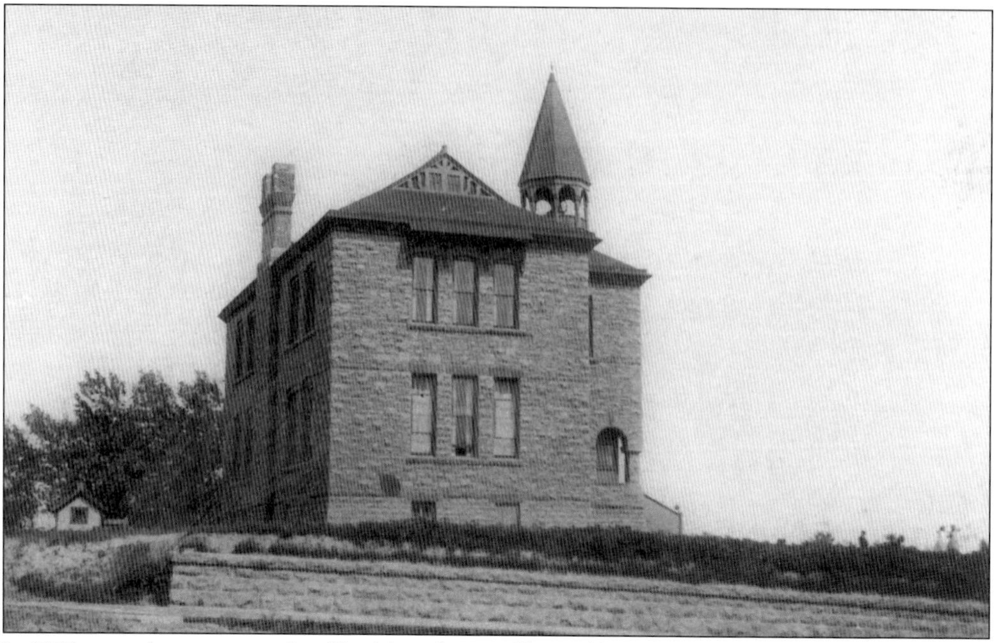

In 1885, a sturdy two-story school building designed by Wallace Dow was erected. Quartzite blocks from the local quarry were cut by hand by master stonecutters from Norway. High school classes were added in 1886, and the first high school graduating class, of five students, was in 1890. The 396-pound bell was added in 1887.

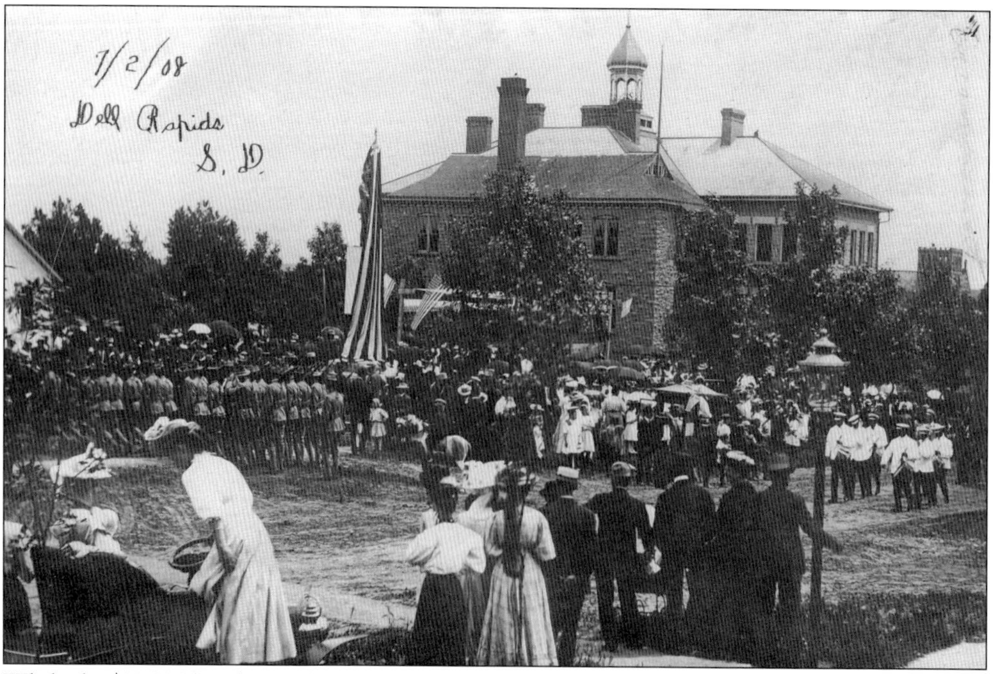

While the $10,000 bond issue for the building of a new school was originally defeated, it eventually passed and construction began in 1905. A large addition was built on the front of the 1885 structure. Three years later, on July 2, 1908, dedication ceremonies were held on the north side of the "old high school."

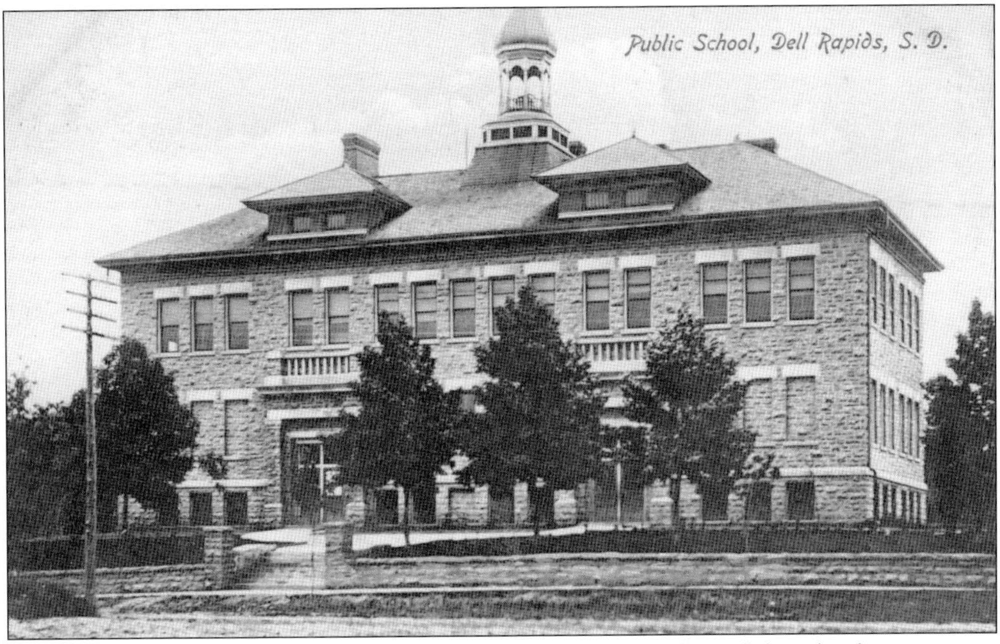

In December 1970, school staff and students boxed up their books and the school's possessions and moved into the new school. The old high school, no longer needed, was boarded up. In 1982, the 97-year-old building was torn down to make room for the next phase of school expansion.

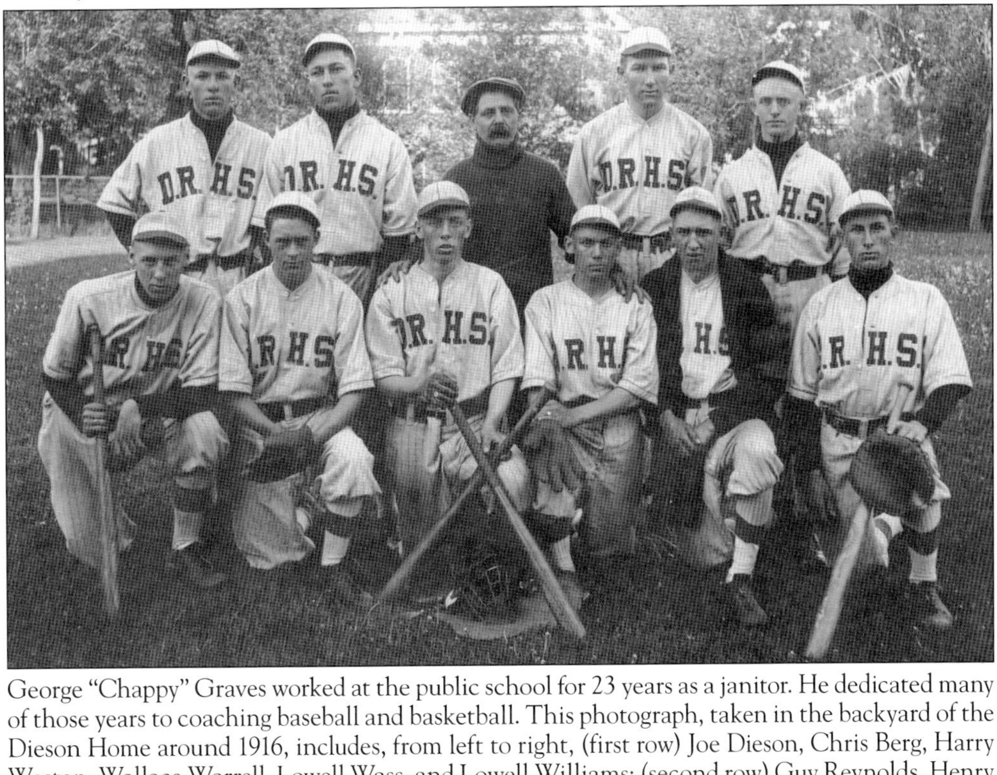

George "Chappy" Graves worked at the public school for 23 years as a janitor. He dedicated many of those years to coaching baseball and basketball. This photograph, taken in the backyard of the Dieson Home around 1916, includes, from left to right, (first row) Joe Dieson, Chris Berg, Harry Weston, Wallace Warrell, Lowell Wass, and Lowell Williams; (second row) Guy Reynolds, Henry Merry, George "Chappy" Graves, Morris Hjort, and Howard Meldrum.

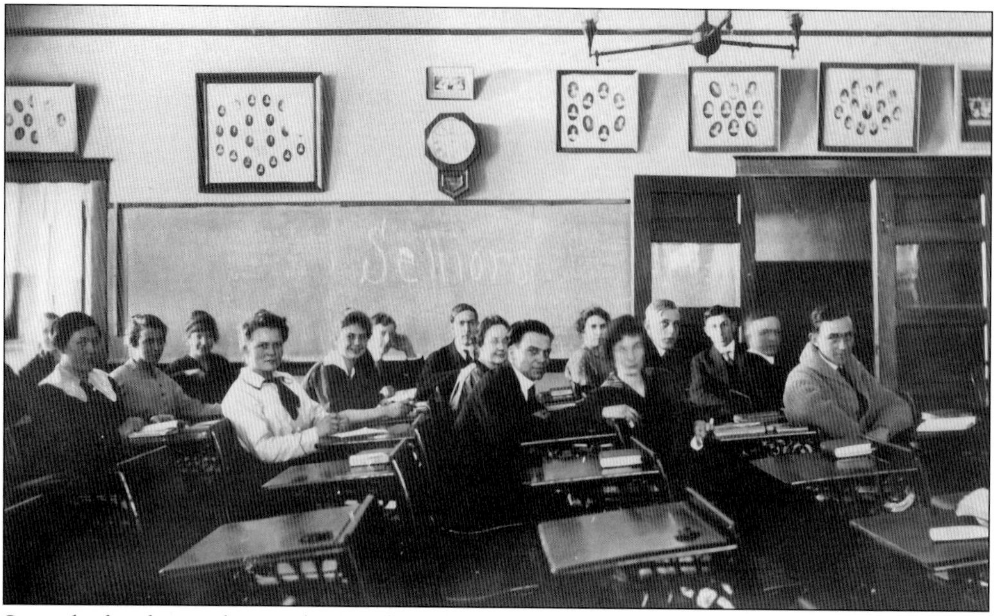

Since the first five-student graduating class of 1890, enrollment has steadily grown. This photograph, taken in the assembly room of the old high school after 1915, shows 17 seniors. Many of the class composites and the clock on the wall are now on display at the Dell Rapids Museum. (Photograph by Lowell Williams.)

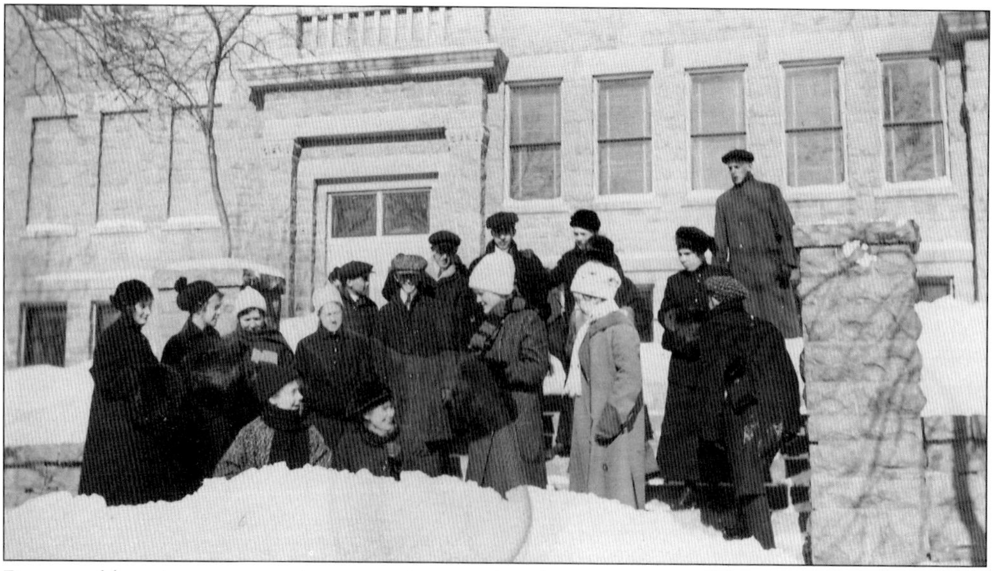

Dates and locations are very important in recording historic events; however, it is moments like this that many reminisce about during reunions. These students appear to be taking a break from their studies and are gathered on the steps leading up to the south side of the high school. All appear to be in a very joyous mood.

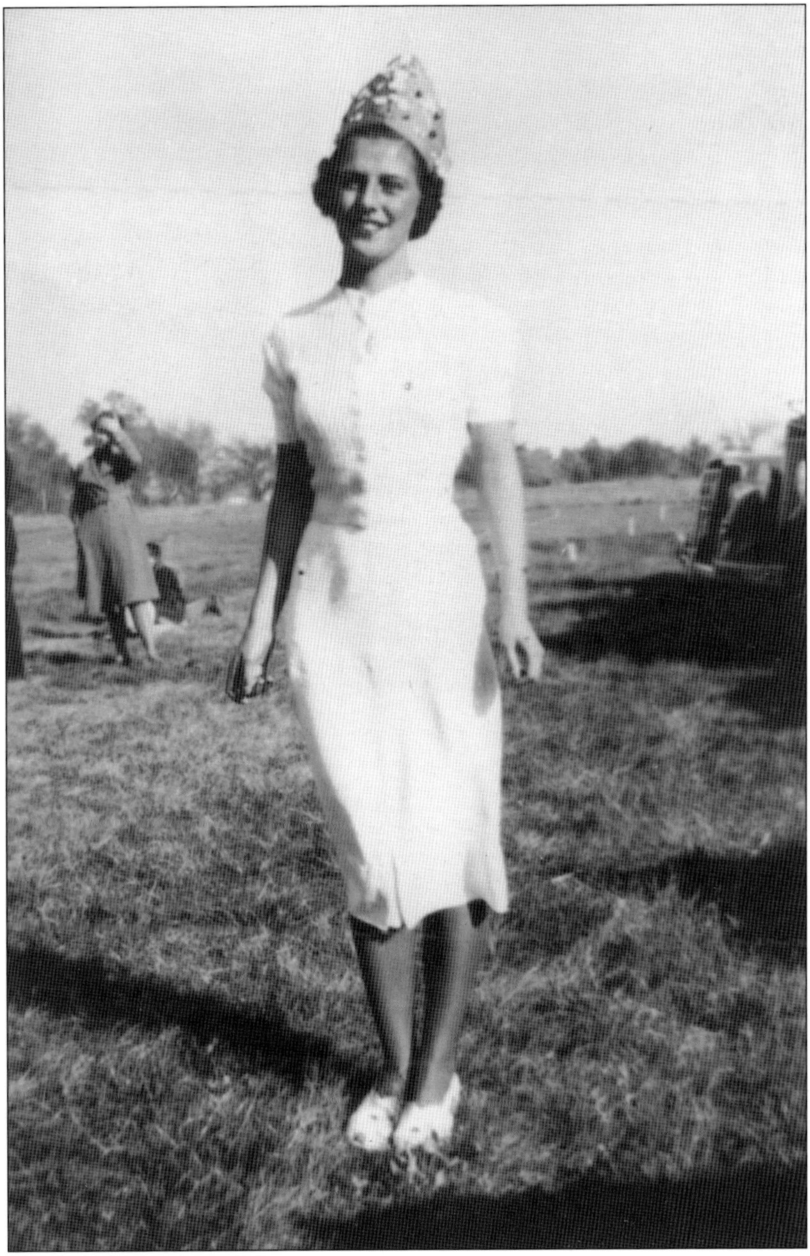

The homecoming queen presided over the celebrations of Dell Rapids High School's first homecoming on October 21, 1938. Excitement and anticipation were at a high as the students began preparing for the parade. At 2:00 p.m., all the businesses in town closed; many of them had entered a float in the parade. Spectators stood on the sidelines cheering and supporting the students. Beginning at the schoolhouse, the parade was led by the Dell Rapids Band, followed by the queen's car and her attendants. The queen was dressed in white and her attendants in black. There were 17 floats entered by various departments of the high school and businesses. The parade journeyed through town to the football field, where the players met their rivals from Garretson. During halftime, there was a special ceremony to crown the queen of the day, Dell Rapids' first homecoming queen, Ethel Lorraine Sagmoe (now Dybvig).

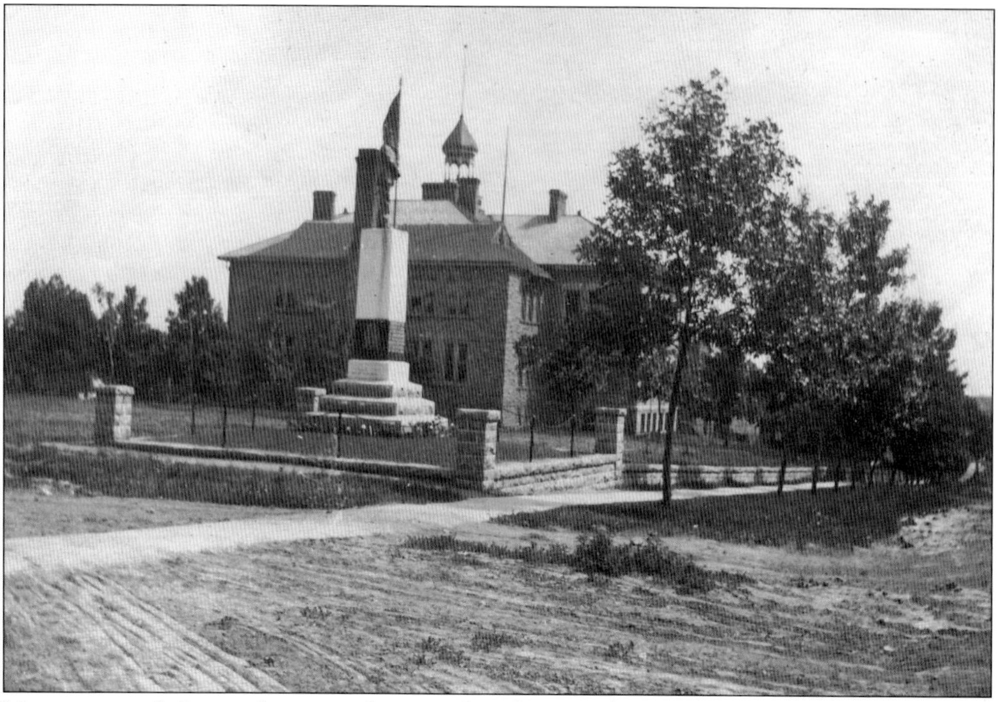

Many years and changes have gone by since this photograph was originally taken, looking south from the corner of Seventh Street and Orleans Avenue. The school has been torn down to make way for a newer building, and the streets have been paved with curb and gutter. Yet, the Civil War statue and the quarry rock retention wall still stand.

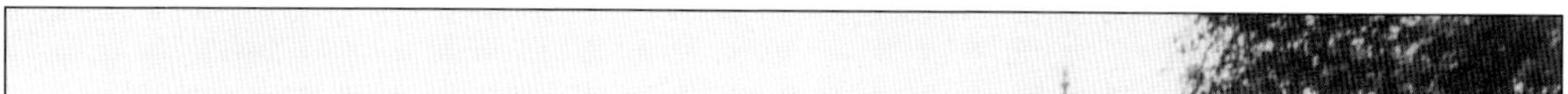

The Veterans Memorial Hall, more commonly known as the City Auditorium, shown here in 1919, was built on the north side of the school in 1914. The building was used for many public events, as well as basketball games, school functions, and classes. In 1971, the old high school was closed, and the auditorium was torn down to provide room for playground space for the elementary students.

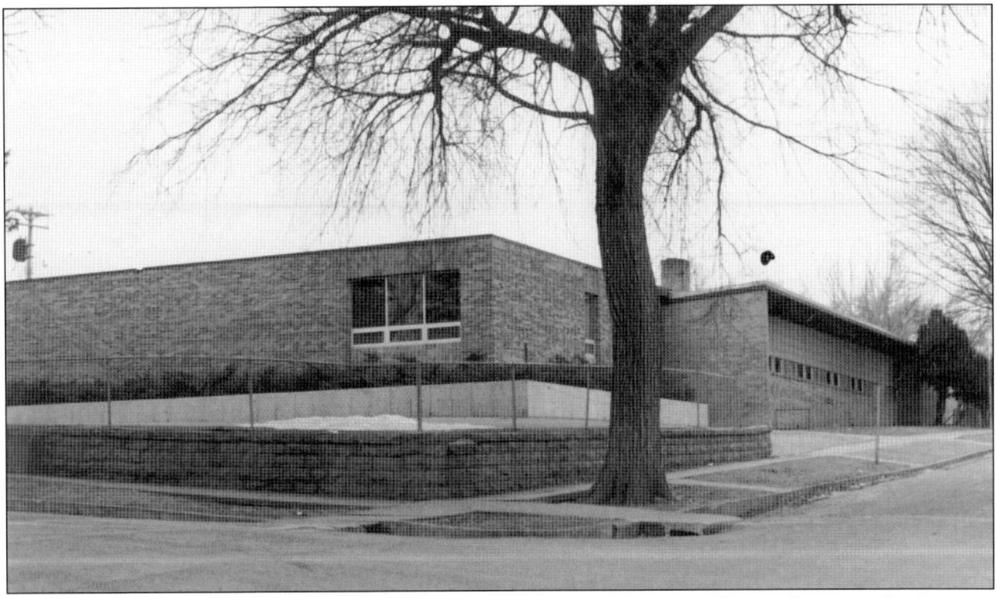

In 1982, the Dieson Home, which had been used for classes, was razed to make room for the new kindergarten addition. Four groups of kindergarten classes—two all-day, every-other-day classes; and two half-day, everyday classes—were taught for many years in this portion of the school. It took nearly 30 years to complete all phases of the four elementary additions.

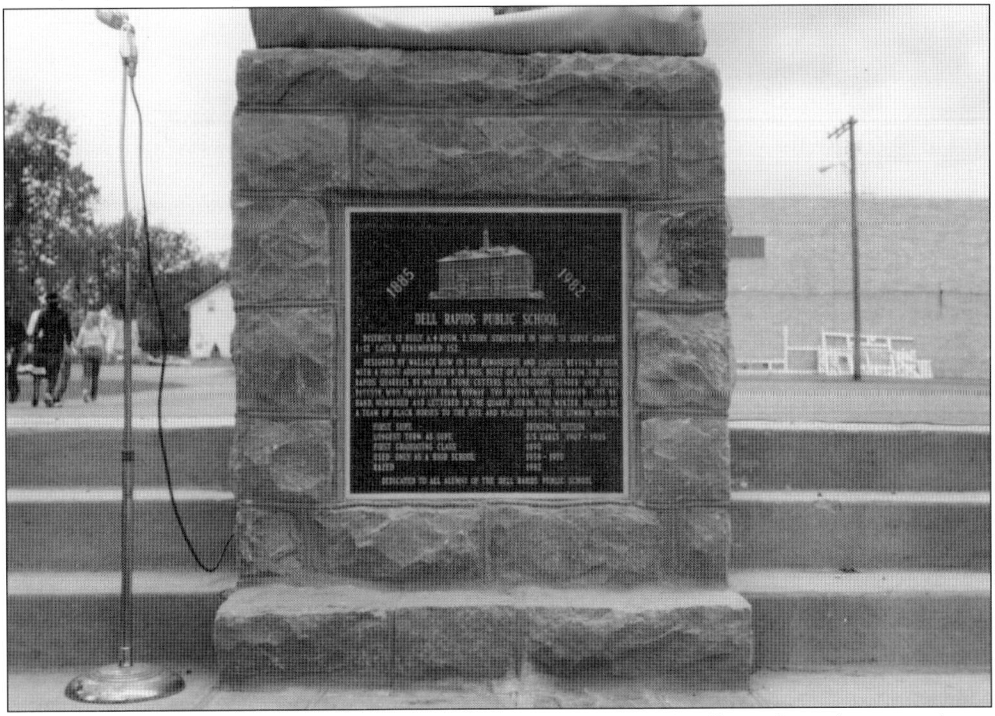

This dedication marker for the original Dell Rapids Public School still stands on the original site. The monument is made from local block that was quarried, cut by hand, numbered, and lettered in the quarry, then transferred to the building site in the summer of 1885. Unveiled on May 30, 1983, it reads: "Dedicated to all alumni of the Dell Rapids Public School."

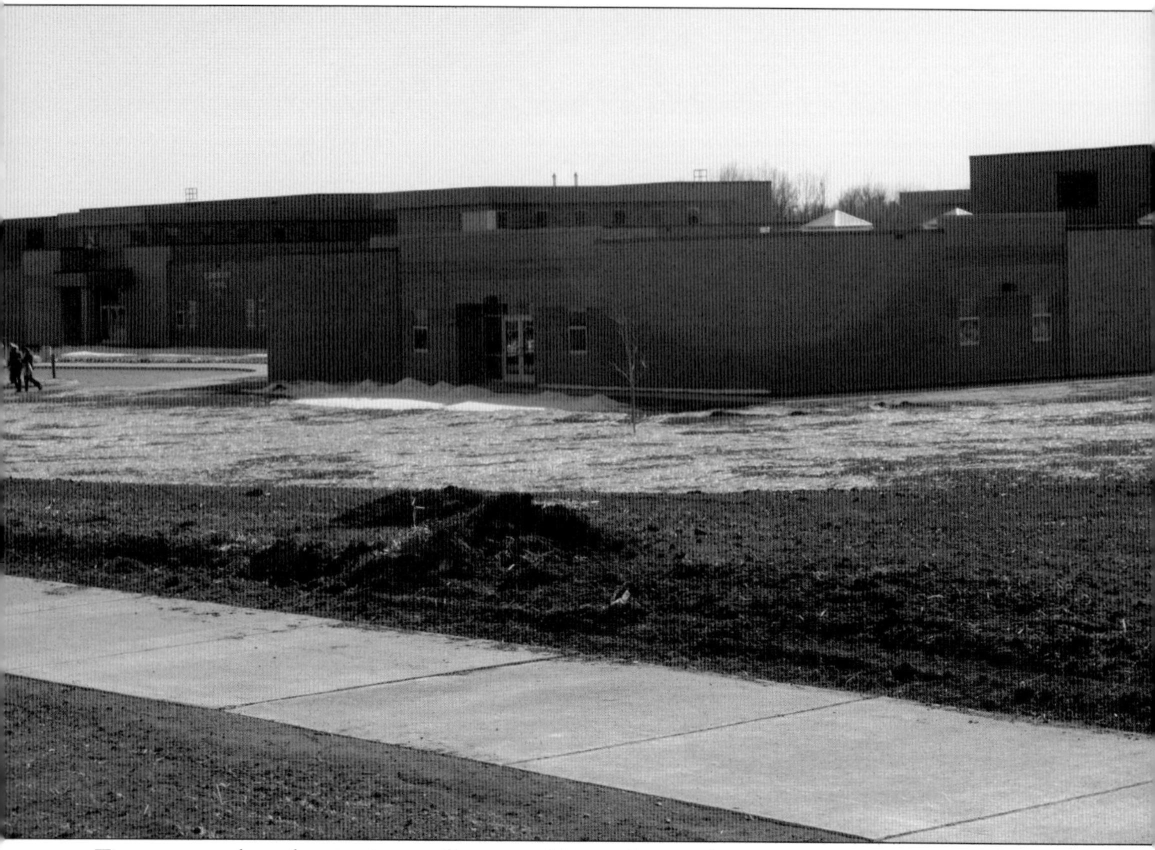

To accommodate the rise in enrollment, additional space became a necessity. In 2001, a new middle school, attached to the high school, was opened for fifth through eighth grades. Projections for enrollment grew quickly as the outdated elementary school could no longer provide proper classroom settings. In 2000–2001, two temporary buildings were added to the elementary school, taking up playground space. The additional space again proved to be inadequate with the addition of two more temporary buildings and classes being held on the stage in the gym, in the basement, and in the library. The need for a new elementary school was immediate. For the first time in 135 years (1876–2011), all three levels of school will take place away from the Seventh Street location. After three years of planning, the new $11 million elementary school opened in January 2012, accommodating kindergarten through fourth grade, with an enrollment of about 300 students and plenty of room for growth.

Seven

Health and Wellness

Now a part of the Avera Medical Group, the Dell Rapids Hospital was once the go-to hospital in the area for procedures and health care and home to one of the most noted operating rooms in the region. Hallmarks of the facility have included its gifted and well-known doctors, such as Drs. Martin Grove and John Eagan, who helped establish the hospital and clinic as a hub for outstanding medical care in South Dakota. Also home to a nurses training program that helped hundreds of people begin their careers as medical professionals, the hospital partnered with a leading Chicago hospital to give nurses the best three-year education they could get in the region. And with the honor of erecting the only Odd Fellows Home, for retirees, in South Dakota, Dell Rapids has stayed active in the areas of elder care and assisted living.

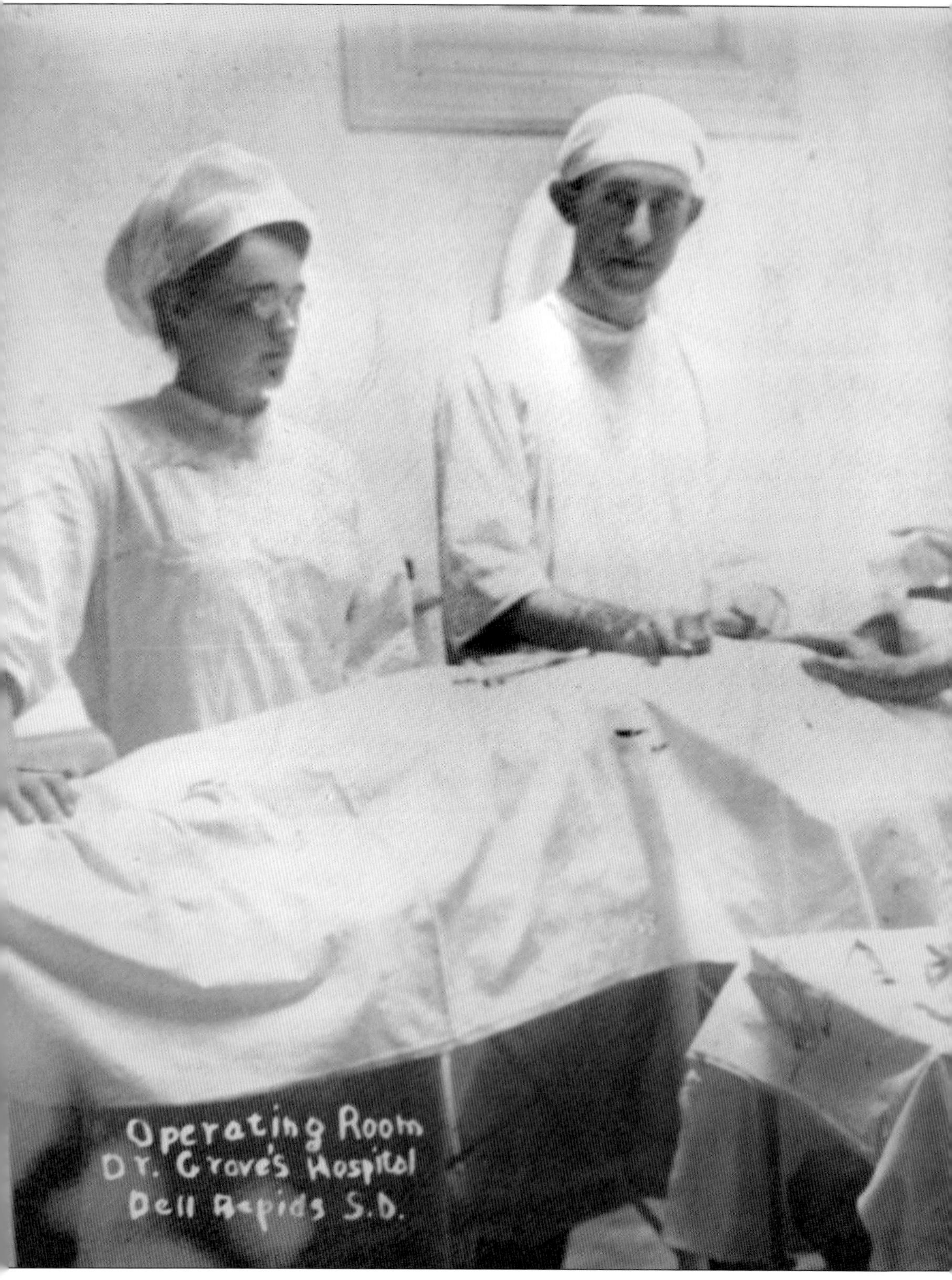
Operating Room
Dr. Grove's Hospital
Dell Rapids S.D.

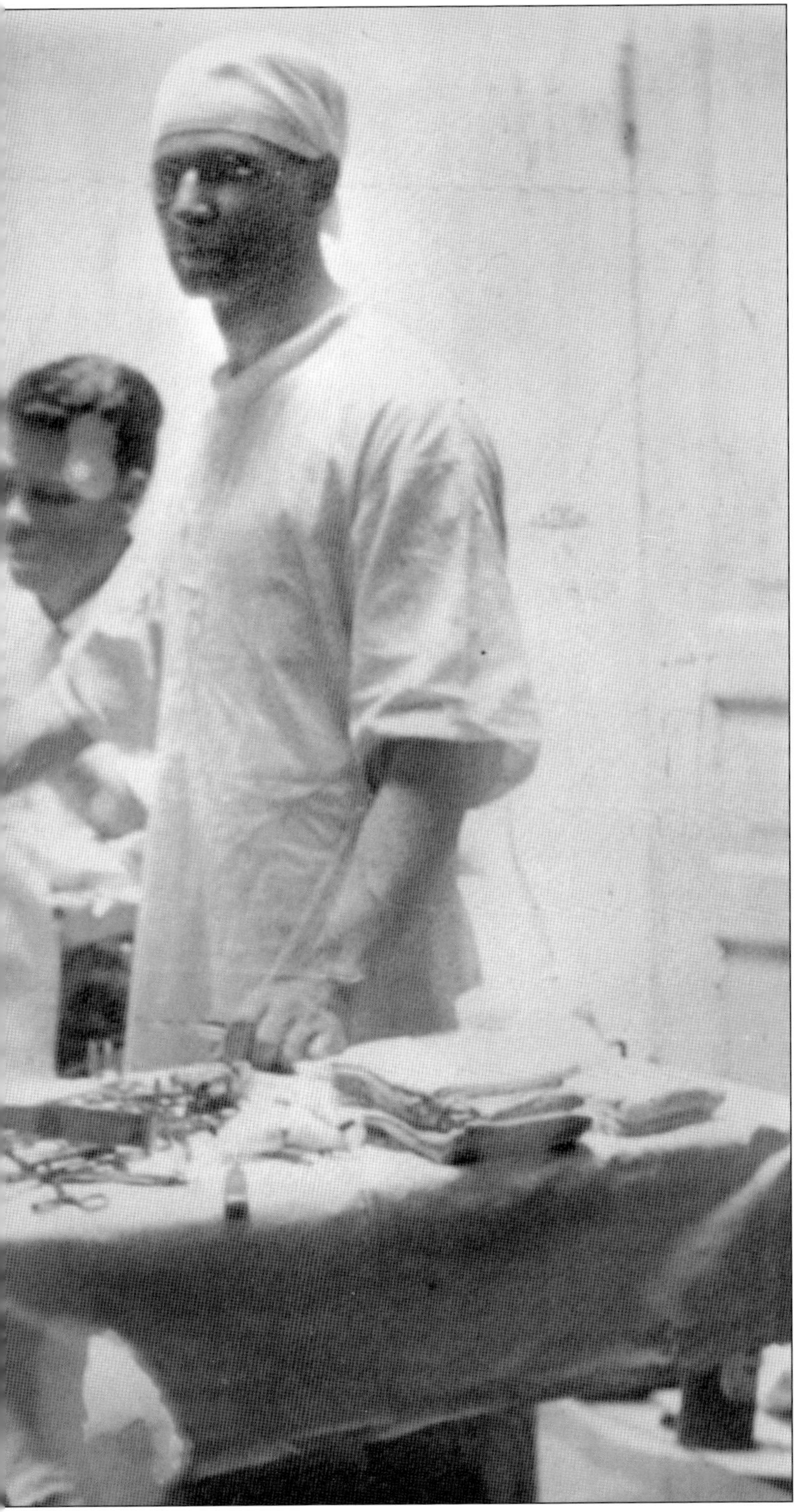

While plans and designs for the new hospital were being made, Drs. Martin Grove and John Eagan expressed the need to have one of the finest operating rooms of any hospital in the region. Established with the latest and best equipment, the operating room provided more expanded services to better treat the hospital's patients. Grove and Eagan carried on a successful general hospital practice with an excellent surgical department. As the hospital flourished, the facility became known as a regional medical center, with many traveling long distances specifically to be treated there.

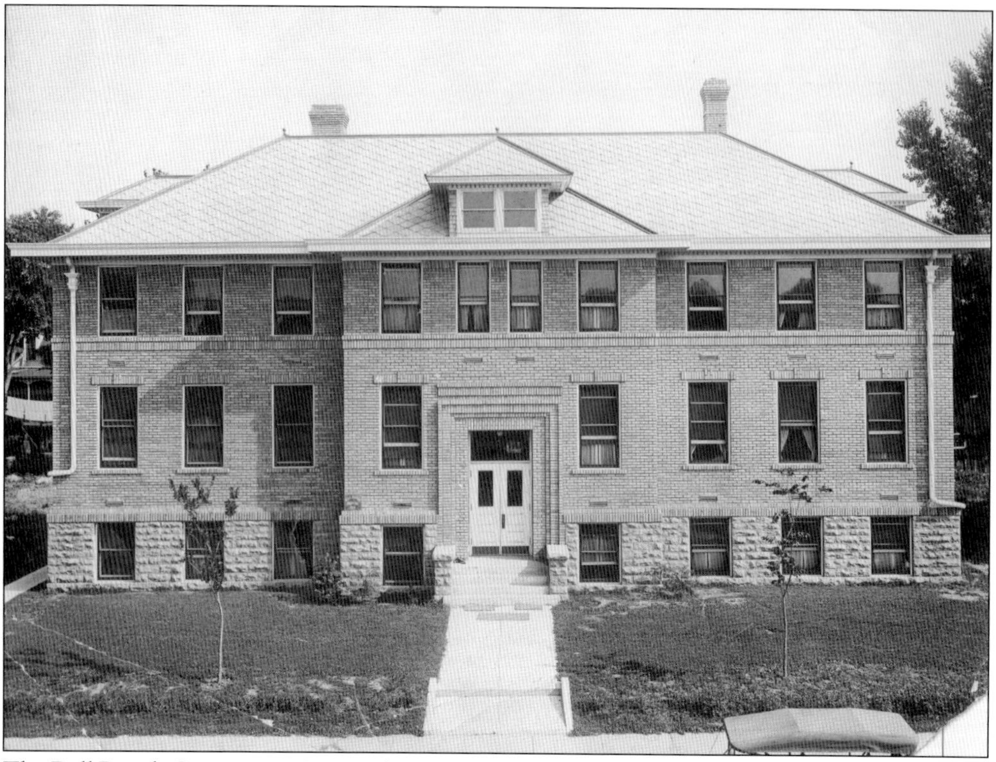

The Dell Rapids Community Hospital opened for patient care on February 10, 1915. The building was 75 feet long and 38 feet wide, with a large waiting room, X-ray laboratory, medicine and linen rooms, bath and toilet rooms, and rooms for patients, all providing the most up-to-date medical needs. This building served as the local hospital until 1960.

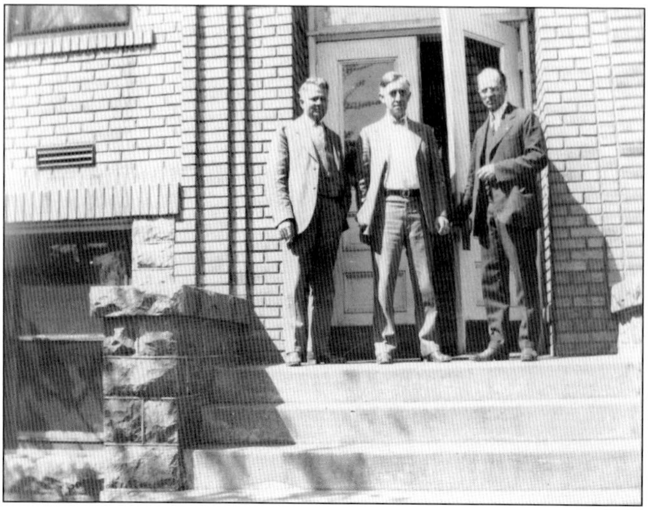

Dr. Martin Grove (right) and Dr. John Eagan (center) had become a very successful medical team in the early 1900s, with the reputation of their services expanding beyond the local community. With the overwhelming increase in the number of patients, Dr. Grove requested the use of an additional physician from the University Medical College in Chicago. He was surprised to learn the new physician was his younger brother, Dr. Arthur Grove (left).

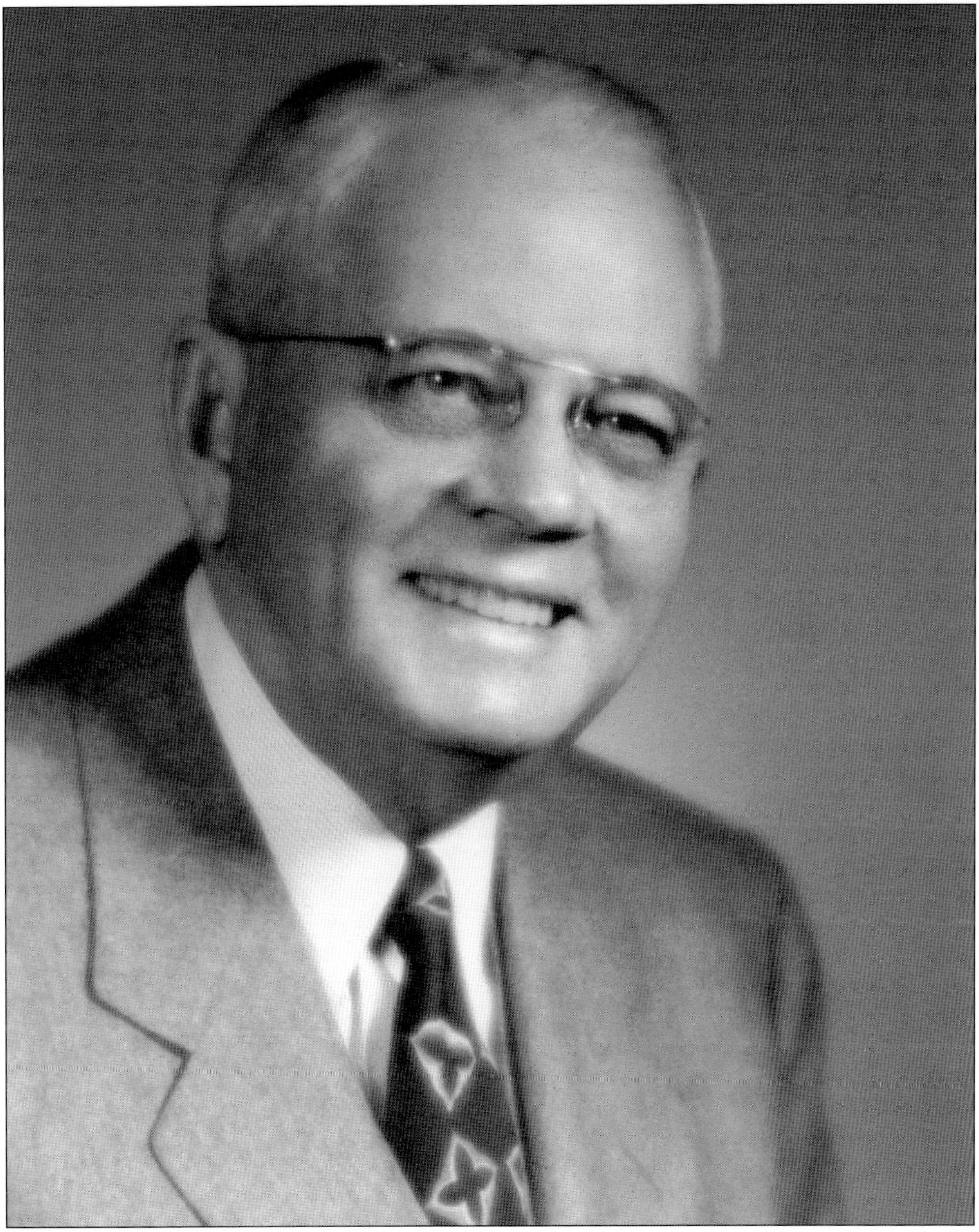

Dr. Arthur F. Grove was born in 1884 on a farm near Plainview, Minnesota, the youngest of eight children. He graduated in premed from the University of Minnesota and from medical school at the University of Illinois before completing a residency in surgery at Cook County Hospital in Chicago. In 1912, Dr. Grove moved to Dell Rapids to practice medicine with his brother, Dr. Martin Grove, and Dr. John Eagan. In the early 1940s, Dr. Eagan was disabled by a stroke and due to the extreme shortage of doctors during the war years, Dr. Arthur Grove carried on the practice alone. His practice was marked by frequent house calls, sometimes two a night. He actively served the community of Dell Rapids and the surrounding area as a physician and surgeon for 40 years. In World War I, he served as a medical officer with an evacuation hospital in France and later with the Army of Occupation in Trier, Germany.

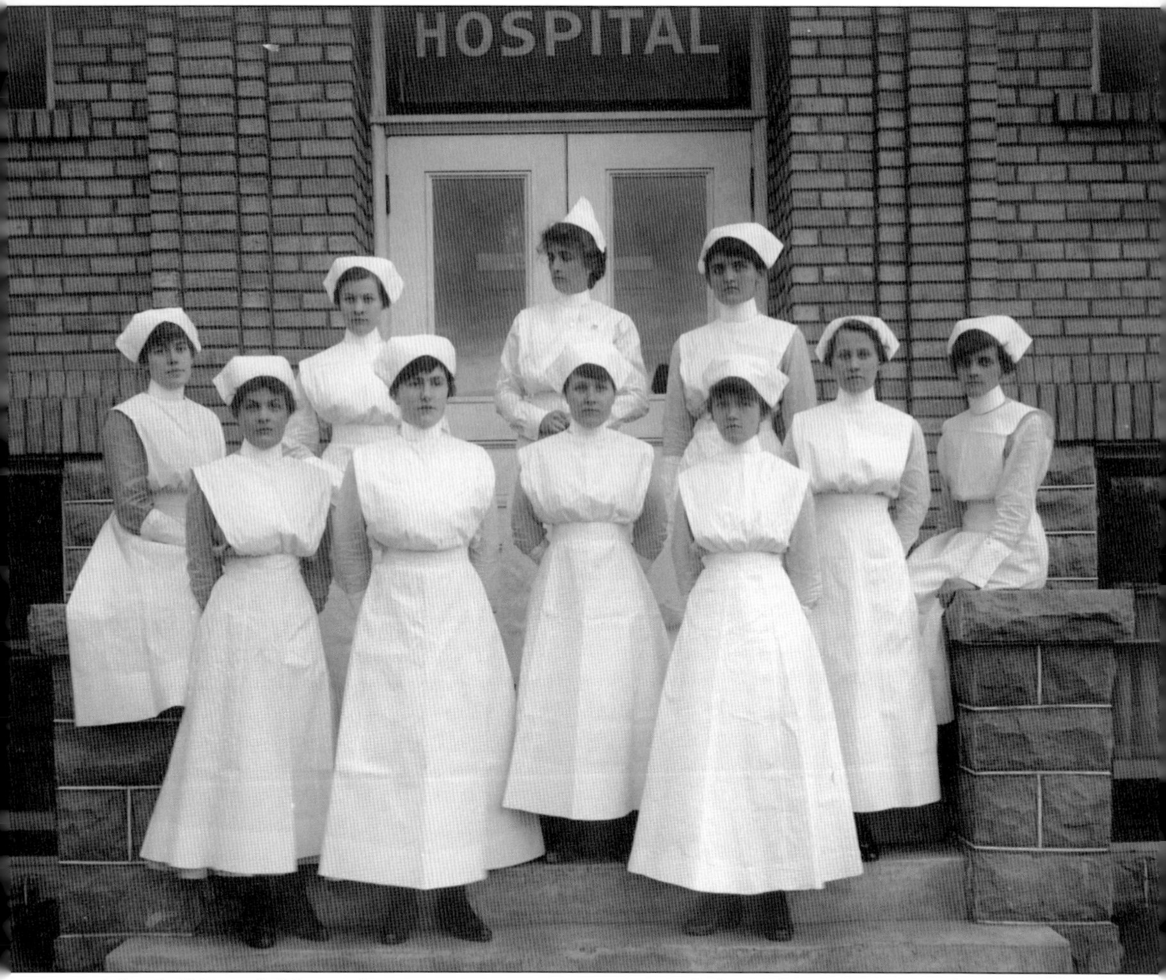

The Dell Rapids Hospital nursing program was organized through Drs. Grove and Eagan. The three-year program offered nurses hands-on training at the hospital, with the strict guidance of a nursing director. A pharmacist at the time, Dr. William Voy instructed thorough classwork. This nursing school was affiliated with one of the leading hospitals in Chicago, and graduates were qualified to take the state board examination to become a registered nurse. In addition to training, the nurses were also provided living quarters, conveniently located a few short blocks away on the corner of Fourth Street and Iowa Avenue. Nine well-trained commitment nurses graduated in the first class. The program continued until 1936, with 65 individuals completing the course.

Dr. Ora Sawyer studied medicine at Rush Medical College and graduated in March 1879, arriving in Dell Rapids a month later. He at once commenced the practice of medicine, demonstrating himself to be a well-qualified physician. In addition, he was a charter member of the old Territorial Medical Society and the Minnehaha County Medical Society, a value to the county as well as Dell Rapids.

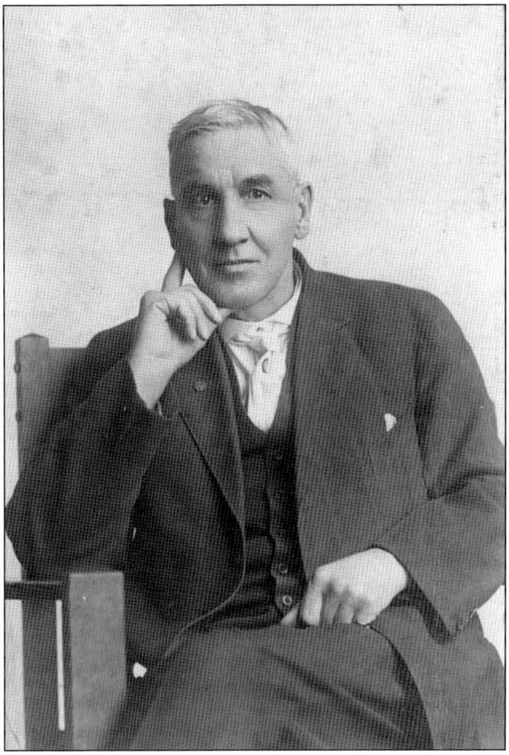

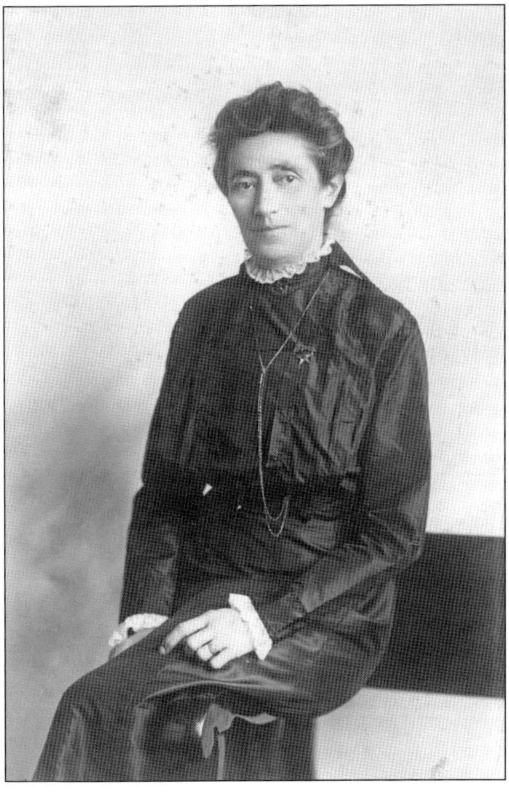

Elizabeth Janette Grow was born in 1858. At 21 years old, she married Dr. Ora Sawyer immediately after he graduated from medical school, and they came to Dakota Territory. At the time, medical facilities were not available for patients, and the use of private homes was often common. Dr. Sawyer became a fine doctor with the home-based assistance of Elizabeth.

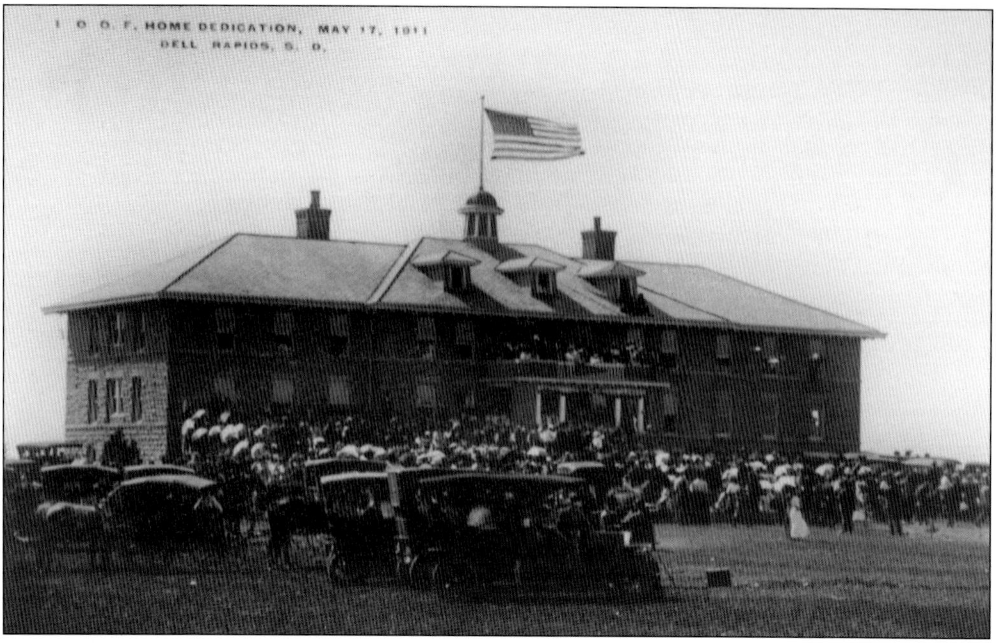

The Dell Rapids Odd Fellows Home was dedicated on May 17, 1911, with 6,000 people gathered on the grounds to witness the ceremony. The idea of a state Odd Fellows Home was suggested in 1892 at the state convention in Hot Springs. After painstaking and careful deliberation, the Odd Fellows Board of Trustees decided that Dell Rapids had made the most attractive offer.

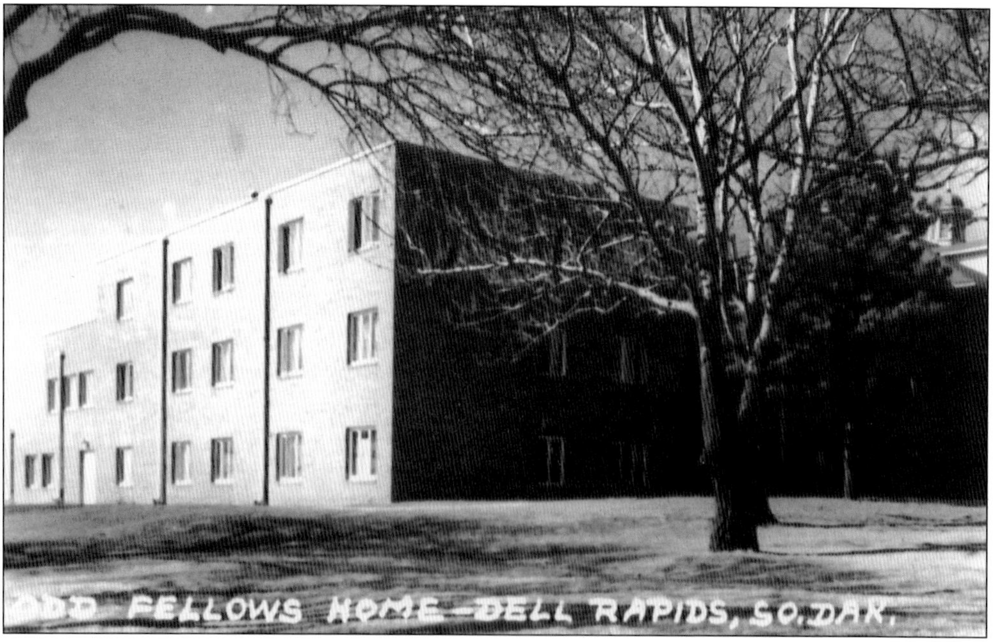

The "home idea" originally provided for dependent children as well as members the Odd Fellows' families. From 1910–1947, many orphaned children found a home at the Odd Fellows. In 1977, the home was declared opened; those who wished to live there did not need to be affiliated with the organization. The home continued to provide assisted and congregated care to residents until it closed in 2003.

Eight

Recreation

The city park has hosted countless events through the years, including Cootie Days, Quarry Days, and Memorial Day services, but the big draw for outsiders has consistently been its namesake – the rocky and picturesque dells that have become the city's calling card. From early youngsters traversing the rocky terrain in feats of one-upmanship, to the Three Sisters outcropping of the Big Sioux, the landscape has served families and residents of the region well. Once the home of a popular bathing beach and boat launch, the river still remains a useful tool for recreational purposes, with ongoing traditions like cardboard boat races and fishing derbies in the summer. Students and adults have kept busy following the many sporting and musical opportunities Dell Rapids offers through its amateur baseball teams and city band.

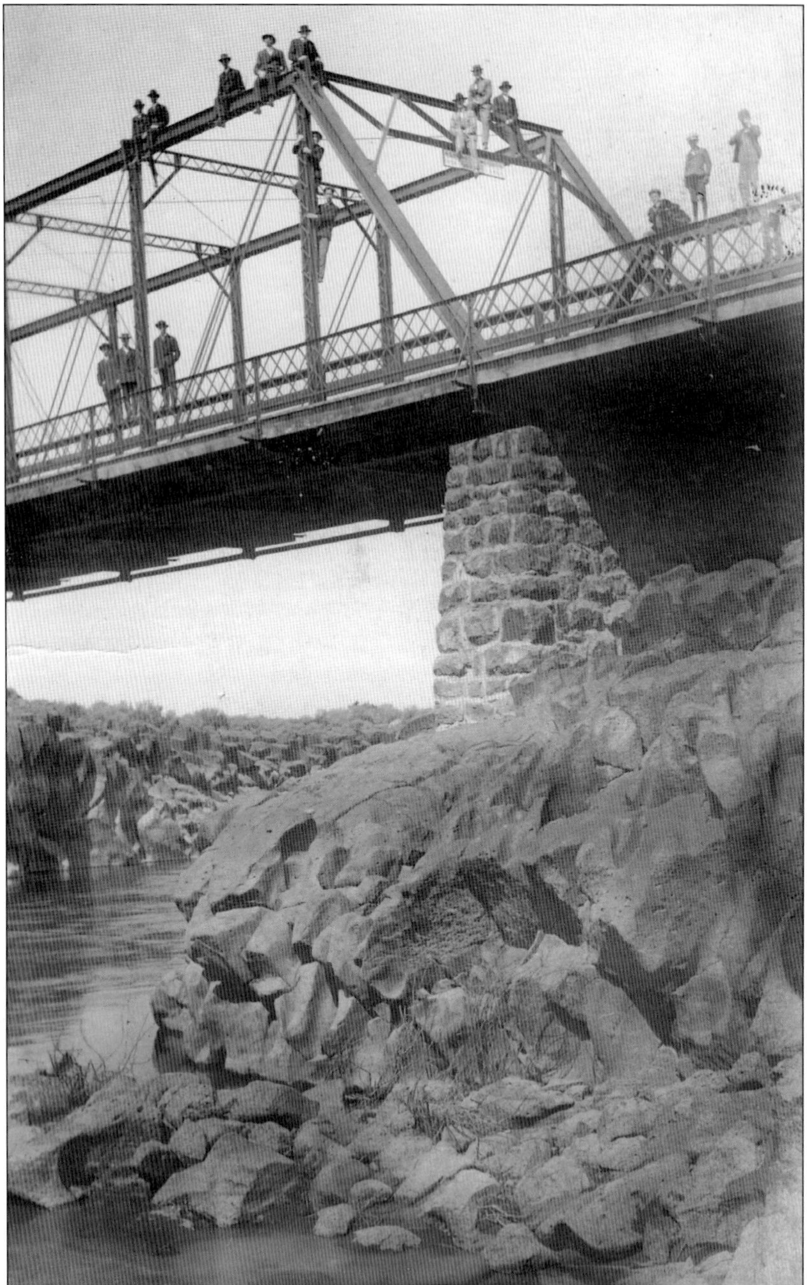

The year 1880 marked the first appearance of the railroad to Dell Rapids. By then, the town consisted of 993 residents, 50 businesses, and three church buildings. It took a lot of hard work to accomplish the early tasks of creating a town. In addition to the labor, the residents had also taken time to rejoice in those achievements, whether it was a town celebration, a military parade, or a simple picnic. The nearby river and the railroad bridge crossing the Big Sioux River west of town were principal points of recreation for many of the city's first residents. The thrill of climbing the cliffs of the dells and the bridge was an enticement for many people young and old, each one attempting to outdo the other, climbing up higher to more perilous locations.

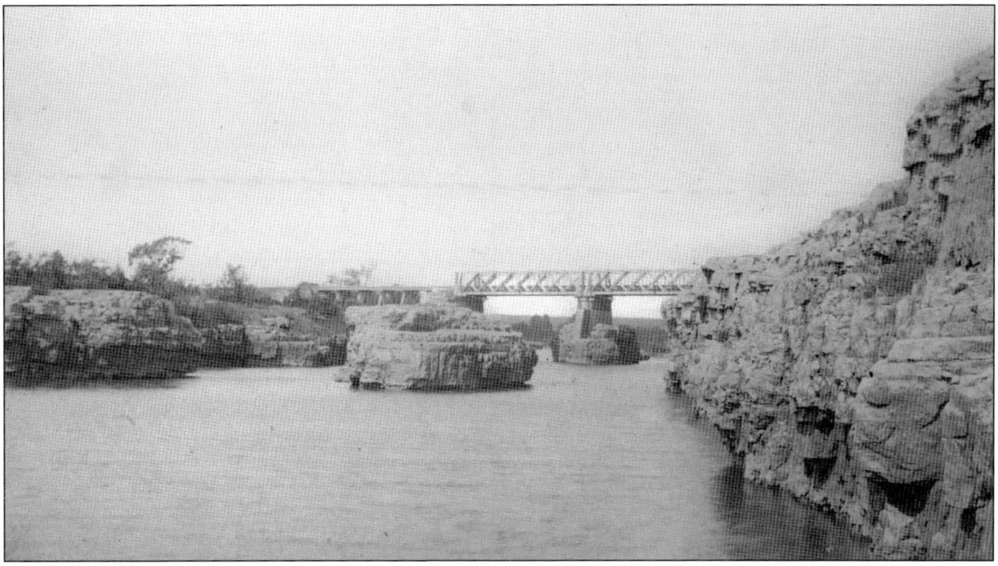

This particular outcropping west of town on the Big Sioux River is called the Three Sisters. The river rises a few miles east of Waubay in Roberts County and flows south, roughly paralleling the eastern boundary of the state to the north line of Lincoln County, from which point it forms the boundary to its junction with the Missouri River at the southeast tip of Union County. The river is 390 miles long and was named for the Sioux Nation, which inhabited the region prior to the white settlers. The Sioux name for this river meant "winding" or "crooked" river.

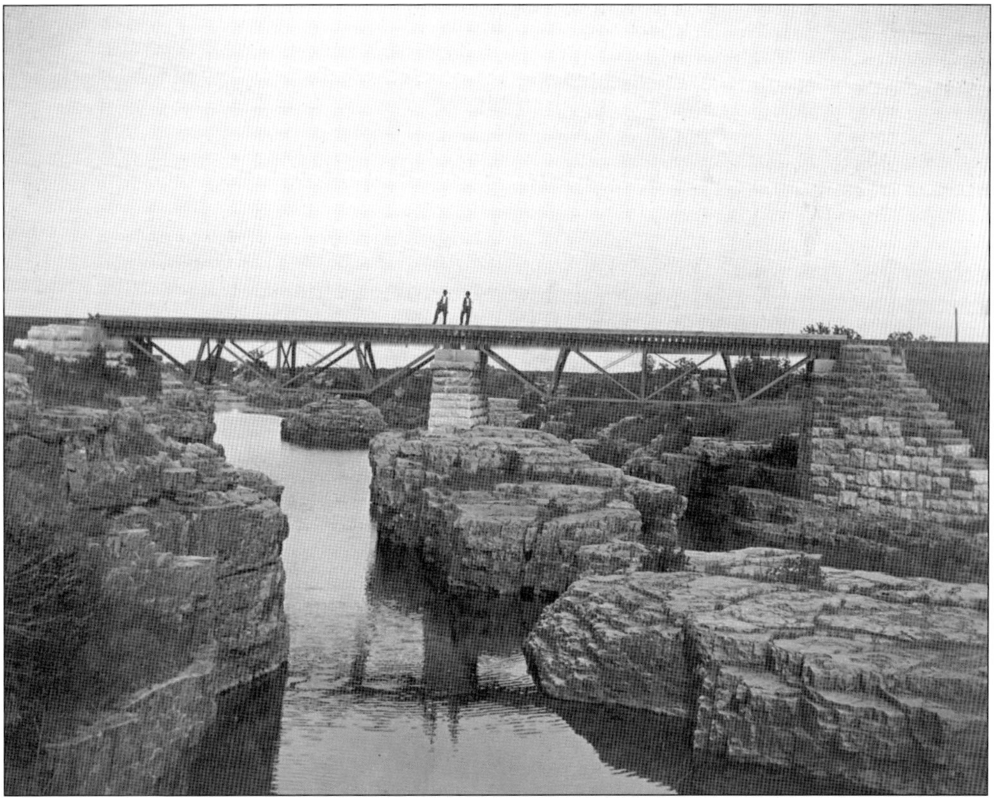

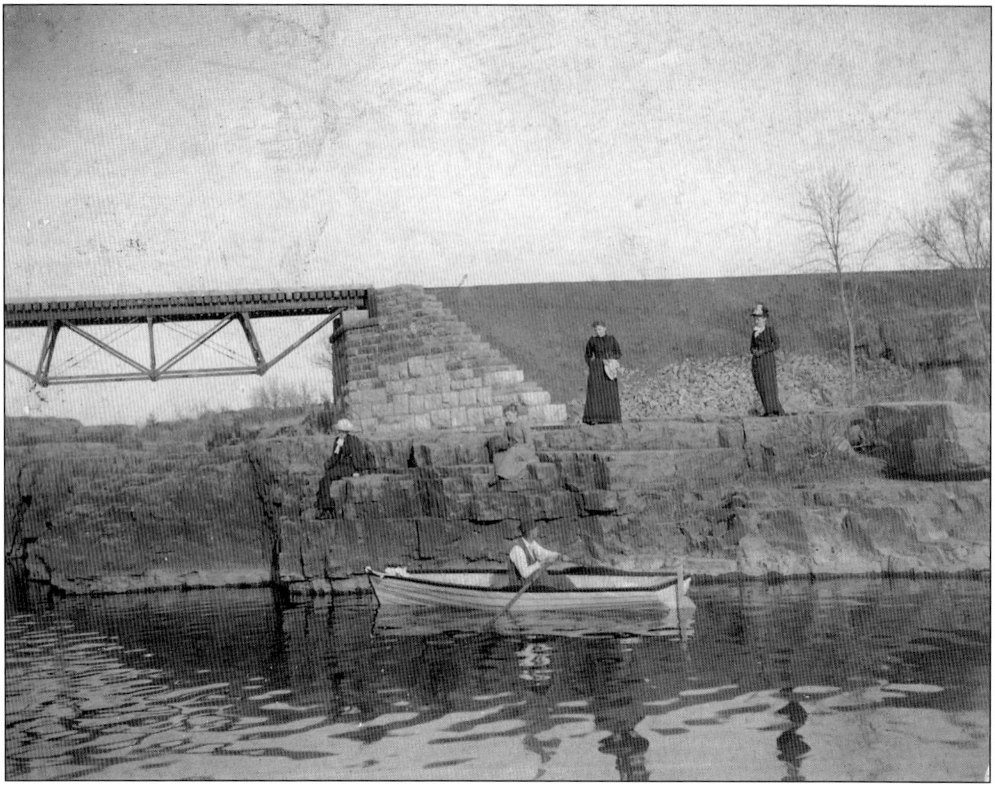

Spending Sunday afternoons at the Big Sioux River was a frequent pleasure for families in the area. Picnicking or climbing the cliffs, parents and children visited this area to take in the unique feature of the town—its namesake, the rapids.

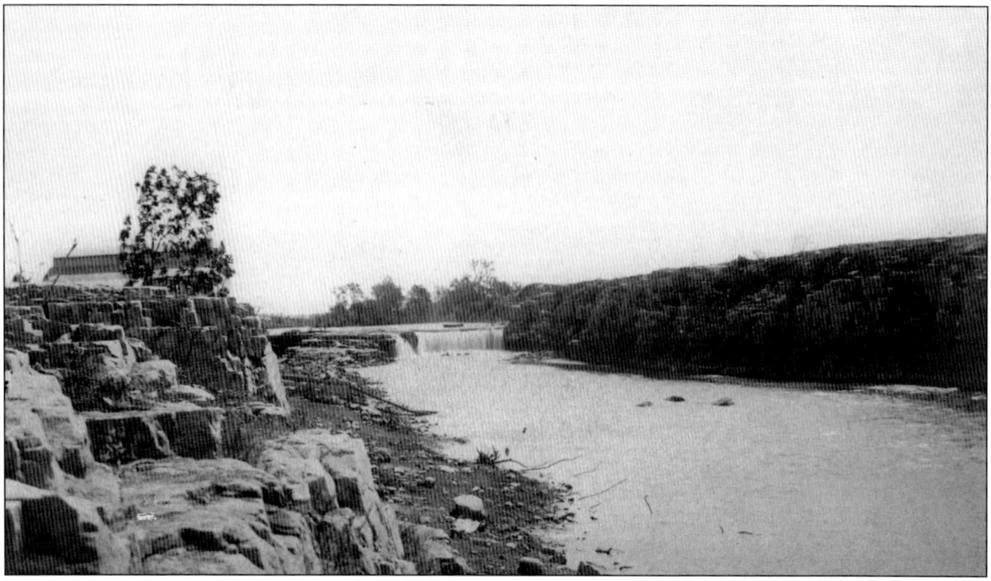

The mill and the dam, two hallmarks of early life in Dell Rapids, are seen in this view of the river. Frank and Dennis Rice built both structures and the area has remained virtually unchanged since, with little known about the dam aside from passed-down stories about its former use.

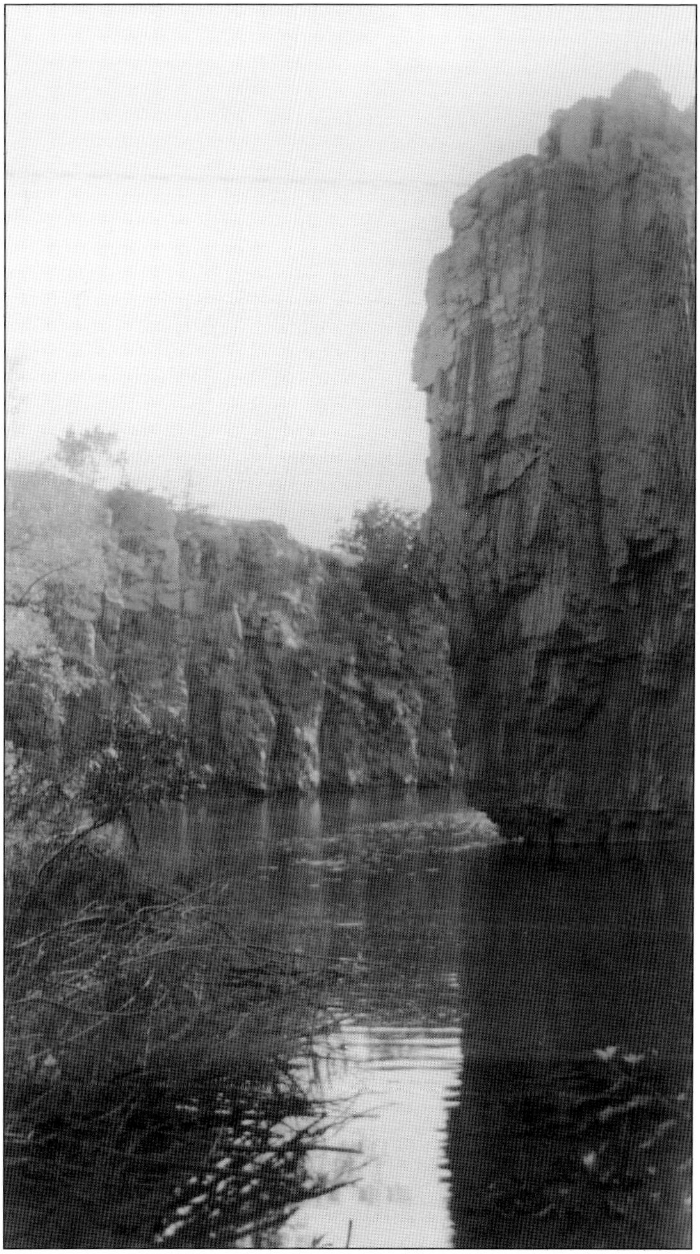

In the early 1870s, Peter Morse was on a leisure traveling expedition. He came upon this breathtaking view of the winding river and the deep-set pink quartzite north of Sioux Falls. He knew then that it was the perfect location for a town. The Dells of the Big Sioux River are part of a rich vein of rose quartzite that runs from the Wisconsin Dells to eastern South Dakota. Geologists have classified the rock formations in the area as part of the Potsdam Formation of rose quartzite, also known as pink quartzite, which runs at least 2,600 feet deep at the Dell Rapids quarries. Thousands of years ago, a shift in the Earth's surface at Dell Rapids caused an enormous fissure, producing the dells. The dells split off from the Big Sioux, ushering visitors into a 40-foot canyon of rose quartzite. With very little change in the river, the view from the dells lookout is still very much the same as when Peter Morse first spied it.

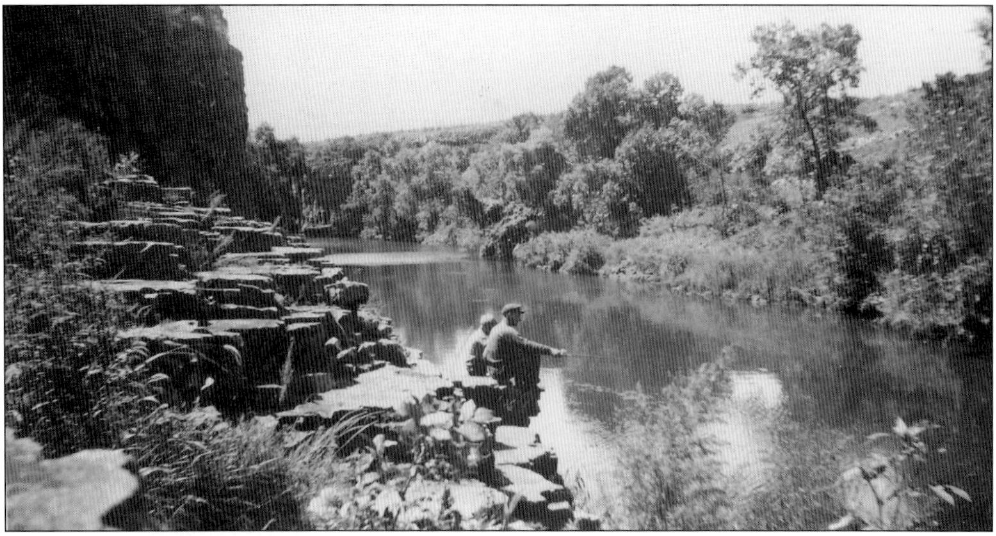

The Big Sioux River produces an abundance of fish for nourishment and sport. Many who camp nearby or leisurely stroll the walking trail are amazed to see fish literally jumping out of the water. A local altar society conducts a fishing derby every year, with a range of prizes.

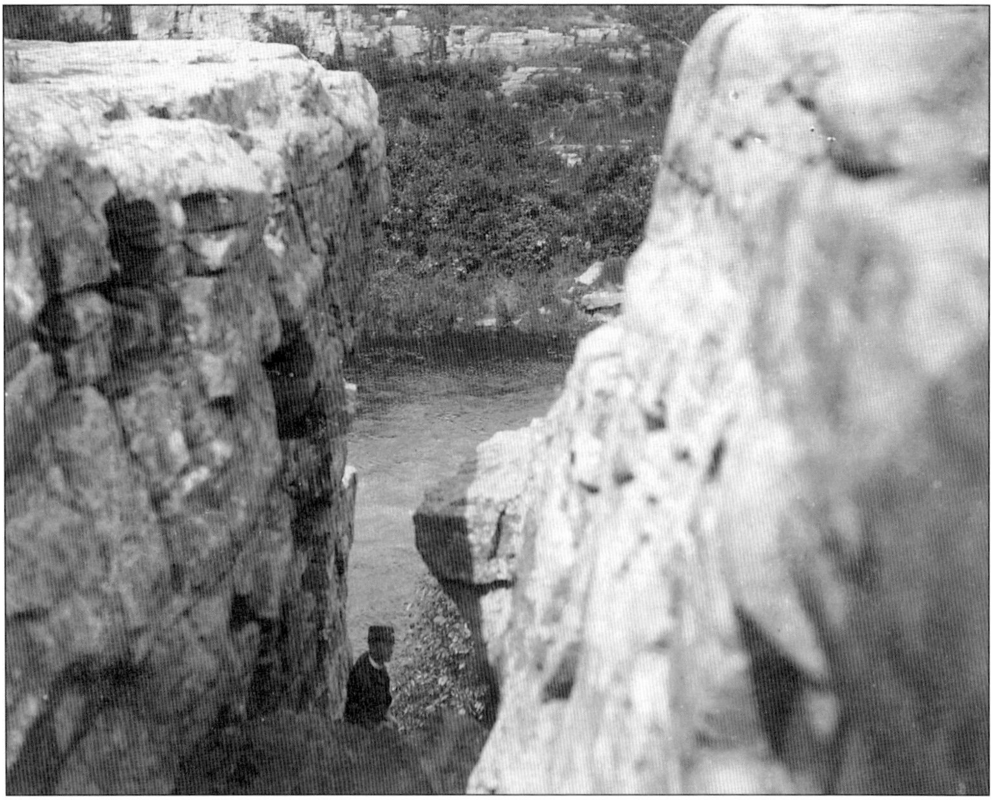

While many local fishermen boast of secret spots that are the best, there is no shortage of locations for fishing along the entire length of the town. The natural cliffs along this portion of the river have formed many layers, providing a series of natural benches, or seats. This determined gentleman has squeezed through the separation in the rock formation to get a closer glimpse of the river.

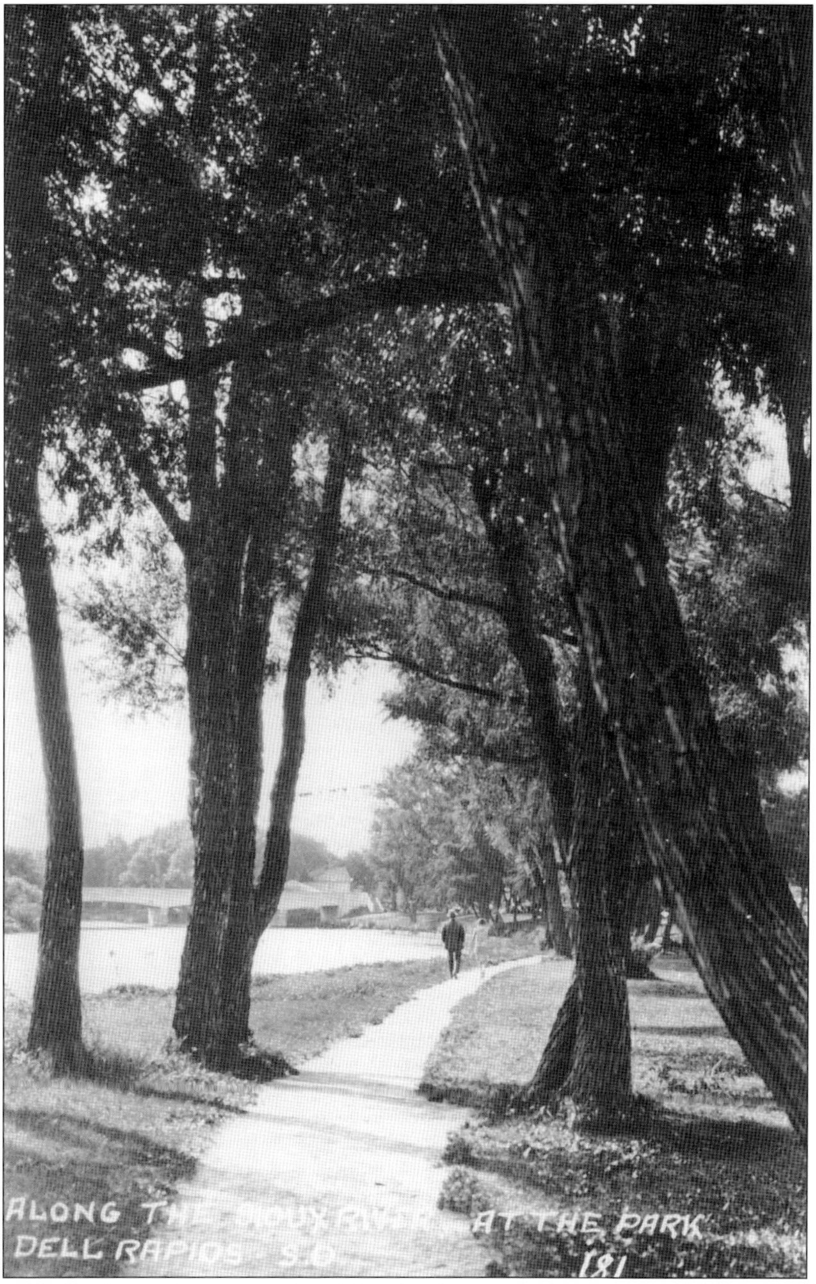

The city park has been the setting for all kinds of entertainment, enjoyment, and relaxation. Streets in the park were laid out in 1917, along with walking paths, a bandstand, a food stand, and a pavilion. During the summer months, weekends are filled with baseball, swimming, fishing, and even a wedding or two. Yearly events at the park, such as Cootie Days and Quarry Days, are filled to the brim with visitors from the southeastern region of South Dakota. Many gather to reminisce of old days while returning home on vacation or attending a high school reunion. Years ago, many enjoyed ice-skating along the river. Nowadays, the familiar sounds of snowmobiles are often heard. The city park, with its beautiful landscape, flowerbeds, and abundance of trees, is truly a city treasure.

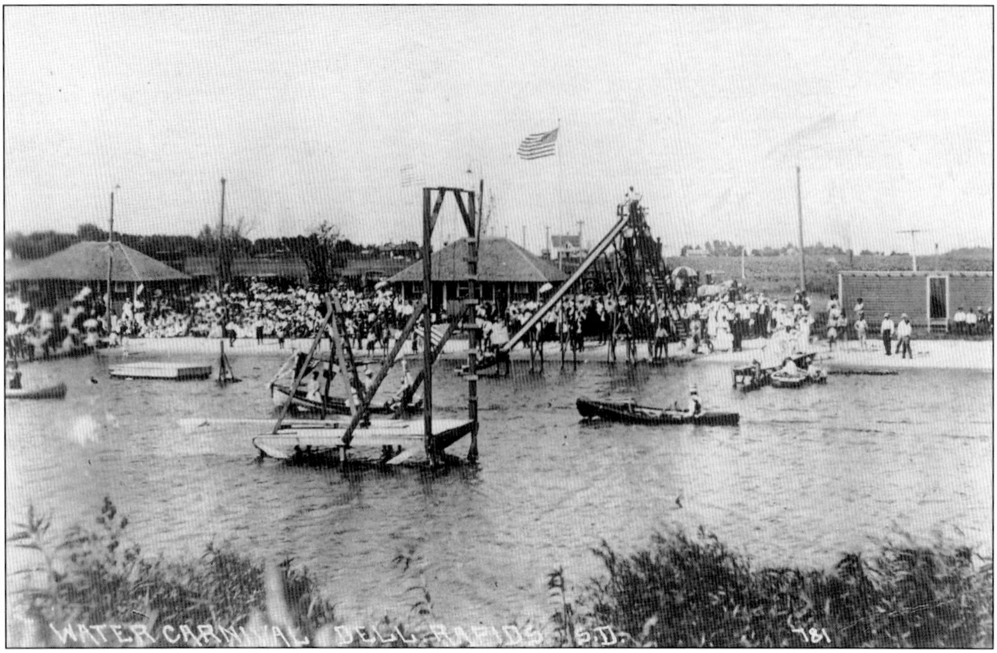

In 1917, the Dell Rapids City Park was credited as being the "best in the area." The second annual water carnival was held the same year and attracted more than 400 people from Sioux Falls alone. It had diving towers, a ring trapeze, floats, safety cables, a 40-foot speed chute, and beautiful sand on the beach.

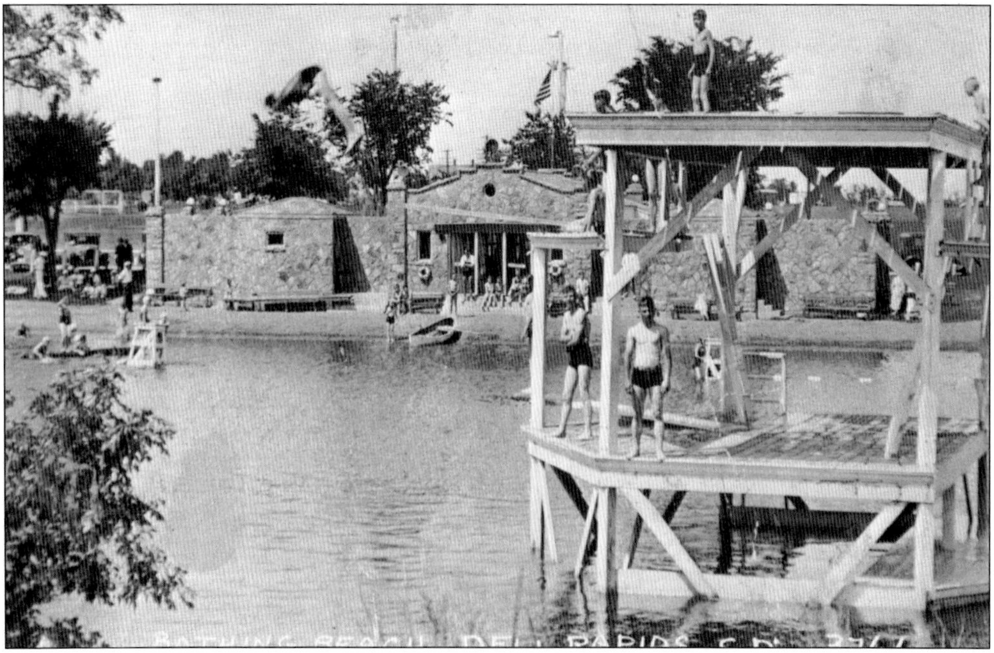

From 1913 to 1960, the Dell Rapids bathing beach was one of the most popular sites in the area for swimming. In a time before rules, regulations, and insurance, the river was a common location for summertime recreation. Here, Tom Merry waits his turn while an adventurous diver takes flight.

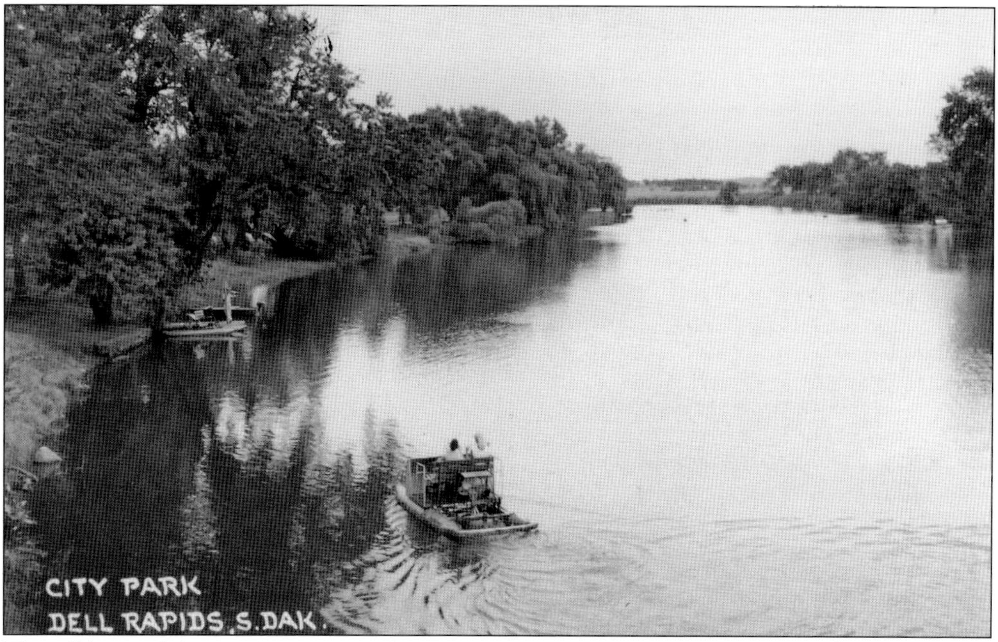

The offshoot of the Big Sioux River flowing past the city park also played host to a boat launch, where visitors entered the water to traverse the sometimes rushing rapids. The city park's stretch of river is the site of the annual cardboard boat races during the Quarry Days celebration.

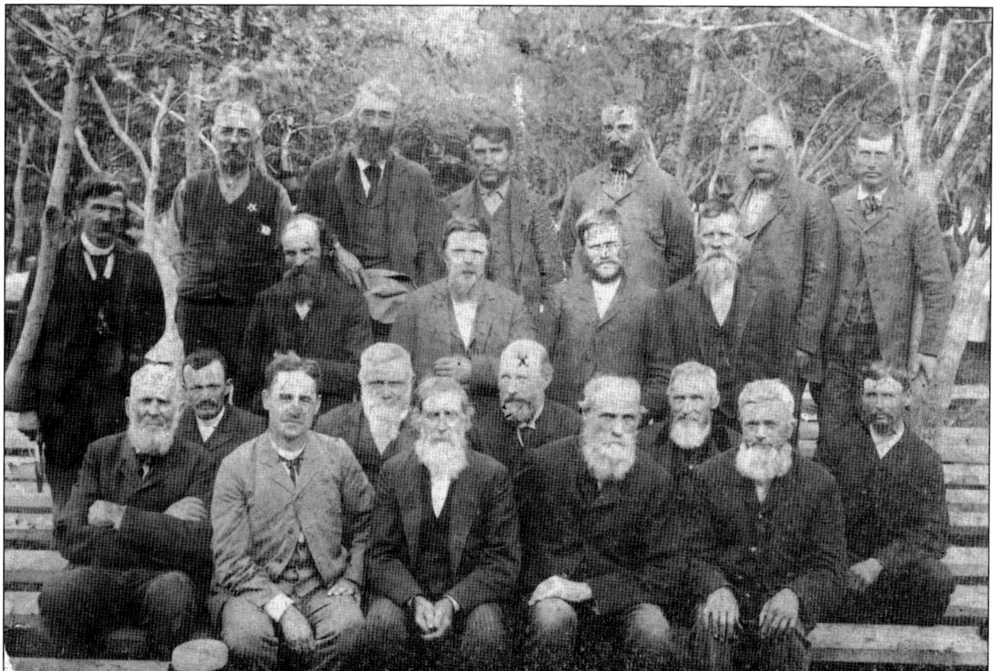

During the 1900 G.A.R. Encampment, members were photographed here in a grove on the grounds of the city water tower, currently located on Tenth Street. The Dell Rapids G.A.R Post, known as Dahlgren Poster No. 20, was organized on May 31, 1883 and at one time was made up of about 70 members. Thomas Lilly (1842–1932) was Dell Rapids' last Civil War veteran.

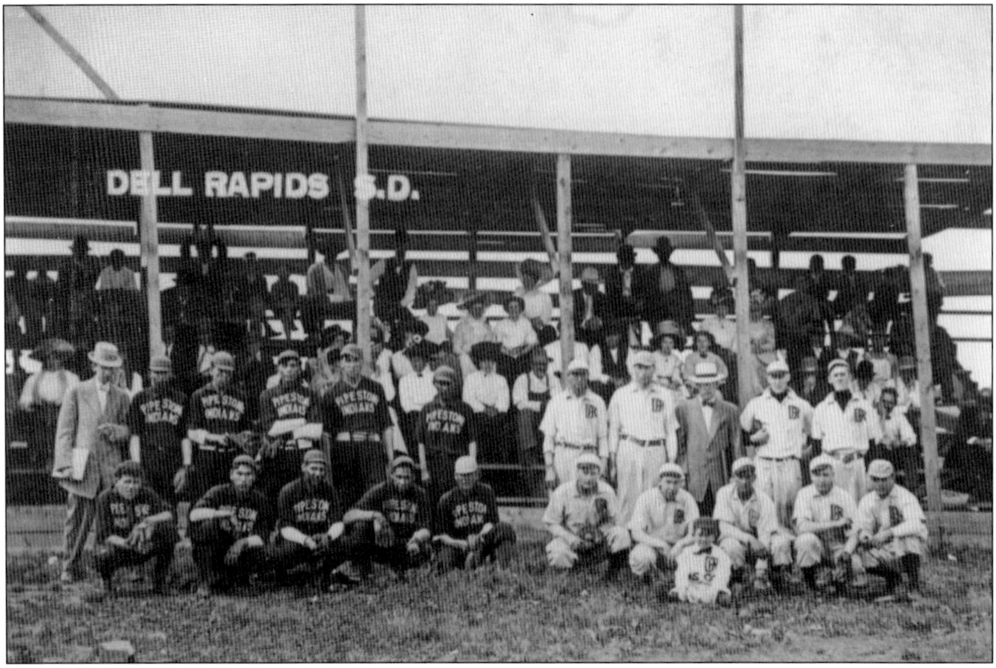

The baseball diamond was once located just east of City Park, and Dell Rapids was on a circuit with other towns. The baseball team was salaried, with outside players and highly talented local men. In addition to the 1915 "salaried" team, the high school had acquired enough young men to form a team of its own. In 1939, new lights were added to the baseball fields. With much enthusiasm and participation, baseball has expanded to include all ages, including T-ball in 1994. Currently, Dell Rapids is the only city in the state to have sent two teams, the Mudcats and Pabst Blue Ribbon (PBR), to the state finals, after the 2001 season left both teams on top. The game-ending score was 8-6, in favor of the longer-running PBR.

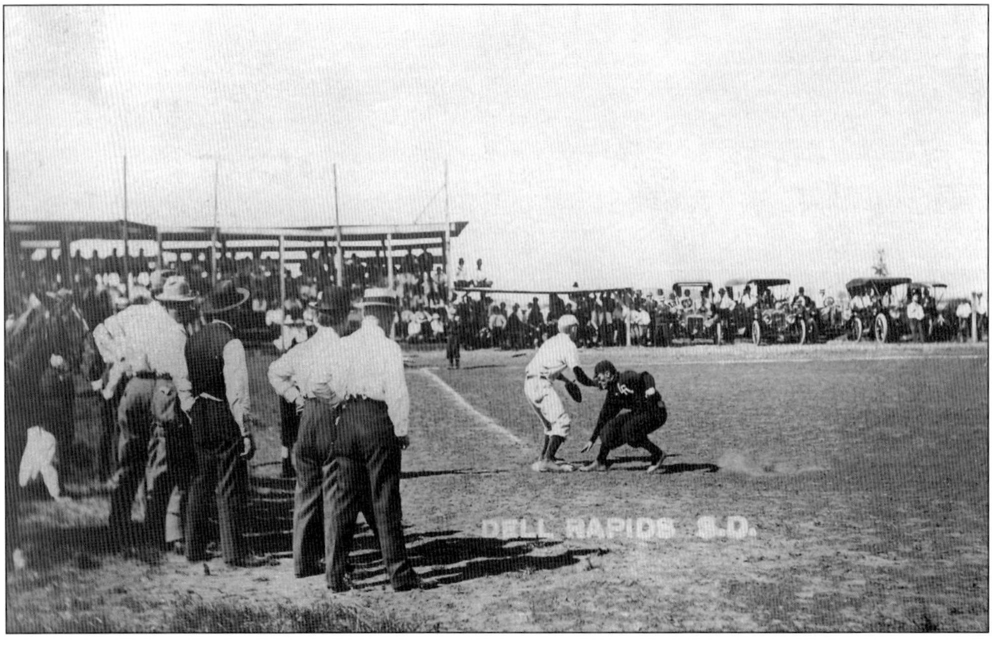

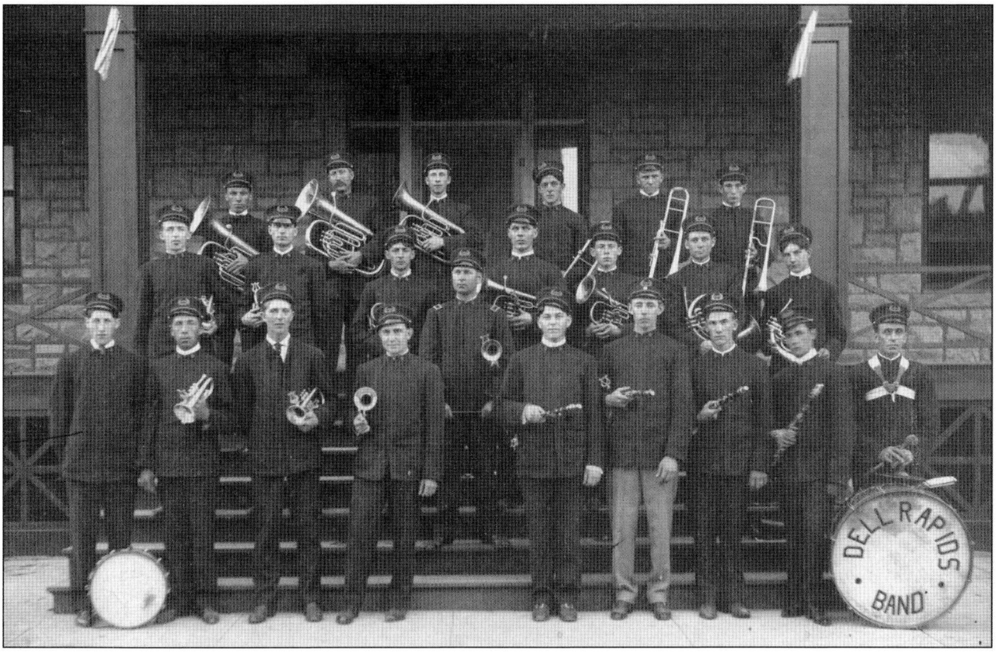

At one time, the Dell Rapids City Band was considered one of the best in the state. It was active in various events in town, from parades and dedications to concerts and baseball games. In addition, the band traveled to many neighboring communities representing Dell Rapids. In 1925, the 22-piece band traveled 170 miles to promote the upcoming Cootie Days.

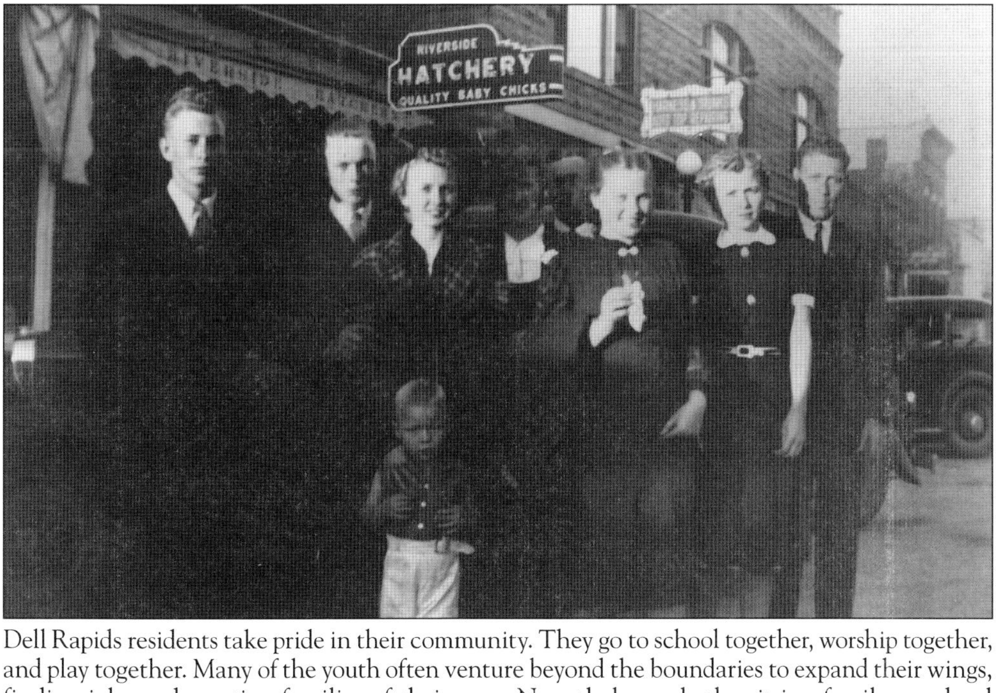

Dell Rapids residents take pride in their community. They go to school together, worship together, and play together. Many of the youth often venture beyond the boundaries to expand their wings, finding jobs and creating families of their own. Nonetheless, whether it is a family or school reunion or a simple vacation, Dells folks always come back to a place they call home. (Courtesy Dan Ahlers.)